P9-CDH-268

what does
god know

and

when does he know it?

MILLARD J. ERICKSON

WHAT DOES GOD KNOW

AND

WHEN DOES HE KNOW IT?

*The Current Controversy over
Divine Foreknowledge*

ZONDERVAN™

GRAND RAPIDS, MICHIGAN 49530 USA

ZONDERVAN™

What Does God Know and When Does He Know It?
Copyright © 2003 by Millard J. Erickson

Requests for information should be addressed to:
Zondervan, *Grand Rapids, Michigan 49530*

Library of Congress Cataloging-in-Publication Data

Erickson, Millard J.
    What does God know and when does he know it? : the current controversy
over divine foreknowledge / Millard J. Erickson.
       p. cm.
    Includes bibliographical references and index.
    ISBN 0-310-24769-1
    1. God—Omniscience.   2. Free will and determinism—Religious aspects—
Christianity. I. Title.
    BT131.E75 2003
    231'.4—dc21

                                            2003013952

Interior design by Michelle Espinoza

Printed in the United States of America

04 05 06 07 08 09 /❖ DC/ 10 9 8 7 6 5 4 3 2

To
Allan Fisher
and Jim Weaver

— ◆ —

Two Christian gentlemen
who made the author-publisher relationship
one of integrity and even of friendship

contents

Preface

October 8, 2000. Two days earlier my wife and I had attended the Passion Play in Oberammergau, Germany, a town in which we had once lived. We then drove north into Luther country, and on this Sunday morning we attended the worship service in the Town Church in Wittenberg, the church where Martin Luther had preached. After the service ended, I sat there for several minutes, reflecting on what Luther had done. Then we strolled past the university where he had taught, the house where he had lived, and the place where he burned the papal bull. We walked past the statues of Luther and Melanchton, and on to the Castle Church, where he nailed his ninety-five theses on October 31, 1517, and beneath the floor of which he lies buried.

I thought of what the Reformation had meant, how Luther had challenged the established teaching of the church by propounding what appeared to be novel and heretical doctrines but which actually called the church back to its source, the Bible. I asked myself, "May it be that a similar reformation is now pressing upon the evangelical church? May the movement called open theism be calling us to abandon traditions that are not really biblically based, in favor of the purer teaching of the Scriptures, long buried under philosophical and theological tradition?" Although I had previously studied the movement at some length, I resolved that, with as open a mind as possible, I would again search through the teachings of the open theists, who have claimed that they are indeed calling for a reformation of the church's theology. This book represents a fresh attempt on my part to explore and answer that question.

My aim in this investigation is to be as fair and impartial as possible. It is important to distinguish between impartiality and neutrality, however. Judges, referees, and umpires are expected to be impartial; they are not expected to be neutral or to refuse to render a judgment. That, after all, is why they are employed. This distinction needs to be asserted again because in today's environment the two are often confused. I will attempt to deal with these issues with an open mind and to listen carefully to the arguments on both sides. I will, however, come to some definite conclusions regarding the relative strengths of two competing views.

This book also grows out of the practical necessity of addressing the debate in a variety of settings. Because the issue has been controversial in the small denomination of which I have been a member most of my life and because of the debate within the Evangelical Theological Society, I have been called on to speak to laypersons, pastors, students, and professors on this subject. Out of these presentations has grown a collection of material that deserves wider dissemination. I have benefited greatly from the comments and questions of those present and have been encouraged to publish this material. Among those occasions were class sessions at Northwestern College, Roseville, Minnesota; Berry College, Mount Berry, Georgia; Toccoa Falls College, Toccoa Falls, Georgia; and Biola University, La Mirada, California; theological and pastors' conferences at Mundelein, Illinois; Edmonds, Washington; Detroit, Michigan; Tuolumne, California; Hyderabad, Bangalore, and Madurai, India; Tokyo, Nagoya, Hamamatsu, Kobe, and Sendai, Japan; church services at Bloomington Baptist Church, Bloomington, Minnesota; Trinity Baptist Church, Maplewood, Minnesota; Berean Baptist Church, Burnsville, Minnesota; and Quamba Baptist Church, Quamba, Minnesota; as a lecture at the Remaking the Modern Mind conference at Union University, Jackson, Tennessee; as a lecture to the Orthodox Faculty of Theology at Sofia University, Sofia, Bulgaria; and the Deere Lectures at Golden Gate Baptist Theological Seminary, Mill Valley, California.

To many pastors, laypersons, and students, this controversy has proved rather bewildering. Wanting to remain true to the teaching of the Bible and also desiring to avoid unnecessary controversy, they have found themselves uncertain what and whom to believe. This book is a small attempt to clarify the issues and guide toward some answers.

We serve a good and wise God. It is my prayer that this book will contribute to readers' coming to know God better and loving him more.

INDtRODUCtION:
wHat's tHis aLL aвout?

Both in popular culture and in conservative Christian circles, a certain idea of God is held, whether it is believed that he exists, as the latter group holds, or whether that question is open, as is generally the case with the former view. The very idea of God seems to include that he is able to do all things and that he knows everything. In these respects, he is different from, and superior to, human beings, and this is in fact the point of having a god: that he is capable of doing, and doing for us, the things we cannot do. The very expression, "the Almighty," is one indication of this widespread conception. Generally, the belief that God knows everything includes the dimension of knowing the future as well.

Sometimes this conception appears in surprising places. In one episode of a long-running, popular prime-time television series, the doctor is asked whether his patient, a young army lieutenant, will regain the use of his legs. The doctor replies, "Contrary to public opinion, we doctors are not God. We have to find out about the future in the same way as everyone else." That statement by Hawkeye Pierce reflects the general idea of what it would mean to be God. In an episode of another longtime series, a group of nuns, having done a great deal to change a small Old West town, head out in their wagons, alone and unarmed, to cross dangerous Indian territory. One man, a thief who has reformed as the result of the influence of the nuns, comments, "How can those women set out alone through that Indian Territory? Why, God knows . . ." Then realizing the import of what he has said, he grabs his gun and runs to join them. I do not know whether the scriptwriters of *MASH* and *Gunsmoke* were Christians, but their characters articulate quite well what most people think of when they think of God. This idea can even be heard on financial programs. On *Wall Street Week with Fortune,* Jean-Marie Eveillard of First Eagle Funds responded to a question from Karen Gibbs on what might happen regarding a possible war with Iraq, the price of oil, and the effect on the stock market: "Nobody knows what is going to happen. Only God knows, and he ain't telling."

Most Christians have assumed this idea of God's knowing the future. To be sure, there were liberal circles where this might not be the case, but in those instances usually other, more basic attributes of God, such as unlimited power or independence of existence, were also not present. Divine foreknowledge was thought of as including free future actions of humans and other free moral agents. This simply was not challenged, in most cases. The question of how one's actions could be free if they were sufficiently definite to be foreknown was not ordinarily raised. While there had been occasional differences of opinion in the history of the church, they were rare and seldom if ever originated from someone who was basically orthodox in conviction.

Most of the discussion centered on the question of *how* God knows the future, and here a number of theories competed for preeminence. One of these was the idea of *simple foreknowledge,* that God simply "sees," as it were, the future. Generally this was allied with a view of God as atemporal, that is, as standing outside of time, so that he sees all points within time as if they were simultaneous with him. The events of history were likened to a parade. To someone watching the parade from a curb at ground level, the elements of the parade come past in succession. A person observing the parade from a high vantage point, however, is able to see the entire parade simultaneously. Thus, to an atemporal God, there is really no past, present, and future. All things simply are simultaneous.

A second conception is known as *middle knowledge.* On this basis, God knows not only all that will be, but all the other possibilities in every possible world. Out of these possibilities, he chooses to bring into existence one possible world, a world in which each person will freely choose to do what God has chosen for that person to do. This is free, but if God had wanted someone to do something differently, he would have actualized that other, slightly different world.

The final widely held view is Calvinism, which holds that God knows everything that will happen because he has *chosen* what is to occur and thus *brings it about* that it actually happens. This makes God's knowledge of the future a function of his will. God's action is not to be understood as some sort of external compulsion. He works in relationship to the person's will in such a way that the person chooses what God has decided. This is compatibilistic freedom, the freedom to do as one chooses; but that choosing is not pure spontaneity or ability to act in ways inconsistent with one's character. As it has sometimes been put, "We are free to do as we please, but not to please as we please." God not only knows each person completely but is involved in that person's being what he or she is.

In approximately the last fifteen years, however, a rather different view has begun to be announced. Several theologians, calling themselves "open theists," have begun to challenge the conventional view. Self-identified as evangelicals, these theologians have agreed that God has complete and perfect knowledge of the past and that he also has exhaustive and accurate knowledge of all present truth. He even knows part of the future. However, there are other future events that God does not know, and these are those that involve free human will. In most cases, God does not know what a given human is going to do until that person actually decides and acts.

These open theists contend that their view is not only in accord with Scripture, but is even more so than the traditional or classical view. They cite several types of texts in support of their view: some in which God claims to discover something he did not know until the action; some in which God expresses regret over his actions in the past; some in which God seems uncertain, saying, "Perhaps." Taking these texts seriously leads us, they assert, to the conclusion that God does not have exhaustive knowledge of future events.

Open theists also assert that this is not some lack in God, however. God knows everything that can be known. The future, however, is not something that has any reality; therefore, there is nothing there to be known. The difference between their view and the traditional view, they declare, is not over the nature of God at all, but over the nature of the future. The issue is not the doctrine of God but the doctrine of creation, of the type of world God has created.

Although the issue of God's knowledge relates especially to the question of freedom of the will, open theists affirm that their starting point is not there. Rather, the core issue and doctrine is *divine love.* The central attribute—in fact, perhaps the very essence of God—is love. God desires his human creatures to love him in return, and consequently he has created them as genuinely free beings, capable not only of loving and obeying him but also of doing the very opposite. He will not coerce his children. But since, if God knows what persons are going to do, it would not be possible for them to do otherwise, his decision to make them genuinely free creatures was also a decision to be unable to know in advance what they would do.

As we noted earlier, this has become a matter of concern for both pastors and laypersons. They are confused as to whether open theism is a departure from biblical teaching, or whether those who oppose it are creating disunity within the church.

More than a century ago, James Orr delivered a series of lectures on the history of dogma. By dogma, he meant critical reflection on the doctrines believed. Over its history, the church has deepened its understanding of its doctrines as challenges to the received view arose. These challenges, however, were generally to one specific doctrine, so theology has unfolded progressively through different doctrines. Orr observed that the order of development historically had followed the same order as the logical order in which the doctrines are customarily considered.[1] So, for example, the first doctrinal dispute and subsequent formulation concerned the doctrine of God, specifically, the Trinity. Then the nature of humanity was worked through in the Augustinian-Pelagian controversy. The nature and status of Jesus was a topic of concern for several centuries, finally coming to virtual completion in the seventh century. Next the work of Christ, specifically the atonement, took up the attention of theologians. The nature of grace and of salvation was the next item, particularly in the Reformation and following, as was the doctrine of the church. Orr believed that the one doctrine that had not previously been thoroughly discussed, which would then become the doctrine of the twentieth century, was the doctrine of the last things, or eschatology.[2]

---

[1] James Orr, *The Progress of Dogma* (Grand Rapids: Eerdmans, n.d.), 21.
[2] Ibid., 29–30.

Interestingly, we have had a revival of interest in the doctrine of God, the first of the doctrines to have been articulated. Yet this time it involves, not the question of God's triunity, but a different aspect of the doctrine, namely, his knowledge, and specifically, divine foreknowledge. It is probably because this has never really been decided definitively that it is now under consideration. It was not as if the issues posed by the open theists had never been raised before. As we shall see in the historical chapters, some of the very issues involved in this dispute, such as the compatibility of human freedom and divine knowledge of those acts, had been debated from very early in the church's history. This was always done by isolated individuals who fell outside the mainstream of the church's life and thought. Now, however, a sizable and articulate group of theologians is pressing the point. It is therefore likely that, as in the debates in the early church, the presentation of a divergent view will lead to a more complete consideration and a more detailed expression of the doctrine.

The doctrine of God proposed by open theists involves much more than just his knowledge. It involves such traditional doctrines as immutability, impassibility, and relationship to time. While open theists insist that these are intertwined, it is not on these other attributes that the dispute ordinarily takes place. In fact, as we shall see, traditional theists do not necessarily differ from open theists on these items as definitely as they do on divine foreknowledge. The issue is not really one of whether God is concerned about and responsive to humans. So, while our discussion will necessarily have to treat the relationship of these attributes to God's foreknowledge, that will not be a primary focus of attention.

Neither is the issue of this book which theory of foreknowledge is correct. Historically, as we noted above, there have been several different views of how God knows the future, but there has been basic agreement among advocates of simple foreknowledge, middle knowledge, and Calvinism that God does know the future. Similarly, the issue is not one of Calvinism versus Arminianism because both agree, as contrasted with open theism, that God does know the future exhaustively.

The issue, then, is the question that was posed regarding President Richard Nixon during the Watergate investigations: What did he know and when did he know it? The question has been repeated in numerous discussions of public figures, most recently Martha Stewart and President George W. Bush. Here the question is: How much does God know about human actions, and when does he know it? In other words, does he know them in advance of their occurrence? Does God know the future, and how much of it does he know?

This is not merely an academic question debated by scholars but unrelated to the life of the ordinary Christian. Important matters of Christian living are involved. When we pray, do our prayers make a difference, or is everything that will happen already determined? If God answers our prayers, is he wise enough to know what will be best in the future, or might he unknowingly grant something that turns out to be evil? Does God have a plan for our lives, and is it based on a knowledge of all that will happen? Are we really free, or are we simply doing what we are programmed to do? And, perhaps most seriously, does God knowingly allow or even cause things that he knows will lead to evil and suffering in the future, or is he unaware of such consequences? In several different ways, from opposite perspectives, the questions come down to this: Can we trust God?

CHapter 1

the biblical basis
of the open view

The starting point for discussion on any matter of evangelical theology must always be, What do the Scriptures say? Open theists have repeatedly described their view as biblically based. This can be seen in the subtitles of some of their most significant books on the subject.[1] They have complained that the traditional view is based on philosophy—or at least on a philosophically based reading of Scripture. They have also protested that their critics have not interacted with the texts to which the open theists have appealed. Similarly, although *Christianity Today* has called for both sides to give more attention to the relevant biblical passages, it is apparent that this concern is especially addressed to traditional theists: "Classical theists, please return to a more robustly biblical approach to talking about God. . . . But the biblical revelation, and not a suspect theological traditionalism, must be the starting point for fresh theological reflection in every generation. If classical theists fail to be biblical, they will surely lose the debate where it counts: in the churches."[2] We will turn first to those passages on which the open theists base their theology.

Repentance Passages

Genesis 6:6, 7. This is one of the most interesting and most frequently cited passages. The open theists are unanimous and

---

[1]Clark Pinnock, Richard Rice, John Sanders, William Hasker, and David Basinger, *The Openness of God: A Biblical Challenge to the Traditional Understanding of God* (Downers Grove, Ill.: InterVarsity, 1994); Gregory A. Boyd, *God of the Possible: A Biblical Introduction to the Open View of God* (Grand Rapids: Baker, 2000).

[2]"God vs. God," *Christianity Today* 44.2 (February 7, 2000):35.

emphatic in their interpretation of this passage. Here God surveys the evil thoughts and actions of humans and contemplates what he will do. The key expression comes in v. 6, where the text says that God "was grieved [or repented] that he had made man on the earth," and v. 7, where God says, "for I am grieved [or repent] that I have made them."

Boyd does very little real exegesis of the passage. He comments: "How can God feel this regret if he knew, even before he created them, that humans would degenerate to this exact condition? . . . Shouldn't we conclude that God *hoped* (but was not certain) things would not have turned out the way they did? And doesn't this imply that the future was not exhaustively settled in God's mind when he created humanity?"[3]

The major issue here is the meaning of the Hebrew word נִחָם *(niham)*. This is in the Niphal stem, the simple passive stem of the verb, which can also carry reflexive meaning.[4] In that stem, it can have several possible meanings, according to Brown, Driver, and Briggs:

1. *be sorry, moved to pity, have compassion,* for others.
2. *be sorry, rue, suffer grief, repent,* of one's own doings . . . for ill done to others.
3. *comfort oneself, be comforted:* . . . concerning the evil.
4. *be relieved, ease oneself,* by taking vengeance.[5]

The problem is determining which of these meanings the word bears in this passage. One of the most complete studies of this verb, by Parunak, says, "Unfortunately, with this root, much recent theology has flowed through a channel tracing it to the Arabic *naḥama* (the snorting of a horse), and thus to a sigh, whether of comfort or pain."[6] The whole etymological approach has been seriously called into question, however, by the work of James Barr and others. More hopeful is attempting to determine the meaning by semantic indicators such as parallelism, context, and idiom. Parunak finds the meaning of the verb in this passage to be "to suffer emotional

[3]Gregory A. Boyd, "The Open-Theism View," *Divine Foreknowledge: Four Views,* ed. James K. Beilby and Paul R. Eddy (Downers Grove, Ill.: InterVarsity, 2001), 26.
[4]A. B. Davidson, *An Introductory Hebrew Grammar* (Edinburgh: T. & T. Clark, 1951), 90.
[5]Francis Brown, S. R. Driver, and Charles A. Briggs, *A Hebrew and English Lexicon of the Old Testament* (Oxford: Clarendon Press, 1955), 637.
[6]H. Van Dyke Parunak, "A Semantic Survey of *NHM,*" *Biblica,* vol. 56, no. 4 (1975), 513.

pain." He finds that the parallelism is particularly significant here, so that it is to be understood as equivalent to the latter part of the verse, "he was grieved at his heart."[7] In terms of idiom, the presence of *kî* here, as in Judg. 21:15, confirms this classification.

Some commentators see a parallel here with Lamech's statement in Gen. 5:29, which shares three words, *niham,* *ᶜāśāh,* and *ᶜāṣaḇ,* with this verse. Wenham speaks of "the ironic punning of the Hebrew text."[8] This parallelism suggests that the meaning of *comfort* in that passage also applies here, but it should be observed that *naham* there is in the Piel (simple active intensive stem). Westermann suggests that the parallelism between אֶל־לִבּוֹ (*ʾel-libbô*) in v. 6 and לְבּוֹ (*libbô*) in v. 5 means that just as God is depicted anthropomorphically in v. 5, where he "sees" human evil, so the statement about him here "shows that this human way of speaking is used deliberately of God."[9] Matthews notes not only the parallel between the two verbs in v. 6 but also the similarity to the painful consequences of sin for the man and woman in 3:16–17 and 5:29. Thus, here God also experiences the painful consequences of the sin of the humans.[10] Matthews maintains that "Genesis 6:6–7 is describing the emotional anguish of God; our verse does not present an abstract statement about God's decision making. This would be altogether out of place for the intention of the passage, which depicts God as wronged by the presumptuous sin of humanity. Moreover, the parameters of this verse have been dictated by the author's intention to imitate 5:29 with its distinctive vocabulary and mood."[11]

1 Samuel 15:11, 35. Here is a statement much like that in Gen. 6:6, in which the Lord says that he is grieved, in this case because he has made Saul king of Israel and Saul has been disobedient. Boyd renders this as "I *regret* that I made Saul king, for he has turned back from following me." He feels that the point is reiterated for emphasis in v. 35.[12]

[7]Ibid., 519.
[8]Gordon J. Wenham, *Word Biblical Commentary,* Vol. 1, *Genesis 1–15* (Waco, Tex.: Word, 1987), 144.
[9]Claus Westermann, *Genesis 1–11* (Minneapolis: Augsburg, 1984), 410.
[10]Kenneth A. Matthews, *The New American Commentary,* Vol. 1A, *Genesis 1–11:26* (Nashville: Broadman and Holman, 1996), 341.
[11]Ibid., 342.
[12]Boyd, *God of the Possible,* 56.

Once again we face the issue of how to translate *niḥam*. Bergen sees definite parallels between this verse and Gen. 6:7, not only in the lexical linkage involving this word but also in the clause and phrase similarities: "The degree of similarity suggests that the writer was making a deliberate connection between the Genesis and Samuel narratives. Certainly similarities exist between the outcomes of the stories."[13] Just as the wickedness of humanity caused God pain and he then destroyed the population but raised up Noah, so here Saul's disobedience caused God pain but led to his raising up David to take his place. The expression *kî* appears again here, as it did in Gen. 6.

One of the problems with the interpretation of vv. 11 and 35 is the presence of v. 29, where the same verb appears regarding God, but the text states that he does not repent. The contradiction requires some explanation or resolution. Fretheim observes that both v. 29 and the similar verse in Num. 23:19 are speaking of God's commitment to David, the latter being a foreshadowing of the relationship that will prevail between them.[14] While Jehovah will never turn from that commitment, vv. 11 and 35 speak of his change of mind with respect to his establishment of Saul as king. Interestingly, however, this is certainly not made explicit in either 1 Sam. 15:29 or Num. 23:19.

In both vv. 11 and 35 it could be argued that the context favors the idea of regret or repenting or changing of the divine mind, for God then goes on to say that he is going to remove Saul from his position. This certainly contrasts with what he has previously done. Yet the arguments from parallelism and idiom cited earlier seem to favor the meaning simply of emotional pain.

Perhaps the most we can say from a direct exegetical treatment of these passages is that they teach that God experiences emotional pain as a result of his having created humans and put certain ones of them in positions of leadership. Whether they teach that God changes his mind, and if so,

[13]Robert D. Bergen, *The New American Commentary*, Vol. 7, *1, 2 Samuel* (Nashville: Broadman and Holman, 1996), 170.
[14]Terence Fretheim, "Divine Foreknowledge, Divine Constancy, and the Rejection of Saul's Kingship," *Catholic Biblical Quarterly* 47 (1985): 595–602.

whether this entails the idea that God must not have known antecedently what was to take place, remains to be decided.

There are at least two possible interpretations of these passages. One is that God, not knowing what would happen when he created humans and when he established Saul as king, was then disappointed and pained when these did not act as God desired them to. He consequently regretted his action, recognizing that it was a mistake, and acted to correct the consequences of his earlier actions. That could have been the case only if God did not have perfect foreknowledge of these human actions. This is the interpretation favored by open theists.

> We must wonder how the Lord could truly experience regret for making Saul king if he was absolutely certain that Saul would act the way he did. Could God genuinely confess, "I regret that I made Saul king" if he could in the same breath also confess, "I was certain of what Saul would do when I made him king"? I do not see how. Could I genuinely regret, say, purchasing a car because it turned out to run poorly if in fact the car was running exactly as I knew it would when I purchased it? Common sense tells us that we can only regret a decision we made if the decision resulted in an outcome other than what we expected or hoped for when the decision was made.[15]

It should be observed that Boyd's analogy is not completely fitting, since this would require that Saul had actually displayed that behavior prior to his being chosen, rather than God's knowing that he would later display it. Nonetheless, the structure of the open theist argument for limited foreknowledge on the basis of these passages is something like this:

1. *niham* here means "to relent or change one's mind or repent."
2. One can only repent of that which one did not know in advance.
3. Consequently, the attribution of *niham* to God here entails that he did not know in advance what the human race (Gen. 6) or Saul (1 Sam. 15) would do.

---

[15]Boyd, *God of the Possible*, 56.

Two issues need to be raised, however. One is whether the verb should carry the meaning of "repent" here. On the basis of the evidence we have cited, it is questionable whether anything more than simply God's feeling pain should be attributed to these statements. The other question, however, is whether the feeling of such pain, occasioned by God's having brought these persons into these positions, implies a surprise or something that he did not know would occur.

Is it the case that if I know that something unpleasant will occur, I do not feel pain when it occurs? If we are to appeal to common sense, as Boyd does, it seems that this is not necessarily the case. For example, one may know that one's parents will someday die and that in all likelihood their deaths will precede one's own, yet grieve and feel deep pain when they actually occur. Similarly, an athlete may choose a training regimen that he or she knows will be painful and exhausting, but that prior knowledge does not diminish the subsequent pain. Knowing that one will experience a particular emotion and actually experiencing it are not the same thing.

CHANGE OF MIND PASSAGES

Genesis 18:20–33. In this passage Jehovah declares his intention to destroy the wicked cities of Sodom and Gomorrah, and nothing conditional is mentioned in his statement. Abraham asks him whether he would destroy the city if fifty righteous people can be found there, and Jehovah responds that he will not. Abraham then proceeds to negotiate further: forty-five, forty, all the way down to ten. This seems to be a clear case of God's changing his mind in response to a human request. Sanders comments on this passage: "The divine decision was yet open, and God invited Abraham into the decision-making process. God chooses not to exercise judgment without the human input of this man he trusts. In cases such as this, it is plain that God considers others as having something significant to say."[16] Keil and Delitzsch summarize well the most obvious explanation of the incident:

> This would indeed be neither permissible nor possible, had not God, by
> virtue of the mysterious interlacing of necessity and freedom in His nature
> and operations, granted a power to the prayer of faith, to which He consents

[16]John Sanders, *The God Who Risks: A Theology of Providence* (Downers Grove, Ill.: InterVarsity, 1998), 53.

to yield; had He not, by virtue of His absoluteness, which is anything but blind necessity, placed Himself in such a relation to men, that He not merely works upon them by means of His grace, but allows them to work upon Him by means of their faith; had He not interwoven the life of the free creature into His own absolute life, and accorded to a created personality the right to assert itself in faith, in distinction from His own.[17]

Presumably, had God known what Abraham was about to do in this situation, it would have affected his intention from the start. This change therefore suggests that the future was open, and God did not take that into account

There is, however, another possible interpretation. This would be that God did not really change his mind. He simply agreed that if X number of righteous persons could be found, he would not execute his intended destruction. Knowing that there were not such righteous persons, he knew from the beginning that he would not end up sparing the city. This would be the case, despite his foreknowing that Abraham would intercede for the city. Abraham's failure to find such was vindication of God's act of destroying the city.

2 Kings 20:1–20. In this passage, King Hezekiah is ill and anticipates dying. He reminds God of his past faithfulness to God, and God decides to increase his life by fifteen years. This was a key passage leading Boyd to the open theist position.[18] It seems clearly to represent a change in what God is going to do because in v. 1 Hezekiah is told to prepare himself, since he will not recover from the illness and will die. The original declaration would not have been made if God knew that Hezekiah would cry out as he did.

Here again, however, a feature of the narrative presents a problem for the open theist position. Bruce Ware in particular points out that Jehovah does not just *tell* Hezekiah that he will extend his life. He is much more specific: his life will be extended *by fifteen years.* Ware says:

Does it not seem a bit odd that this favorite text of open theists, which purportedly demonstrates that God does not know the future and so

---

[17]C. F. Keil and F. Delitzsch, *Biblical Commentary on the Old Testament,* Vol. 1, *The Pentateuch* (Grand Rapids: Eerdmans, 1956), 231–32.
[18]Boyd, *God of the Possible,* 8.

changes his mind when Hezekiah prays, also shows that God *knows precisely and exactly how much longer Hezekiah will live?* On openness grounds, how could God know this? Over a fifteen-year time span, the contingencies are staggering! The number of future freewill choices, made by Hezekiah and by innumerable others, that relate to Hezekiah's life and well-being, none of which God knows (in the openness view), *is enormous.*[19]

GOD TESTS PEOPLE

<u>*Genesis 22:1–19,*</u> Here is one of the most commonly cited passages. In it we are told that God tested Abraham (v. 1), although Abraham is not told that this is a test. Abraham is asked to sacrifice his son Isaac and proceeds to do so, but he is stopped by the angel of the Lord, who says, "Do not lay a hand on the boy. Do not do anything to him. Now I know that you fear God, because you have not withheld from me your son, your only son" (v. 12). This seems to be a clear case of God not knowing what Abraham would do until the test was complete. Boyd says of this text, "The verse clearly says that it was *because* Abraham did what he did that the Lord *now* knew he was a faithful covenant partner. The verse has no clear meaning if God was certain that Abraham would fear him before he offered up his son."[20] Similarly, Sanders comments, "If one presupposes that God already 'knew' the results of the test beforehand, then the text is at least poorly worded and at most simply false."[21]

Nothing in the text suggests that this was for Abraham's benefit so that he might know that he loved God this much. There also is nothing here to suggest that God already knew the outcome of the test. Taken at face value, this text certainly seems to teach that God used this test to discover something that he did not know, that he could not be sure that Abraham would indeed obey his command.

Note, however, exactly what is said here. God does not say, "Now I know what you would do in such a situation." Rather, he says, "Now I know that you fear me." While this may seem to be a small matter of difference,

---

[19]Bruce A. Ware, *God's Lesser Glory: The Diminished God of Open Theism* (Wheaton, Ill.: Crossway, 2000), 95–96.
[20]Boyd, *God of the Possible,* 64.
[21]Sanders, *The God Who Risks,* 52.

it will be worth bearing in mind. Apparently, Jehovah did not simply not know what Abraham would do. If one interprets this text in a literal fashion, then one has also established that, at least in this case, Jehovah did not really know the heart of the person involved. The problem comes from the fact that the open theists believe that God knows persons completely, all of the personality and character of each person, all of the thoughts of the heart. It is only on this basis that God is able to make the predictions he does of what persons will do.

Boyd also appeals to 2 Chron. 32:31. Here, according to the text, "God left him [Hezekiah] to test him and to know everything that was in his heart." Boyd comments, "Again, if God eternally knew how Hezekiah would respond to him, God couldn't have *really* been testing him in order to gain this knowledge. Unfortunately for the classical view, however, *this is exactly what the text says.*"[22] Boyd does not, however, call attention to the fact that the text says God's testing was to "know everything that was in his heart." If the passage is to be interpreted literally, then the entire passage must be taken so, and it teaches that God did not know the heart of Hezekiah any more than he did that of Abraham. This teaching will need to be retained when further theological explanation is given.

Testing of Israel. In several passages this action of testing is extended to the entire covenant nation of Israel. In Deut. 8:2, Moses says, "Remember how the LORD your God led you all the way in the desert these forty years, to humble you and to test you in order to know what was in your heart, whether or not you would keep his commands." Similarly, in Deut. 13:3, the people of Israel are warned that if a prophet prophesies things that come to pass but he then asks the people to follow a false god, they are not to follow him because "the LORD your God is testing you to find out whether you love him with all your heart and with all your soul." Also in Judg. 3:4, God is said to have left Israel's enemies alone, to "test the Israelites to see whether they would obey the LORD's commands, which he had given their forefathers through Moses."

Certainly these passages, like the Abraham passage, seem to indicate that the test had to be performed so that Jehovah could know what they

---

[22]Boyd, "The Open-Theism View," 32.

would do, implying that he did not know what they would do until the moment actually came. Boyd, as usual, puts the case quite directly: "How are these passages to be reconciled with the classical assumption that God never 'really' comes to know anything, for supposedly his knowledge is eternally settled? These verses can only be accepted straightforwardly if we accept that God and humans face a partly open future."[23]

There are other ways of reading these texts. God had found it necessary to humble them for their lack of love for him and obedience to him. They might have complained about God's unjustness in doing this. Here he was publicly revealing what their true hearts and attitudes were. The justice of any punishment that might come would be clear. Keil and Delitzsch describe the Deut. 8 passage as a means by which God sought to prevent them from "falling into pride and forgetfulness of God, when enjoying the abundant productions of that land." Moses was here reminding them of how God had trained them to obey. So he recalls for them this humbling and testing. Keil and Delitzsch comment, "נִסָּה , to prove, by placing them in such positions in life as would drive them to reveal what was in their heart, viz., whether they believed in the omnipotence, love, and righteousness of God, or not."[24]

Adam Clarke, sometimes appealed to as a commentator who held a view similar to that of the open theists, gives a somewhat similar interpretation: "*The Lord your God proveth you.* God permits such impostors to arise to try the faith of his followers, and to put their religious experience to the test; for he who experimentally knows God cannot be drawn away after idols. He who has no experimental knowledge of God, may believe any thing. Experience of the truths contained in the word of God can alone preserve any man from Deism, or a false religion."[25]

Keil and Delitzsch interpret the Judg. 3 passage by calling attention to the fact that this testing involved the men who had not previously gone to war. So they comment,

---

[23]Ibid.

[24]C. F. Keil and F. Delitzsch, *Biblical Commentary on the Old Testament,* Vol. 3, *The Pentateuch* (Grand Rapids: Eerdmans, 1956), 330.

[25]Adam Clarke, *Commentary on the Holy Bible*. Abridged from the original six-volume work by Ralph Earle (Grand Rapids: Baker, 1967), 214.

In this respect, learning war, *i.e.*, learning how the congregation of the Lord was to fight against the enemies of God and of His kingdom, was one of the means appointed by God to tempt Israel, or prove whether it would listen to the commandments of God (v. 4), or would walk in the ways of the Lord. If Israel should so learn to war, it would learn at the same time to keep the commandments of God. But both of these were necessary for the people of God. For just as the realization of the blessings promised to the nation in the covenant depended upon its hearkening to the voice of the Lord, so the conflicts appointed for it were also necessary, just as much for the purification of the sinful nation, as for the perpetuation and growth of the kingdom of God upon the earth.[26]

Clarke comments, "*That . . . Israel might know, to teach them war*— This was another reason why the Canaanites were left in the land, that the Israelites might not forget military discipline, but habituate themselves to the use of arms, that they might always be able to defend themselves against their foes. Had they been faithful to God, they would have had no need of learning the art of war; but now arms became a sort of necessary substitute for that spiritual strength which had departed from them."[27]

FAILED PROPHECIES

If God indeed knows the future and inspires prophets to declare this, then those prophecies should certainly come to pass. Indeed, that was the test of the genuineness of a prophet and, as we shall see in the following chapter, a major distinguishing mark of the true God in Isa. 41–48. If, then, some of these claimed prophecies never were fulfilled, that would certainly be a telling consideration against the traditional view of foreknowledge.

Genesis 37:9–11. John Sanders has especially called attention to such phenomena. Of Joseph's dream he says, "But neither Jacob nor the brothers believe they have to do what the dream describes (37:8, 10; Joseph's parents never do bow down to him)."[28] Sanders does not offer

---

[26]C. F. Keil and Franz Delitzsch, *Biblical Commentary on the Old Testament: Joshua, Judges, Ruth* (Grand Rapids: Eerdmans, 1950) 274–75.
[27]Clarke, *Commentary on the Holy Bible*, 268.
[28]Sanders, *The God Who Risks*, 75.

any documentation for this statement, however. Presumably, he is arguing from the silence of the biblical text about any such parental subjugation. There is quite a difference, however, in saying that the Bible does not *say* that they bowed down, and in saying that they did *not* bow down. Since such an act would presumably have occurred after Joseph was revealed as the second in command in Egypt, it does seem particularly unlikely that his mother would have personally bowed down to him, since she was dead by that time. It is strange, however, that Sanders, who makes much of the Hebrew culture, does not consider the fact that in that culture, a husband could be assumed to act on behalf of his wife. If a husband bowed down to someone, it would be unheard of for his wife to refuse to do so. She would be considered to have done so in his act. This could be the case even if she were now deceased. So Sanders's contention regarding this prophecy does not carry much weight.

Sanders cites two examples of prophecies not coming to pass: Jonah's prophecy against Nineveh, and the death of Hezekiah in 2 Kings 20. These, however, are correctly understood as conditional in nature. The cases where the fulfillment is not exactly as prophesied are more significant.

One of these is in Acts 21:11, where Agabus prophesied that the Jews would bind Paul and hand him over to the Gentiles. This, Sanders claims, did not come to pass because "actually, the Roman authorities rescued Paul from the mob and they, not the Jewish authorities, bound him."[29] Apparently Sanders bases this assertion on the statement in v. 33, "The commander [of the Roman troops] came up and arrested him and ordered him to be bound with two chains." This, however, assumes that the Jews who had seized Paul and were beating him had not bound him (with something other than chains) and that Agabus's prophecy requires that the Jews initiate the turning over of Paul to the Romans. Actually, Agabus's words do not require either of these.

---

[29]Ibid., 296, n. 134. Sanders does concede, "Of course, one could argue that the prediction did come true in a 'general' sense. I agree, but those who affirm divine foreknowledge are the ones using such prophecies to claim God knows the future in detail. If so, then either God or the prophet cannot get the details straight." In fairness, it should be observed that those who hold that God possesses exhaustive divine foreknowledge do not insist that God necessarily makes every one of the prophecies specific in the maximum degree.

Sanders's other example of this type is Gen. 27:27–40, where he says, "Jacob's blessing is qualified by Esau's blessing."[30] Apparently Sanders has in mind v. 29, where Isaac says to Jacob, "Be lord over your brothers, and may the sons of your mother bow down to you," and v. 40, where he tells Esau, "You will live by the sword and you will serve your brother. But when you grow restless, you will throw his yoke from off your neck." Actually, the second blessing, which includes "you will serve your brother," seems to confirm the first. The second statement, "you will throw his yoke from off your neck," contradicts the first only if the first is thought of as "you will be lord over your brother forever." If one wishes to take the prophecies as completely literal and detailed, then one should find the contradiction as being, instead, in the plural "sons" and "brothers." Here again, however, it appears that the interpretation is a bit forced. Sanders comments, "One would think that a God with foreknowledge would get such details straight."[31]

Later in the book, Sanders seems to take back some of the force of this argument when he says, "Strictly speaking, God would make a mistake if he declared infallibly that something would come to pass and it did not."[32] This specification sounds like the Roman Catholic statement that papal pronouncements are only infallible if they are made ex cathedra in matters of faith and practice. He does add, "Using the term more loosely, we might say that God would be mistaken if he believed that X would happen (for example, Israel in Jeremiah's day would come to love him), and in fact, X does not come about. In this sense the Bible does attribute some mistakes to God."[33]

Boyd, however, is not willing to call these mistakes. In fact, he chides Ware for accusing open theists of holding that God makes mistakes and says of Jer. 3:6–7, 19–20, "Passages such as these need not imply that God was caught off guard as though he didn't anticipate the *possibility* of the improbable. Nor do they imply that God was mistaken in thinking people would do one thing when it turns out they did another."[34] In fact, he says

---

[30]Ibid., 75.
[31]Ibid.
[32]Ibid., 132.
[33]Ibid.
[34]Boyd, *Satan and the Problem of Evil,* 101.

that "only a most unsympathetic reading of Jeremiah's and Isaiah's language—and of the open theists who simply repeat it—would conclude that this language entails that God holds false beliefs."[35] A more sympathetic reading, says Boyd, would be this:

> When God says he "thought" or "expected" something would take place that did not take place, he is simply reflecting his perfect knowledge of probabilities. When the improbable happens, as sometimes is the case with free agents, God genuinely says he "thought" or "expected" the more probable would happen. Because God is infinitely intelligent, we cannot conceive of God being altogether shocked, as though he did not perfectly anticipate and prepare for this very improbability (as much as if it was a certainty from all eternity). But *relative to the probabilities of the situation,* the outcome was surprising [*viz.* improbable].[36]

The problem with this approach is that there is nothing in the text that suggests that God was making a probability statement. It appears that Boyd has significantly departed from his principle of taking a text "at face value" or in "its plain sense" for the sake of avoiding the implications of his hermeneutic.

GOD'S APPARENT IGNORANCE ABOUT THE FUTURE

Boyd proposes that a further indication of a partially open future is that God sometimes expresses uncertainty about it by asking questions. He asks Moses, "How long will these people treat me with contempt? How long will they refuse to believe in me, in spite of all the miraculous signs I have performed among them?" (Num. 14:11). God also asks Hosea, "How long will they be incapable of purity?" (Hos. 8:5). Boyd also mentions 1 Kings 22:20 without developing it further: "And the LORD said, 'Who will entice Ahab into attacking Ramoth Gilead and going to his death there?'"[37]

Boyd acknowledges that some will treat these as rhetorical questions, much like Gen. 3:8 and 9, where God asks Adam and Eve where they are. Yet, he says, "This is a possible interpretation, but not a necessary one. Unlike

---

[35]Gregory Boyd, "Christian Love and Academic Dialogue," *Journal of the Evangelical Theological Society* 45.2 (June 2002): 237.
[36]Ibid.
[37]Boyd, *God of the Possible,* 58–59.

God's question about location in Genesis, there is nothing in these texts or in the whole of Scripture that requires these questions to be rhetorical. Moreover, the fact that the Lord continued for centuries, with much frustration, to try to get the Israelites not to 'despise' him and to be 'innocent' suggests that the wonder expressed in these questions was genuine. The duration of the Israelites' stubbornness was truly an open issue."[38]

Is this an accurate assessment of the comparative texts, however? Speech-act theory may assist us here. In general, a rhetorical question is considered to be one to which no answer is expected. In the case of "Adam, where are you?" (Gen. 3) there could be an answer because Adam knew where he was. In the case of Num. 14:11 and Hos. 8:5, there could be no answer, because they did not know when they would change. Rather than calling for a verbal answer, these seem to call for a response of action. It is something like a question, "Did you leave that door open?" which is actually a suggestion that the person addressed close the door. In the case of 1 Kings 22:20, this appears rather clearly to be a request, not for information but for a volunteer. It is interesting that none of the other open theists cite this type of textual consideration and that Boyd does not include this argument in his later essay in *Divine Foreknowledge*. It may be that the open theists have concluded that this is not a credible argument.

One other instance of this type is Jehovah's statement in Jer. 7:31: "They have built the high places of Topheth in the Valley of Ben Hinnom to burn their sons and daughters in the fire—something I did not command, nor did it enter my mind." Here, according to Boyd, is a case of God's being unable to know what was to happen. "However we understand the phrase 'nor did it enter my mind,'" he says, "it would at the very least seem to preclude the possibility that the Israelites' idolatrous behavior was eternally certain in God's mind. If the classical view is correct, we have to be willing to accept that God could in one breath say that the Israelites' behavior 'did not enter my mind,' although their behavior 'was eternally in my mind.' If this is not a contradiction, what is?"[39]

---

[38]Ibid., 59.
[39]Ibid., 61–62.

It is quite possible to take this statement in a different fashion. This probably should be understood, not as a declarative sentence, but as an expression of rebuke. When one says, "I never thought you would do that!" it often is a means of indicating how "unthinkable" the action is. In fact, an unthinkable action is usually understood, not as literally impossible to think, but as something that is so outrageous or scandalous that one would not seriously consider doing it.

Those who hold the traditional view point out another problem with the open theists' interpretation of this passage. The open theists, and especially Boyd, hold that God knows all the possibilities that may occur but does not know which of these will actually come to pass. So he says, in the analogy of the chess master, "This chess master does not foreknow exactly what moves her opponent *will* make, but she perfectly anticipates all the moves her opponent *might* make. And on the basis of this superior intelligence, she is confident of victory."[40]

Traditional theists have pointed out the inconsistency of this approach. Ware puts it clearly: "First, since open theists affirm God's awareness of all possibilities (i.e., omniscience is defined as God's comprehensive knowledge of everything past and present, of everything logically entailed from the past or present, and of all possible states of affairs), it cannot literally be the case that 'it never entered God's mind' that Israel would behave as she did. God has known from eternity that this could happen, even on openness criteria."[41]

FRUSTRATION STATEMENTS

Another type of Scripture claimed by Boyd is the situations in which God expresses or experiences frustration. One of these is Ezek. 22:30–31, where Jehovah says, "I sought for anyone among them who would repair the wall and stand in the breach before me on behalf of the land, so that I would not destroy it; but I found no one. Therefore I have poured out my indignation upon them" (NRSV). Now, comments Boyd, "It is difficult to understand how God could have sincerely 'sought for' someone to

---

[40]Boyd, "The Open-Theism View," 45.
[41]Ware, *God's Lesser Glory*, 78.

intercede if he had been certain all along that there would be no one, as the classical view of foreknowledge must contend."[42] If he had, would one consider him all wise for so doing?

An even more serious variety of this problem is to be found in the fact that God has created persons who, on the classical view, he knew would not be saved. It is clear from biblical statements such as 2 Peter 3:9 that God is "not wanting anyone to perish, but everyone to come to repentance." How then can it be that he creates some who he knows will freely choose to reject his offer of grace? Boyd comments, "Why would God strive to the point of frustration to get people to do what he was certain they would never do before they were even born: namely, believe in him? Doesn't God's sincere effort to get all people to believe in him imply that it is not a foregone conclusion to God that certain people would *not* believe in him when he created them? Indeed, doesn't the fact that the Lord *delays* his return imply that neither the date of his return nor the identities of who will and will not believe are settled in God's mind ahead of time?"[43]

In general, the classical view has not offered much response to this interpretation. Keil finds hints that this may not be a literal searching in Ezek. 22:

> For although וָאֶשְׁפֹּךְ [*wā'ešpōk*] expresses the consequence of Jehovah's seeking a righteous man and not finding one, it by no means follows from the occurrence of the preterite מָצָאתִי [*māṣā'tî*] that וָאֶשְׁפֹּךְ [*wā'ešpōk*] is also a preterite. וָאֶשְׁפֹּךְ [*wā'ešpōk*] is simply connected with וָאֲבַקֵּשׁ [*wā'ăbaqqēš*] as a consequence; and in both verbs the *Vav consec.* expresses the sequence of thought, and not of time. The seeking, therefore, with the result of not having found, cannot be understood in a chronological sense, *i.e.*, as an event belonging to the past, for the simple reason that the preceding words do not record the chronological order of events. It merely depicts the existing moral condition of the people, and v. 30 sums up the result of the description in the thought that there was no one to be found who could enter in the gap before God. Consequently, we cannot determine from the imperfect with *Vav consec.* either

---

[42]Boyd, "The Open-Theism View," 28.
[43]Ibid., 29.

the time of the seeking and not finding, or that of the pouring out of the wrath.[44]

For the most part, the traditional view has taken this statement as an anthropomorphism, simply expressing the idea that there was no one willing to intercede the way Abraham and Moses had done.

The creation of those God knows will reject him is a larger issue. On this model, God wills to create persons, even though he knows they will not exercise saving faith. We should draw a distinction between God's desire or preference and his actual willing. In reality, all of us do things like this. We may choose to do something that we do not really want or wish to do, but we will to do it nonetheless. This is what moral character involves. "Frustration" is a term chosen by Boyd, but it is not necessarily an appropriate term. If God were incapable of accomplishing something that he wills to do, that would be frustration, and that would be more applicable to God as Boyd conceives him than as traditional theism does.

CONDITIONAL STATEMENTS

Another type of argument advanced by open theists is that God sometimes speaks of future actions in a conditional or uncertain fashion, such as that "they may do such and such." Certainly, these must indicate uncertainty on God's part.

Exodus 4:5–8. Initially, God tells Moses that the elders will listen to his voice (Ex. 3:18). Moses, however, has some doubts, and asks, "What if they do not believe me or listen to me?" (Ex. 4:1). Boyd suggests that Moses must not believe in the classical view of divine foreknowledge or he would not question God's statement, and then he says: "God's response to him suggests that God doesn't hold to this view of foreknowledge either."[45] Jehovah performs a miracle "so that they may believe that the LORD . . . has appeared to you" (4:5). When this does not satisfy Moses, God performs a second and suggests even a third miracle, saying, "If they will not

---

[44]Carl Friedrich Keil, *Biblical Commentary on the Prophecies of Ezekiel* (Grand Rapids: Eerdmans, 1950), 320.
[45]Boyd, *God of the Possible,* 67.

believe you or heed the first sign, they may believe the second sign" (v. 8, NRSV) and then, "If they will not believe even these two signs or heed you, you shall take some water from the Nile and pour it on the dry ground; and the water that you shall take from the Nile will become blood on the dry ground" (v. 9, NRSV). Boyd's comment on the second sign is, "How can the Lord say, 'they *may* believe'? Isn't the future behavior of the elders a matter of certainty for the Lord? Apparently not." He adds, regarding the third sign, "If the future is exhaustively settled, God would of course have known exactly how many miracles, if any, it would take to get the elders to believe Moses. In that case, the meaning of the words he chose ('may,' 'if') could not be sincere. If we believe that God speaks straightforwardly, however, it seems he did not foreknow with certainty exactly how many miracles it would take to get the elders of Israel to believe Moses."[46] Boyd holds that God knew the ultimate outcome but not the exact number of miracles it would take to accomplish that outcome.[47]

Boyd cites several other examples of this type, including Ex. 13:17; Ezek. 12:3; Jer. 26:3 and 19. The most interesting, however, is Jesus' prayer in the Garden of Gethsemane. Jesus prayed, "My Father, if it is possible, let this cup pass from me" (Matt. 26:39, NRSV). Boyd comments: "Jesus' prayer presupposes that divine plans and possible future events are, in principle, alterable. In short, Jesus' prayer evidences the truth that the future is at least partly open, even if his own fate was not."[48]

Is there another way of viewing these seemingly hypothetical passages? In the case of the Old Testament passages, much rests on the nature of Hebrew conditional sentences. The Hebrew language does not have the finely developed distinctions of classes of conditionals that Greek has. Nonetheless, as A. B. Davidson puts it, "The verbal forms vary according as the mind presents to itself the condition as fulfilled and actual (perf.) or to be fulfilled, and merely possible (impf.)."[49] The type of sentence that might resolve the problem here would be a conditional assuming the truth of the supposition—in other words, "If they do not believe you (and they

---

[46]Ibid.
[47]Ibid., 67–68.
[48]Ibid., 71.
[49]A. B. Davidson, *Hebrew Syntax,* 3rd ed. (Edinburgh: T. & T. Clark, 1902), 175.

will not)." Such a type of conditional would be one in which "the mind may conceive or imagine the condition as realised and actual."[50] In such a case, the protasis, or if-clause, would be in the perfect, and the apodosis, or then-clause, would be in the perfect or the simple imperfect.[51] This is not the case in Ex. 4:8, however, since the conditional clause is in the imperfect and the apodosis, or conclusion clause, is in the perfect. This is the type of conditional described by Davidson as "when the supposition expresses a real contingency of any degree of possibility," and is the most common form of that.[52] Thus, Boyd can legitimately appeal to this passage in support of his thesis. Boyd's suggestion that Moses apparently did not hold to the classical view is not relevant, however, for Moses' words are not always to be taken as divinely inspired and authoritative. Here, as in several other places, Moses' lack of trust in God and perhaps even lack of complete understanding of God is what we would expect from a sinful human being.

The Ex. 13:17 text does not seem to serve well the use to which Boyd puts it. This is a "lest" passage, involving the conjunction פֶּן־ (pen-), which always occurs with the makkeph.[53] This is actually an instrumental construction, which one could render "so that." Thus, this verse could be translated, "so that they do not repent." This does not require that God did not know what they would do. It could well be a case of his knowing that they would relent or change their minds (which does seem to be the meaning of the Niphal of נָחַם [niham] here), so he took that action to prevent it.

More promising for Boyd's use is Ezek. 12:3. Here the word is אוּלַי (ʾûlay), which is an adverb usually translated "perhaps." Ordinarily it expresses hope, but it can also express a fear or a doubt and can even be used in mockery, as in Isa. 47:12 and Jer. 51:8. It seems likely that here it expresses genuine contingency. The Jer. 26:3 text also involves this same word, אוּלַי (ʾûlay); consequently, it implies this same contingency.

Ware suggests that there may be another reason why God puts this in this modal fashion: "Although he knows what will occur, he may be

[50]Ibid., 177.
[51]Ibid.
[52]Ibid., 176.
[53]Brown, Driver, and Briggs, *Hebrew and English Lexicon,* 814.

purposely withholding this information from others. Now, granted, God sometimes tells people precisely what will occur (as stated above). But in other cases God may think it best that they do not know." For example, in the case of Moses and the response to the divine signs, God could have told Moses at exactly what point the people would believe. But, says Ware, "Had God said this to Moses, Moses would not have had to trust God through the whole experience in the same way he did, not knowing how the people might respond. So, the 'perhapses' and 'maybes' may be for our sake; they do not necessarily indicate that God does not know."[54]

When we come to Jesus' prayer in the Garden of Gethsemane, however, we face a rather different situation. In Matthew's account, there are actually three prayers. In the first, "he fell with his face to the ground and prayed, 'My Father, if it is possible, may this cup be taken from me. Yet not as I will, but as you will'" (26:39). In the second, v. 42, Jesus prays, "My Father, if it is not possible for this cup to be taken away unless I drink it, may your will be done." The third, v. 44, says simply that "he prayed the third time, saying the same thing." In Mark 14:35–36, we are told, "Going a little farther, he fell to the ground and prayed that if possible the hour might pass from him. '*Abba*, Father,' he said, 'everything is possible for you. Take this cup from me. Yet not what I will, but what you will.'" Verse 39 says that "he prayed the same thing." In Luke, the situation is given an interpretation. Only one prayer is mentioned, and here Jesus says, "'Father, if you are willing, take this cup from me; yet not my will, but yours be done" (Luke 22:42). While one might argue on the basis of Luke that the question was not about possibility but about divine willingness, the implication is still the same: Jesus did not seem to regard the future as fixed.

Looking at this somewhat differently, however, one might say that Jesus was not questioning whether what was to happen was certain but only what that will was. If God had already determined that his plan involved Jesus dying, then in a sense it was not "possible" for him not to. We should bear in mind, however, that this was part of Jesus' period of earthly incarnation, during which he said of his second coming, "No one knows about that day or hour, not even the angels in heaven, nor the Son, but only the Father"

---

[54]Ware, *God's Lesser Glory*, 81.

(Matt. 24:36). It should not therefore be thought surprising if Jesus did not know whether the fulfillment of the divine plan necessitated his death but was willing to submit to whatever was involved. There seem to be no implications as to whether the future was certain to the Father or not, or the degree to which the details were fixed.

We have looked at a number of passages that the open theists use in support of their contention that God does not know the future. Some of these do not appear to carry the weight that the open theists attach to them. Others, however, on a straightforward or plain sense reading, appear to support the open view more fully than they do the traditional view. Advocates of the traditional view are able to give some explanation or interpretation of these, often by suggesting that they are anthropomorphic or phenomenological. They describe things in terms of the hearer or reader, and how things appear to such. The bigger issue on which the traditional view stakes its claim is a hermeneutical one: In what sense or as what type of literature should these passages be regarded?

We observed at the beginning of the chapter that open theists maintain that others have not examined and interacted with the Scriptures they cite. Whether or not the complaint is fully justified, the next chapter should help to remedy the problem.[55]

---

[55]For example, Boyd says, "What is particularly sad about the current state of this debate is that Scripture seems to be playing a small role in it. Most of the published criticisms raised against the open view have largely ignored the biblical grounds on which open theists base their position. For example, in his recent book, *God the Father Almighty*, Millard Erickson devotes an entire chapter to refuting the open view, but he never once interacts with any of the biblical arguments that support the open theist position. Unfortunately, this is typical of literature that critiques the open view" (*God of the Possible*, 12). Comparing Boyd's comments with the actual content of the book he mentions, A. B. Caneday concludes that they are inaccurate and adds, "It is not readily apparent that Boyd has read the entire book" ("The Implausible God of Open Theism: A Response to Gregory Boyd's *God of the Possible*," *Journal of Biblical Apologetics* 1 [2000]:84, n.4).

CHAPTER 2

THE BIBLICAL BASIS
OF THE TRADITIONAL VIEW

The traditional view is, even by the admission of the open theists,[1] able to muster a large number of biblical passages in support of its position. These are of several types: didactic, narrative, and prophetic.

DIDACTIC PASSAGES

There are passages that make statements about God's knowledge of the future. These didactic passages are found in various parts of the Bible.

Psalm 139. This is a passage in which the psalmist expresses wonderment at the extent of God's knowledge and especially God's knowledge of him. In v. 4 he says: "Before a word is on my tongue you know it completely, O LORD." The point of the passage is that God knows the psalmist exhaustively, and this is offered as an example or illustration. That even before he speaks, God knows every word, the noun כֻּלָּהּ *(kullāh)* meaning "both all of it and every one,"[2] is seen as a clear indication of divine foreknowledge. Ware contends that this advance knowledge of what we are going to say cannot simply be reduced to what he considers to be "informed guesses as to what we will say."[3]

---

[1]Richard Rice, "Biblical Support for a New Perspective," in *The Openness of God: A Biblical Challenge to the Traditional Understanding of God,* by Clark Pinnock, Richard Rice, John Sanders, William Hasker, and David Basinger (Downers Grove, Ill.: InterVarsity, 1994), 15.

[2]Franz Delitzsch, *Biblical Commentary on the Psalms* (Grand Rapids: Eerdmans, 1955), 3:346.

[3]Bruce A. Ware, *God's Lesser Glory: The Diminished God of Open Theism* (Wheaton, Ill.: Crossway, 2000), 123.

Open theists would contend that God knows us completely in our present state, including all our thoughts and feelings, and since the thought and decision to speak precedes the speaking, he knows what we will say before we say it: "This may be explained by divine foreknowledge or by God's knowing the psalmist so well that he can 'predict' what he will say and do."[4] Ware, however, contends that "We all say surprising things—surprising sometimes even to ourselves. No amount of past or present knowledge of individuals could predict with complete accuracy the words they will speak next."[5]

This part of the traditional view's argument may not be as strong as claimed because of the rather limited assertion of this specific verse. The psalmist does not say that God has always, from all eternity, known what he would say. What the Hebrew here says literally is "when the word is not on my tongue," which could be any time until the actual utterance. Furthermore, Ware's contention does not seem to me to be cogent, for presumably sometime prior to the actual utterance of the word, we decide to speak it, even if that is just a microsecond in advance, which is all that this statement by the psalmist entails. So on this consideration, the verse could be accounted for simply by the complete present knowledge of the person (in this case, "I decide to say the following: . . ."), which open theists hold God has (with the possible inconsistency pointed out in chapter 1). Ware's claim about our doing and saying unforeseen things also fails to take into account the possibility that God's knowledge of us is more exhaustive than our own self-knowledge or any knowledge that any other human might have of us.

This might be sufficient if the verse were taken out of its context. When viewed in context, however, it becomes clear that this is an assertion of foreknowledge. For this is part of a statement in which the psalmist declares God's complete knowledge of him, and as part of that listing, he gives this item. The divine knowledge of the psalmist is a result of this searching of him, in which the various activities that the psalmist does that are known by God are in the infinitive rather than in the first person singular inflected

---

[4]John Sanders, *The God Who Risks: A Theology of Providence* (Downers Grove, Ill.: InterVarsity, 1998), 130.
[5]Ware, *God's Lesser Glory,* 123.

WHAT DOES GOD KNOW AND WHEN DOES HE KNOW IT?

form, as one would expect. Whereas the personal suffix ׳ (î). [in this case ׳נִ (nî)] "me" or "of me," is attached to "search," it is not attached to "know," but to each of these several activities. Delitzsch comments that these are therefore to be understood as "the sum of the human conditions or states."[6] According to Delitzsch, the passage affirms that the divine knowledge is the result of the divine scrutiny. He then goes on to say of this divine scrutiny that it is "a scrutiny that is never unexecuted, and the knowledge is consequently an ever-present knowledge. מֵרָחוֹק is meant to say that He sees into not merely the thought that is fully fashioned and matured, but even that which is being evolved."[7] His comment, "In v. 4 this omniscience of God is illustratively corroborated with כִּי"[8] confirms Ware's comment that "this declaration that God knows our every word before we utter it is merely an example of the general principle, stated in the early verses of the psalm, that God knows and oversees every aspect of our lives."[9]

As one continues reading in the psalm, however, the meaning becomes clearer. In v. 13, the psalmist speaks of God's intimate involvement with him, even in his coming into being within his mother's womb. Verses 14–16 indicate the knowledge of him that God has as a consequence of this creative activity. Verse 16 is a particularly interesting one: "All the days ordained for me were written in your book before one of them came to be." The verb יִכָּתֵבוּ (yikātēbû) is the Niphal imperfect third person plural of כָּתַב (kātab) "to write." The Niphal is the simple passive stem and the imperfect is the tense denoting uncompleted action. This might lead one to interpret the statement as "all my days … are being written," which could suggest that they are appearing there as the psalmist himself writes them, by doing these things. Two considerations in the text militate against such a rendering, however. The first is that tense in Hebrew is time-independent, indicating status of the action (completed or uncompleted), rather than time. Time must be determined from context. Here it is apparent from the context, where all that precedes refers to a past time, that this should also be considered past action. Beyond that, however, is the verb יֻצָּרוּ (yuṣṣārû),

[6]Delitzsch, *Psalms*, 345.
[7]Ibid.
[8]Ibid., 346.
[9]Ware, *God's Lesser Glory*, 123.

which means in the Qal, when applied to a human, a potter forming the pot, a woodworker carving an object, or a person forming an idea or a plan. When applied to divine activity, the Qal stem speaks of God as a potter and "fig. for *frame, pre-ordain, plan* (in divine purpose), of a situation; . . . of an occurrence."[10] In the Pual, which is the intensive passive stem, it refers only to God and means "*pre-ordained* (in the divine purpose) [Ps. 139:16]."[11] The conclusion from this text seems to be quite clearly that God knows and even has formed the future days of the person.

Isaiah 41–48. Here is certainly one *locus classicus* of the traditional view of divine foreknowledge. Ware refers to it as an "astonishing portrayal of God's foreknowledge."[12] The extended section of Scripture includes several separate passages, with differing emphases.

> "Present your case," says the LORD. "Set forth your arguments," says Jacob's King. "Bring in [your idols] to tell us what is going to happen. Tell us what the former things were, so that we may consider them and know their final outcome. Or declare to us the things to come, tell us what the future holds, so we may know that you are gods. Do something, whether good or bad, so that we will be dismayed and filled with fear. But you are less than nothing and your works are utterly worthless; he who chooses you is detestable.(Isa. 41:21–24)

Here Jehovah gives a challenge to the idols that claim to be gods. They are to tell what the former things were, but more than that, they are to declare the future, what is to happen. A very direct tie is established between foreknowledge and deity: "Declare to us the things to come, tell us what the future holds, so that we may know that you are gods." It is apparent that they will be unable to do so, for Jehovah then declares, "But you are less than nothing and your works are utterly worthless; he who chooses you is detestable." The challenge by God is general. If the open theists are correct, there are some things about the future that he does not know, so that the challenge would have to apply only to certain areas.

---

[10]Francis Brown, S. R. Driver, and Charles A. Briggs, *A Hebrew and English Lexicon of the Old Testament* (Oxford: Clarendon, 1955), 427.
[11]Ibid., 428.
[12]Ware, *God's Lesser Glory,* 101.

In verses 25–29 of chapter 41, Jehovah repeats the challenge but makes much of the fact that he has fulfilled this criterion, but the idols have not:

> "I have stirred up one from the north, and he comes—one from the rising sun who calls on my name. He treads on rulers as if they were mortar, as if he were a potter treading the clay. Who told of this from the beginning, so we could know, or beforehand, so we could say, 'He was right'? No one told of this, no one foretold it, no one heard any words from you. I was the first to tell Zion, 'Look, here they are!' I gave to Jerusalem a messenger of good tidings. I look but there is no one—no one among them to give counsel, no one to give answer when I ask them. See, they are all false! Their deeds amount to nothing; their images are but wind and confusion."

God emphasizes his own activity, giving virtually a causal explanation to what happens: he has stirred up the one who comes and acts (v. 25). Then, however, he repeats his challenge, asking who has foretold this, so that it could be said, "He was right." He answers his own question: "No one told of this, no one foretold it" (v. 26). Boldly, he then declares: "I was the first to tell Zion" (v. 27) and affirms that he does not draw his knowledge from anyone else (v. 28). His final denunciation is powerful: "See, they are all false! Their deeds amount to nothing; their images are but wind and confusion" (v. 29).

To my knowledge, no open theist discusses this problem, restricting the treatment to portions of chapters 46 and 48. Yet here is a challenge that some would see to relate directly to the legitimacy of the God that they claim to find in Scripture. Particularly in view of Boyd's complaint (recounted at the end of chapter 1) that critics of open theism do not interact with the passages advanced by the open theists, this omission is, at the very least, puzzling.

The next passage, 42:8–9, builds on the preceding as the doctrine is progressively assembled:

> "I am the LORD; that is my name! I will not give my glory to another or my praise to idols. See, the former things have taken place, and new things I declare; before they spring into being I announce them to you."

Here is Jehovah's clear declaration of his uniqueness. He will not share his glory with any of these idols, whose emptiness has been demonstrated. The proof that he is the Lord, the only true god, is that he "declares new things, announcing them before they spring into being." One can hardly conceive of a clearer description or even definition, of foreknowledge.

This theme is continued into chapter 43:

> All the nations gather together and the peoples assemble. Which of them foretold this and proclaimed to us the former things? Let them bring in their witnesses to prove they were right, so that others may hear and say, "It is true." "You are my witnesses," declares the LORD, "and my servant whom I have chosen, so that you may know and believe me and understand that I am he. Before me no god was formed, nor will there be one after me. I, even I, am the LORD, and apart from me there is no savior. I have revealed and saved and proclaimed—I, and not some foreign god among you. You are my witnesses," declares the LORD, "that I am God." (vv. 9–12)

The challenge to the idols is repeated: "Which of them foretold this and proclaimed to us the former things?" (v. 9). They are challenged to produce the witnesses to what they have done, and the Lord declares that his hearers are his witnesses (v. 10). He then goes on to broaden the testimony, not only to what he has foretold but also to his saving and delivering action.

Isaiah 44:6–8 repeats these same themes. "Who is like me?" asks the Lord. If any is, "Let him proclaim it. Let him declare and lay out before me what has happened since I established my ancient people, and what is yet to come—yes, let him foretell what will come" (v. 7). There is a generalized dimension to this, calling for a complete accounting of the events in order: וְיַעְרְכֶהָ (wĕya'rĕkehā), the word translated "and lay out," עָרַך ('āraḵ), actually means in the Qal stem "to arrange or set in order," such as building seven altars in a row or arranging a table.[13] This is not only something they are to do with what has already happened, involving memory, but what is to come, involving foreknowledge, and accurate foreknowledge at that.

---

[13]Brown, Driver, and Briggs, *Hebrew and English Lexicon,* 789.

Once more, in Isa. 45:18–25, these motifs are repeated like themes in a symphony. Verse 21 says, "Declare what is to be, present it—let them take counsel together. Who foretold this long ago, who declared it from the distant past? Was it not I, the LORD? And there is no God apart from me, a righteous God and a Savior; there is none but me." While the force of a teaching is not measured simply by a count of the number of times it occurs, the sheer amount of repetition of this theme suggests that it was very clear and definite, and certainly it was very important for God's people to understand.

In Isa. 46:8–11, a new dimension of the claims is introduced:

> "Remember this, fix it in mind, take it to heart, you rebels. Remember the former things, those of long ago; I am God, and there is no other; I am God, and there is none like me. I make known the end from the beginning, from ancient times, what is still to come. I say: My purpose will stand, and I will do all that I please. From the east I summon a bird of prey; from a far-off land, a man to fulfill my purpose. What I have said, that will I bring about; what I have planned, that will I do."

The familiar theme of God's foretelling the future is found here. In addition, however, God's purpose and his execution of the plan he has formed is prominent. This feature is appealed to by open theists in their explanation of this passage. So Boyd, for example, says, "The Lord is not appealing to information about the future he happens to possess; instead, he is appealing to *his own intentions* about the future. He foreknows that certain things are going to take place because he knows *his own purpose and intention* to bring these events about."[14] He then contends that the next sentence is even more emphatic: "He declares that the future is settled to the extent that he is going to determine it, but nothing in the text requires that we believe that *everything* that will ever come to pass will do so according to his will and thus is settled ahead of time. Indeed, if everything came to pass according to his will, one wonders why God has to try to overcome the obstinacy of the Israelites with these assertions about particular future intentions. Wouldn't the Israelites' obstinacy itself be controlled by God?"[15]

---

[14]Gregory A. Boyd, *God of the Possible: A Biblical Introduction to the Open View of God* (Grand Rapids: Baker, 2000), 30.

[15]Ibid.

Similarly, Sanders says of this passage, "Sometimes God simply discloses what God is going to do irrespective of creaturely decision. God can bring some things about on his own if he decides to do so (Is 46:9–11). But this does not require foreknowledge, only the ability to do it."[16] Rice states, "If God's will is the only condition required for something to happen, if human cooperation is not involved, then God can unilaterally guarantee its fulfillment, and he can announce it ahead of time. This seems to be the case with a number of prophecies, including the famous passage in Isaiah.... (Is 46:10–11). Of course, God can predict his own actions."[17]

Ware challenges this interpretation, however. While the principle might be appropriate in the type of situation the open theists describe, this is not one of these, according to Ware: "We dare not miss the point that *his own purpose and intention* includes a multitude of future free choices and actions both of this man himself and of all the surrounding network of individuals whose choices would relate to his being placed in the position where he then carries out specifically what God has intended that he do."[18]

Ware calls attention to one other feature of this passage: "Remember the former things, those of long ago; I am God, and there is no other; I am God, and there is none like me" (v. 9). What, he asks, is the point of introducing these former things? They are offered as additional proof of the reality and uniqueness of God. That, however, in the larger context of this text, is a result of God demonstrating that he knows the future. To Ware the answer is obvious: "The confidence that God in fact will accomplish in the *future* what he here declares, is based on retelling the multitude of ways that God in the *past* has declared what will come to be and has then brought those things to pass just as he had said."[19]

The final text that we will examine in this section of Isaiah is 48:3–6:

I foretold the former things long ago, my mouth announced them and I made them known; then suddenly I acted, and they came to pass. For I knew how stubborn you were; the sinews of your neck were iron, your forehead was bronze. Therefore I told you these things long ago; before

[16]Sanders, *The God Who Risks*, 130–31.
[17]Rice, "Biblical Support," 51.
[18]Ware, 116.
[19]Ibid., 117.

they happened I announced them to you so that you could not say, 'My idols did them; my wooden image and metal god ordained them.' You have heard these things; look at them all. Will you not admit them? From now on I will tell you of new things, of hidden things unknown to you.

Ware believes that this is a powerful testimony to both God's massive foreknowledge and his absolute accuracy and that neither can be accounted for by open theism: "The general term 'former things,' as observed earlier, is purposely broad, encompassing a multitude of times that God has spoken and his word can be shown to have come true. And, because God wants Israel to come back to him, he now proclaims new things . . . *God's designated authenticating sign of his deity is the reality and truthfulness of his foreknowledge.* To diminish this reality or to qualify its truthfulness is to make a mockery of God and the stated purpose for his futuristic declarations."[20]

Neither Rice nor Sanders discusses this passage, presumably because this is another example of the type of passage in which God declares what he is going to do unilaterally. Boyd does treat the passage, taking that very approach: "Again, this is not simply a matter of the Lord possessing information about what was going to take place. It was rather a matter of the Lord *determining* what was going to take place and telling his children ahead of time. The verse doesn't support the view that the future is exhaustively settled in reality, and thus exhaustively settled in God's mind."[21]

As plausible as Boyd's explanation may seem, there is a problem with it, and that may be why Rice and Sanders do not use it here. This passage is part of a promise of deliverance from the Babylonian captivity, as seen clearly in v. 20: "Leave Babylon, flee from the Babylonians! Announce this with shouts of joy and proclaim it. Send it out to the ends of the earth; say, 'The LORD has redeemed his servant Jacob.'" In between these verses he makes the same claim to uniqueness and the same challenge as to which idol has foretold this (vv. 12–17). If, however, this declaration was indeed long before the fact, then it presupposed the condition of their hearts described in v. 4, which was the reason God allowed them to be taken off into captivity. Although God could indeed decide unilaterally to allow

---

[20]Ibid., 119.
[21]Boyd, *God of the Possible,* 31. Cf. Gregory A. Boyd, "The Open-Theism View," *Divine Foreknowledge: Four Views,* ed. James K. Beilby and Paul R. Eddy (Downers Grove, Ill.: InterVarsity, 2001), 17.

them to be taken into captivity and to deliver them, considerable free human actions were involved. God had to know that they would at this point indeed be of this character, that they would not repent or reform. He also knew the actions of numbers of persons involved in the Babylonians' carrying them off into captivity and then releasing them. Whether one says that he caused or directed these Babylonians, there certainly was a knowledge of their human choices and actions, just as there was with the Israelites. While we will discuss this type of explanation at greater length when we examine actual instances of prophecy in a more formal way, it appears that the situation is not as simple as Boyd supposes.

The Terminology of Foreknowledge. While there really is no Hebrew word for *foreknow* or *foreknowledge,* the New Testament vocabulary is rich on this subject. The primary verb is προγινώσκω *(proginōskō),* with the noun form being *prognōsis. Proginōskō* means simply to know in advance. It is used twice of humans having known previously (Acts 26:5 and 2 Peter 3:17). It is used of divine foreknowledge, referring to persons; and here it seems to carry something of the Old Testament term *yāḏaʿ,* which was used of intimate knowledge, even of the most intimate relations of husband and wife. Thus, it appears to carry something of the idea of choosing or electing. The noun, *prognōsis,* also conveys this idea of choosing or election in Acts 2:23 and 1 Peter 1:2. In addition, some other terms—most notably προορίζω *(proorizō),* sometimes cited as indications of divine foreknowledge—actually refer to foreordination and therefore are evidence for the Calvinist view. If foreordination is correct, then of course God also foreknows what he has foreordained. I have omitted such from this consideration, limiting the textual evidence to those ideas accepted by both Calvinistic and Arminian views of full divine foreknowledge.[22]

Another verb, προοράω *(prooraō),* means to "see up ahead" in Acts 2:25, and to "have previously seen" in Acts 21:29. The verb προμαρτύρομαι *(promartyromai)* means "to foretell" in 1 Peter 1:11: "the time and circumstances to which the Spirit of Christ in them was pointing when he predicted the sufferings of Christ and the glories that would follow." The verb

---

[22]Interesting, William Lane Craig, although not a Calvinist, cites several of these instances as evidence for his conviction of exhaustive definite foreknowledge (*The Only Wise God: The Compatibility of Divine Foreknowledge and Human Freedom* [Grand Rapids: Baker, 1987], 31–35).

WHAT DOES GOD KNOW AND WHEN DOES HE KNOW IT?

προκαταγγέλλω *(prokatangellō),* means "to foretell or to predict," and refers to prophecy in Acts 3:18, "But this is how God fulfilled what he had foretold through all the prophets, saying that his Christ would suffer," and in Acts 7:52, "Was there ever a prophet your fathers did not persecute? They even killed those who predicted the coming of the Righteous One. And now you have betrayed and murdered him." While this does not directly assert foreknowledge, it certainly seems to presuppose it.

NARRATIVE PASSAGES

By "narrative" here, we are referring to a particular type of narrative, namely a prophetic narrative, or one written before the occurrence of the events described. These are actual prophecies, which traditionally have been considered one of the most powerful evidences of divine foreknowledge and even of the inspiration of Scripture. Although these passages do not assert that God knows the future, they imply that he does, or they demonstrate that foreknowledge by correctly predicting that which ordinarily humans would be unable to do. The number of such passages is literally immense.

Pre-identified Individuals. In at least two instances, God foretells through his prophets something that will be done by a person not yet born and even gives the name of the individual. One of these is 1 Kings 13:1–3:

> By the word of the LORD a man of God came from Judah to Bethel, as Jeroboam was standing by the altar to make an offering. He cried out against the altar by the word of the LORD: "O altar, altar! This is what the LORD says: 'A son named Josiah will be born to the house of David. On you he will sacrifice the priests of the high places who now make offerings here, and human bones will be burned on you.'" That same day the man of God gave a sign: "This is the sign the LORD has declared: The altar will be split apart and the ashes on it will be poured out."

This seems like a rather clear prophecy, even naming the person who was to perform this particular act. This prophecy cannot simply be dismissed as general or as something that could be brought about by human effort to fulfill it.

A similar prophecy is found in the extended passage we examined earlier, Isa. 41–48, which contains both didactic portions and actual prophecy. In Isa. 44:28, the prophet speaks of Jehovah, "who says of Cyrus, 'He is my shepherd and will accomplish all that I please; he will say of Jerusalem, "Let it be rebuilt," and of the temple, "Let its foundations be laid."'" While one might argue that Josiah as king deliberately desired to fulfill the prophecy and did so, this could not be the case with Cyrus, who likely would have neither knowledge of the prophecy nor desire to fulfill it. These seem to be predictions that can only be reasonably accounted for on the basis of a God who knew the future in detail, a knowledge finite humans could not exercise.

Neither Sanders, Pinnock, nor Rice deal with these two prophecies. Boyd, however, does discuss them. He says, "This decree obviously set strict parameters around the freedom of the parents in naming these individuals (see also Luke 1:11–23). It also restricted the scope of freedom these individuals could exercise *as it pertained to particular foreordained activities.* In other respects, however, these individuals and their parents remained self-determining agents."[23]

Boyd feels that too much has sometimes been concluded from passages such as this: "To conclude from these two examples that the names and activities of *all* people are settled from eternity is unwarranted. They certainly show that Yahweh is the sovereign Lord of history and can predetermine (and thus foreknow) whatever he pleases, but they do not justify the conclusion that he has settled the entire future ahead of time."[24]

In a later chapter we will examine the contention that the Bible never overtly asserts God's total foreknowledge. Here we may simply note that if God can know future events like this, which involve so many free human actions, there is no real reason in principle why he could not foreknow all events. Boyd would, of course, say that God simply did not, but it appears that the principle of partial definiteness of the future has been modified. Previously, he had taught that some parts of the future, those that do not involve free human actions, are definite and therefore knowable, but that those involving human will are indefinite and therefore unknowable. Here,

---

[23]Boyd, *God of the Possible,* 34.
[24]Ibid.

however, the principle seems to be that some free human choices and actions are definite and knowable, while others are not.

Prophecies of Specific Actions of Individuals. Among the more striking prophecies in Scripture are those that foretell in great detail actions that particular individuals will take. Two of the best known of these are Jesus' prediction of Judas's betrayal and Peter's denial of him.

The report of Peter's denial is especially detailed. Matthew's account of the incident reads like this:

> Peter replied, "Even if all fall away on account of you, I never will." "I tell you the truth," Jesus answered, "this very night, before the rooster crows, you will disown me three times." But Peter declared, "Even if I have to die with you, I will never disown you." And all the other disciples said the same. (Matt. 26:33–35)

The fulfillment of this prediction comes in vv. 69–75, with the culminating portion reading as follows:

> Then he began to call down curses on himself and he swore to them, "I don't know the man!" Immediately a rooster crowed. Then Peter remembered the word Jesus had spoken: "Before the rooster crows, you will disown me three times." And he went outside and wept bitterly. (vv. 74–75)

It is difficult to imagine a more detailed prediction of the future action of a human being and fulfillment of the prediction. If there ever was a case of Jesus knowing the future as it pertains to human willing and acting, this must be it. There certainly was no desire on Peter's part to fulfill this prophecy, to say the least. Thus, Jesus must have had foreknowledge that Peter obviously did not have.

As seemingly conclusive as this incident is, Boyd is not about to concede that it establishes divine foreknowledge in the traditional sense. Rather, he believes that this is a case of God so knowing the present situation that he could predict what would happen. In this case, Jesus knew Peter's personality and character so extensively and accurately that he could predict just what Peter would do in a situation such as this. "We don't need to suppose that the future is exhaustively settled in God's mind to explain this prediction," he says. "We only need to believe that God the Father knew and revealed to Jesus one solidified aspect of Peter's character that was predictable in the immediate future. Anyone who knew Peter's character perfectly could have predicted that under certain highly pressured circumstances (which God could easily orchestrate, if he needed to), Peter would act the way he did."[25]

Even if one were to grant this general point of Peter's cowardice beneath the external bravado, that would seem to guarantee simply that Peter would buckle under pressure. This situation is much more detailed than that. It involves not one but three denials. How could Jesus (or the Father who revealed this to Jesus) have known that Peter would deny Jesus, not simply once, but three times? There would seem to be nothing about Peter's character that would indicate this or even that the occasion would arise three times.

Boyd has an answer for this problem as well: God orchestrated the threefold temptation in order to teach Peter an important lesson. Boyd says, "We do not know how much, if any, supernatural intervention was behind the events of that evening. But the outcome was just as God anticipated. Three times Peter's true character was squeezed out of him so that, after the resurrection, Christ could squeeze his character into him three times."[26] So the full explanation, as far as Boyd is concerned, involves a settled character of Peter, which the Father, knowing Peter perfectly, revealed to Jesus, enabling him to predict what Peter would do in a given situation. Combined with this is God "orchestrating" or setting the circumstances in such a way that Peter's character would be manifested or "squeezed out of him" three times. Boyd comments: "In any event, we are clearly going beyond the evidence if we conclude that the future is exhaustively settled from all eternity on the grounds that Jesus knew what Peter would do in the next twelve hours. The only conclusions justified by this episode are that *God possesses perfect knowledge of the past and present* and that some of the future is settled, either by present circumstances (Peter's character) or by God's sovereign design."[27]

---

[25]Boyd "The Open-Theism View," 20.
[26]Ibid., 21.
[27]Ibid.

WHAT DOES GOD KNOW AND WHEN DOES HE KNOW IT?

Is this an adequate alternative explanation of the incident, however? Ware does not think so. He notes several unusual features of the account. Many factors had to fit perfectly. What if Peter had become so confused, frightened, shocked, and bewildered that he had run away after the first encounter rather than remaining to have the second and third? What if those who were there had seized Peter and taken him before the authorities, where he might have repeated the denial several times? What if another disciple had been with him, shaming him so that he did not deny Jesus? What if those who questioned him had either asked him several times in rapid succession or delayed part of their questioning so that the cock crowed before three denials? The prediction of what Peter would do involved not only the knowledge of Peter's character but also that of several other persons whose action bore upon the outcome of the incident. Since God allows free choices, and since he does not rescind that freedom, and since he cannot foreknow free human actions, it would seem to require quite a lot of intervention or "orchestration" on God's part to bring about the fulfillment of this prophecy. Ware says, "In the open view, since Jesus (or the Father) does not know the future free actions of people, he could not have known whether any of these possible and reasonable scenarios (or innumerable others) might have occurred. Honestly, I am simply incredulous that the proposal would be seriously made that Jesus could accurately predict that *Peter would deny him three times,* based on God's perfect knowledge of Peter's character."[28]

The problem is even more complex than Boyd's version of the account would have us believe, however. For not only did Jesus predict what Peter would do in this situation, but he also predicted what he would do subsequently. In Luke 22:32, Jesus declares that Peter will return again, thus not totally and finally denying Jesus, and that he will then be used to strengthen the believers. Ware points out how serious was Jesus' deed in prophesying Peter's future actions: "Given Peter's libertarian freedom, how could Christ possibly have known with such certainty that Peter would in fact return? Knowing the penalty for prophesying falsely, and staking his own claim to deity on announcing in advance what will occur, Jesus would have taken

---

[28]Ware, *God's Lesser Glory,* 128.

an enormous risk to make such a specific prediction unless he knew precisely what Peter would do."[29]

Another major prediction of human behavior, textually located in very close approximation to the prediction about Peter, was Jesus' declaration of Judas's future betrayal of him. The several Gospels give somewhat varying (but not necessarily inconsistent) versions of what happened that evening at the Last Supper. John gives the clearest (for our purposes) description. According to that account, after Jesus announces that one of the gathered disciples will betray him, they all wonder who it will be, and Peter asks John to ask Jesus. At that point, "Jesus answered, 'It is the one to whom I will give this piece of bread when I have dipped it in the dish.' Then, dipping the piece of bread, he gave it to Judas Iscariot, son of Simon" (John 13:26).

Presumably, the open theists could argue that Jesus made this prediction on the basis of his thorough knowledge of Judas's character. What makes such an explanation more difficult, however, is that in 6:64 John reports Jesus as saying, "'Yet there are some of you who do not believe.' For Jesus had known from the beginning which of them did not believe and who would betray him," and then follows this with the following report and explanation: "Then Jesus replied, 'Have I not chosen you, the Twelve? Yet one of you is a devil!' (He meant Judas, the son of Simon Iscariot, who, though one of the Twelve, was later to betray him)" (vv. 70–71). This seems to indicate, not simply that Jesus, at the time of the betrayal, knew Judas's character so well that he knew that Judas would be the one to do it, but that he seemed to know this "from the beginning" *(ex archēs)*.

Boyd does not think the text requires such a meaning. He contends that the phrase *ex archēs* "does not imply that Jesus knew who would betray him from a time *before* the person decided, in his heart, to betray him (let alone that he knew from all eternity, as the classical view of foreknowledge requires). It can more plausibly be taken to mean that Jesus knew who would betray him *early on* (cf. Phil. 4:15), either from the moment this person resolved it in his heart to betray him or from the time Jesus chose him to be his disciple."[30]

---

[29]Ibid., 129.
[30]Boyd, "The Open-Theism View," 21.

Boyd's position is that "Judas fulfilled Scripture, not that Judas was the individual who *had* to fulfill Scripture." This gives a very different cast to the whole picture. According to Boyd, "Judas could have and should have chosen a different path to his life than the one he chose. But as a free moral agent, Judas tragically chose a path of self-interest and ultimately self-destruction (John 17:12). If his choices had been more godly, he would not have been a candidate for fulfilling the prophecy of the Lord's betrayal. In this case, the Lord would have found someone else to fill this role."[31] In fact, Boyd contends that this is the way to understand "the wicked activity of all the individuals who played foreordained roles in the death of Jesus."[32] While the prophecies necessarily had to be fulfilled, they did not have to be fulfilled by the specific persons who did them, nor perhaps at the time or in the way that they were.

How well does this explanation account for the phenomenon of this specific prophecy? Certainly, the most "straightforward" or "face value" explanation of what happened is the traditional view, that God foreknew, perhaps from all eternity, that this person Judas would betray Jesus. But what of this alternative view? Is it acceptable?

The first thing to notice is the expression in John 6:64, *en archē*. The meaning seems to be simply "beginning."[33] There is little lexicographical support for as mild and general a meaning as "early on." Even if one were to take it in Boyd's sense, however, his explanation is interesting: "either from the moment this person resolved it in his heart to betray him or from the time Jesus chose him to be his disciple." The expression does not unequivocally mean "from all eternity," although it seems to carry that meaning in a number of places.[34] Even if this knowing by Jesus was "from the time Jesus chose him to be his disciple," that suggests that this element of the future was settled quite some time in advance. This in itself would appear to breach or at least strain the principle underlying the open theist position.

[31]Ibid., 21–22.
[32]Ibid., 22.
[33]William F. Arndt and F. Wilbur Gingrich, *A Greek Lexicon of the New Testament,* 2nd ed. (Chicago: University of Chicago Press, 1979), 111–12.
[34]Ibid.

Second, the prophecies involved in the death of Jesus, which Boyd says had to be fulfilled but did not have to be fulfilled by these exact people, involve some rather specific details. For example, Jesus' side was pierced (John 20:34–37, cf. Zech. 12:10), and his cloak was not divided, the soldiers casting lots for it instead (John 19:24, cf. Ps. 22:18). Once the right person comes along to fulfill the betrayal prediction, the number of possibilities for fulfilling the other details is fewer. Now the number of persons who might fulfill these other prophecies was rather limited, and the time when they were to do it was also rather severely circumscribed. This required a considerable amount of knowledge, several centuries in advance, of who would be the soldiers serving at the crucifixion, their characters, and how they would react in a specific situation of this type.

There is a further problem here, which also attaches to Boyd's explanation of the prediction of Peter's denial. This accurate foretelling is based on a very thorough knowledge of the character of the individual involved—a knowledge so complete that God could know what he would do and, in the case of Peter, what he would do in great detail, even extending to the number of times that he would do it. There does seem to be a problem with relating this to one of the other explanations open theism gives, namely, the testing of Abraham. Somehow Jehovah did not know Abraham's character well enough to know what he would do in the situation of testing, where God "orchestrated" the circumstances in such a way as to "squeeze his character out of him." Note that the text specifically says, not "to know what he would do," but to "know that he feared God"—in other words, not an action, but his character.

The question then becomes how God could know the character of Peter and Judas so well but not the character of Abraham. Abraham had walked with God for many years (he was 100 when Isaac was born, and Isaac was now a young man). How could it be that Abraham, who had trusted God on several occasions, had a character that God apparently still did not know very well? This is not to say that there could not be some exempting reason why what applied to Peter and Judas was not true of Abraham, but the point is that the open theists do not propose such a distinction. In the absence of some such explanation, it appears that we have either an ad hoc exception or a contradiction within the open theist view.

Other prophecies. We have sampled only a few of the fulfilled predictive prophecies found in Scripture. There are literally hundreds of them, concerning the sojourn of the people of Israel in Egypt, specifying even the length of time that this would involve; the captivity, including the name of one king who would lead them away into captivity; the return from the captivity; the details of the life of Jesus; and countless other matters. Matthew alone repeatedly says, "This was done to fulfill that which was written." This virtual avalanche of prophecies has been traditionally taken to be a powerful evidence of God's foreknowledge.

OPEN THEISM AND PROPHECY

It should be apparent that prophecy is perhaps the most difficult single element in Scripture for open theism to account for, as some of them acknowledge.[35] It is therefore crucial that they offer a credible explanation of this phenomenon. The several open theists agree that prophecies can be classified into three types, which can be accounted for without resorting to the traditional view of foreknowledge: unilateral divine action, conditional prophecies, and predictions based on knowledge of the past and present.

Unilateral Divine Action. On this model, some of the prophecies concern actions that God knows will happen simply because he has willed to do them. Jesus' birth and resurrection would be outstanding examples of this. No human free will is involved here, only God's self-knowledge of his self-willing. Certainly, many of the prophecies are of this nature, including the deliverance of his people out of bondage in Egypt and out of captivity.

There are some problems with this explanation, however. Even where the action is unilateral, God's decision to do them is affected by the future actions of humans. For example, the place of Jesus' birth was to be Bethlehem, not Nazareth, where his parents lived. The fulfillment of this prophecy required something to occur that would cause Mary to be in Bethlehem when Jesus was born. This circumstance came about through the census, but the fact that the census was to be taken and in

---

[35]Rice, "Biblical Support," 46.

the fashion that it was (with each person returning to his ancestral home) required considerable knowledge of the persons who would exercise their free will in this fashion. Now it can, of course, be argued that there were several ways in which this could come about and that God simply waited until one of these occurred and then unilaterally established that this was to be when Mary would become pregnant, but this is not the most straightforward reading of the text. In the case of Jesus' second coming, Jesus seems to imply that this is sufficiently established so that the Father knows the time (Matt. 24:36). Yet several conditions had to be met before this could occur, such as the preaching of the gospel in the whole world (Matt. 24:14), which required knowledge of the free actions of numerous individuals.

There are some problems with the concept of knowing who will do what far in advance, as this prophecy seems to require. It is important to remember how many events in history involve human free will. With the exception of events involving physical objects alone, virtually all of what we usually term history involves human willing. Thus, human free choices and actions in one way or another affect much of what God decides to do.

There is one additional problem. It may well be that on the free will theists' understanding of will, God himself is not free if it can be known (by him) what he will do and when he will do it. This is an issue that will be pursued more fully in the discussion of philosophical issues later.

Conditional Prophecies. Another type of prophecy is the conditional prophecy. Here the prophecy is in the form of "I will do such and such if [or unless] you do such and such." On this model, God does not know what the person addressed or described will do, so the prophecy is not definite. It is hypothetical, and the condition may be either expressed or implied.

It seems to me that there are indeed prophecies of this type, and the traditional view has generally acknowledged this in the case of the prophecy of the destruction of Nineveh and other similar declarations. So, for example, Ware says, "*explicitly* conditional prophecies are not problematic for either classical or open theism ... when prophecies are *implicitly* conditional, there are often clues in the contexts of these prophecies as to what the unstated, implicit condition may be." Referring to Jonah's message to Nineveh, Hezekiah's extended life, and Noah's intercession for Israel, he says, "There are good reasons for thinking that God's *stated prediction* was given to elicit some response, after which God then did what he *secretly intended to do all* along."[36] This suggests that even those passages that permit the open theist explanation do not require it. Open theists, of course, suggest that such a message from God would be insincere on the traditional view.

Prediction Based on Knowledge of the Past and Present. The third type of explanation of prophecy proposed by open theists is that God, on the basis of his complete knowledge of the past and of the present, is able to calculate what will happen in the future. The particularly relevant version of this is that God knows Peter's present character so well that he can predict what Peter will do in the future.

While this may serve to account for some prophecies, it faces real difficulties when the prophecy occurs before the birth of the person, in some cases perhaps several centuries before that birth. For until the person is at least conceived, God does not really know that this person will even be. He also does not know, once the person is born, what influences will bear upon his developing the character that he will come to have by the time of the predicted event, since many of them in turn are the results of free human actions, involving complex matrices of huge numbers of people. None of these actions can be foreknown by God except by the same method used to know this person's action, and for the most part, only the possibilities can be known, not which of these possibilities will become actual.

To be sure, if God is indeed infinite, he can know all the immense numbers of possibilities of who will be and what they will do. Yet at best, he can only calculate probabilities as to what will happen.

---

[36]Ware, *God's Lesser Glory,* 132–33.

We have looked at two types of explanation of certain biblical considerations, especially of predictive prophecy. We have seen that each can account for these phenomena. Yet surely the traditional approach must be considered the simpler and more natural one. The open theist attempt to account for some of these at times becomes so involved as to resemble the epicycles that were created to preserve a Ptolemaic account of the observed movements of planets and stars.

In general, a principle classically called the Law of Ockham's Razor, or in science called the law of parsimony, is a good one to follow. In brief, this principle says that of two explanations, all things being equal, the simpler is to be preferred. This rule is not to be followed to the ignoring of all factors. The simpler answer is not always the best, as H. L. Mencken's maxim reminds us: "There's always an easy solution to every human problem— neat, plausible, and wrong." The theory must account for more of the phenomena to be explained, and with less distortion, than the competitive explanation. Thus, a more complex theory that accounts for all of the phenomena must be preferred to a simpler one that does not really cover all of the territory. Since the open theist view accounted for the type of biblical material described in this chapter at least as adequately as did the traditional view and is simpler, we face a problem. We must decide which of the two theories, or perhaps yet some other, handles the material of both types better, and with less complication.

CHAPTER 3

the Hermeneutical
issues in the Debate

At the very core of the current debate is the hermeneutical question. We have seen in earlier chapters that both sides in the debate can cite scriptures in support of their view, sometimes at rather great length. The question, then, becomes how to decide which view is the more faithful to the teaching of Scripture.

IDENTIFYING THE HERMENEUTICAL ISSUES

Traditional theism has a long history of developed hermeneutic, which has been discussed in numerous hermeneutics texts.[1] When we examine the extensive writings of the open theists, it is striking to observe how little discussion of the methodology of interpretation there is. In order to be able to place the hermeneutical issues before us properly, it will be necessary to examine closely the actual hermeneutical practices of the open theists.

In fact, one principle that definitely emerges is that, in general, open theists are inclined to interpret literally certain passages that traditional theists have often treated as anthropomorphisms and anthropopathisms. Thus, when God says that he *now* knows that Abraham loves him (Gen. 22:12), that statement is taken literally as an actual

---

[1] A sampling of these includes Bernard L. Ramm, *Protestant Biblical Interpretation: A Textbook of Hermeneutics* (Grand Rapids: Baker, 1970); A. Berkeley Mickelsen, *Interpreting the Bible* (Grand Rapids: Eerdmans, 1963); J. Robertson McQuilkin, *Understanding and Applying the Bible* (Chicago: Moody, 1983); Earl D. Radmacher and Robert D. Preus, eds., *Hermeneutics, Inerrancy, and the Bible* (Grand Rapids: Zondervan, 1984); Grant R. Osborne, *The Hermeneutical Spiral: A Comprehensive Introduction to Biblical Interpretation* (Downers Grove, Ill.: InterVarsity, 1991); Robert H. Stein, *Playing by the Rules: A Basic Guide to Interpreting the Bible* (Grand Rapids: Baker, 1994).

discovery of something that God previously did not know. These are the types of passages in which the differences in interpretation are clearest. The other type of statement, such as Jesus' prediction of Peter's threefold denial, are not matters of difference on the level of primary interpretation. Both parties agree that Jesus actually forecast what Peter was to do. The difference is rather at the level of secondary interpretation, namely, an explanation of how it was that Jesus could correctly anticipate what Peter would do.

The Literal Interpretation of Actions of God. At a number of points, it is apparent that open theism brings to its study of Scripture a rather literal hermeneutic, including its treatment of those passages that traditionally have been understood as anthropomorphic descriptions of God. This is not presented in a formal fashion, but rather, as Bruce Ware points out, it is an "underlying hermeneutic"[2] that is, however, referred to from time to time. It is Boyd who refers to this principle most frequently. He insists that the verses that speak of God changing his mind, discovering, being surprised, or repenting are to be treated "just as literally"[3] or "every bit as literally"[4] as those that speak of a settled or determined future. He also speaks of taking such passages "at face value,"[5] or interpreting them "straightforwardly."[6] What this means is that these statements are to be taken just as they appear, as in some way giving an exact description of God rather than being understood as anthropomorphic, anthropopathic, or metaphorical. Boyd, in fact, denies that open theists have defined a unique hermeneutic: "Where have we ever espoused a unique hermeneutical theory? Openness theologians utilize the same hermeneutical principles as everyone else. We seek to interpret a passage according to the author's intended meaning. We simply do not see anything in narratives that describe God as thinking about the future in terms of what may or may not happen . . . or changing his mind . . . or expecting something to happen that does not come to pass . . . that suggests that they are anthropomorphisms."[7]

---

[2]Bruce Ware, *God's Lesser Glory: The Diminished God of Open Theism* (Wheaton, Ill.: Crossway, 2000), 65.
[3]Gregory A. Boyd, *God of the Possible: A Biblical Introduction to the Open View of God* (Grand Rapids: Baker, 2000), 54.
[4]Ibid., 120.
[5]Ibid., 60, 71–72.
[6]Ibid., 67.
[7]Gregory A. Boyd, "Christian Love and Academic Dialogue: A Reply to Bruce Ware," *Journal of the Evangelical Theological Society* 45.2 (June 2002): 240.

To a degree Boyd is correct that this general approach to hermeneutics is the common one used by evangelical biblical interpreters. Usually such hermeneutics do not use the term *literal,* but rather use something like *natural,* so that parables, metaphors, and other figures of speech do not have to be forced to the most literal possible sense. In general, this usually means that one takes the literal sense unless there is good reason for doing otherwise. The question then becomes whether there is good reason for giving some other interpretation of a given passage rather than the most literal one possible. It is here that open theists and traditional evangelicals differ.

Consistency of the Hermeneutic. The principle can perhaps be best assessed by examining the result if it is applied to other passages that are similar in nature to those used by the open theists but not cited by them. We have noted that open theists hold that God is omniscient, in the sense that he knows everything that can be known. This means that although he does not know everything about the future, he does know the past and the present exhaustively and correctly. What happens to the understanding of God's past and present knowledge if we apply the literal hermeneutic to some of these other passages?

It would appear that such an endeavor takes us to conclusions that the open theists would not want to accept. For example, in Gen. 3:9, God comes to the Garden of Eden and calls out to Adam, "Where are you?" Taken at face value or straightforwardly, this indicates that God did not know the whereabouts of Adam. Furthermore, he seems on this basis to lack some knowledge of past events as well. In this same context, God asks Adam, "Who told you that you were naked? Have you eaten from the tree that I commanded you not to eat from?" (v. 11). Apparently, God did not know what had transpired.

Other instances can be found throughout Scripture. One of the most interesting is the instance of Abraham and Isaac in Gen. 22, which has been the centerpiece of much open theist argument. Here God says, "Now I know that you fear God" (v. 12). Apparently, taking this passage straightforwardly, until the moment of Abraham's action, God did not know the present state of his heart, whether he truly loved God. God's present knowledge was incomplete. Scripture does not say that now God knew what Abraham would do, but rather that he now knew that Abraham loved him. God was ignorant, not just of Abraham's future action, but of his present condition. The time reference of the verb is significant here. It appears that the open theist hermeneutic, if it proves what they claim it does, actually proves more than they claim or than they want proved about God's knowledge.

There is another dimension to this argument, however. For the open theists, in their early writings, have contended that while God does not know the future, this is an ignorance, not an erroneous knowledge. But what about the statement cited from Jer. 3:7, "I thought that after she [Israel] had done all this she would return to me but she did not, and her unfaithful sister Judah saw it." If we use the open theist literal hermeneutic here, must we not conclude that God is not simply ignorant of the future, but that he is actually mistaken about it?

Open theists have responded to this criticism that God apparently was in error. In order to be an error, says Sanders, God must have "declared infallibly that something would come to pass and it did not. God would never be mistaken so long as he never said that X (for example, Adam will not sin) would infallibly come to pass and it did not."[8] But under what conditions would God so believe and declare? Sanders is definite: "God will not *definitely believe* that something will occur unless it is *certain* to occur. If an event is not certain to occur, then God knows the degree of probability that something will happen in a particular way. But God will not hold that belief as absolutely certain if human freedom is involved, because our decisions, though somewhat predictable, are not absolutely so."[9] Although Sanders does not say so explicitly, he seems to be saying that in those cases where God expresses belief that something would occur that subsequently did not, he was making a probability statement.

Boyd takes a similar approach. He says that open theists take the text at face value, but he advocates a more sympathetic reading of the Jeremiah passage than that God was mistaken. He says, "When God says he

[8]John Sanders, *The God Who Risks: A Theology of Providence* (Downers Grove, Ill.: InterVarsity, 1998), 132.

[9]John Sanders, "Be Wary of Ware: A Reply to Bruce Ware," *Journal of the Evangelical Theological Society* 45.2 (June 2002): 224.

'thought' or 'expected' something would take place that did not take place, he is simply reflecting his perfect knowledge of probabilities. When the improbable happens, as sometimes is the case with free agents, God genuinely says he 'thought' or 'expected' the more probable would happen."[10] In other words, what God is apparently saying is, "I know all the possibilities that may occur, and this one seems somewhat more likely to occur than do the alternatives." The reader must decide whether this is really taking the text at face value. Since God does not seem to differentiate his beliefs in terms of certainty, this seems like an ad hoc solution. As is the case with the Roman Catholic dogma of papal infallibility, it is difficult to find passages in which God overtly states, "I am now making an infallible statement of my infallible knowledge."

This principle may also be applicable to other attributes of God. For example, in Gen. 18:20–21 Jehovah considers the condition of Sodom and Gomorrah so that he may take appropriate action. The text reports, "Then the LORD said, 'The outcry against Sodom and Gomorrah is so great and their sin so grievous that I will go down and see if what they have done is as bad as the outcry that has reached me. If not, I will know.'" If we interpret this text using the usual open theist hermeneutic of the natural meaning or the face value meaning, then some interesting facts emerge. For one thing, God does not know the present spiritual condition of these two cities or their past actions. Beyond that, however, this seems to deny God's omnipresence, for God has to "go down" in order to make such a discovery. The same is also true of the passage where God says, "Come, let us go down and confuse their language so they will not understand each other" (Gen. 11:7). This seems to be a use of the hermeneutical principle analogous to that previously employed by open theists. The same type of problem can be found in Gen. 3:8–9, where God comes walking in the Garden, looking for Adam and Eve. They hear him walking and attempt to hide from him. Apparently they are successful in doing so, because God had to inquire where Adam was: "But the LORD God called to the man, 'Where are you?'" (v. 9).

---

[10]Boyd, "Christian Love and Academic Dialogue," 237.

The principle can be taken even further, however. Following the great flood, God surveyed the situation and made a covenant with the human race. He would never again send a flood of this scope. As a sign of this covenant, he set his rainbow in the clouds. The sign was not merely to remind the people of this promise, however. God says, "I have set my rainbow in the clouds, and it will be the sign of the covenant between me and the earth. Whenever I bring clouds over the earth and the rainbow appears in the clouds, I will remember my covenant between me and you and all living creatures of every kind. Never again will the waters become a flood to destroy all life. Whenever the rainbow appears in the clouds, I will see it and remember the everlasting covenant between God and all living creatures of every kind on the earth" (Gen. 9:13–16). Taken literally, or straightforwardly, or at face value, this suggests that God needs the rainbow in order to remember his promise. Thus, God's memory is faulty. While it might be responded that God's statement, "then I will remember," does not mean he would not have remembered it otherwise, the same could be said of God's statement, "now I know," in Gen. 22.[11]

Another interesting instance of this principle can be found in the creation account in Gen. 1:1–2:3. According to the narrative, God did the creative work in six days, each one dealing with a distinctive type of object. Then, however, the narrator adds, "By the seventh day God had finished the work he had been doing; so on the seventh day he rested from all his work" (Gen. 2:2). It might be argued that this means merely to cease working rather than actually resting. In Ex. 20:9–11, however, the statement "For in six days the LORD made the heavens and the earth, the sea, and all that is in them, but he rested on the seventh day," is offered as the reason for "Six days you shall labor and do all your work, but the seventh day is a Sabbath to the LORD your God. On it you shall not do any work." On the basis of the straightforward hermeneutic, God literally rested, and that implies that he literally was fatigued. Perhaps God did all the creating he was capable of doing, at least in one week, and was exhausted as a result.

---

[11]Interestingly, Sanders appears to take this verse literally, saying, "The sign of the rainbow that God gives is a reminder to himself that he will never again flood the earth and providing [sic] sign as a promise (9:11–12)." Yet he makes no further comment on this in terms of the implication for the understanding of God (*The God Who Risks*, 50).

WHAT DOES GOD KNOW AND WHEN DOES HE KNOW IT?

One other type of text needs to be examined. In Mal. 1:2–3, God says, "Yet I have loved Jacob, but Esau I have hated, and I have turned his mountains into a wasteland and left his inheritance to the desert jackals." Paul quotes this statement in Rom. 9:13, "Just as it is written: 'Jacob I loved, but Esau I hated.'" If taken literally, God actually hates someone, in this case, Esau. This would seem to be a particularly troublesome attribute for open theists, who regularly emphasize the love of God as the supreme attribute—or even more than that, the very definition of God.

In these cases, it would appear that the application of the open theists' hermeneutical principle yields results in excess of what they would wish to endorse. This should create a serious problem for open theism. What sort of response have open theists made to avoid this conclusion?

Boyd, who has most fully articulated and defended this literal hermeneutic, has made several types of responses. One of these is the use of the idea of rhetorical questions. Those cited above (e.g., Gen. 3:8, 11) are not to be taken literally because they are rhetorical in nature. He comments on Num. 14:11 and Hos. 8:5: "Some suggest that in these verses the Lord was asking rhetorical questions, just as he had done when he asked Adam and Eve where they were (Gen. 3:8–9). This is a possible interpretation, but not a necessary one. Unlike God's question about location in Genesis, there is nothing in these texts or in the whole of Scripture that requires these questions to be rhetorical."[12] Unfortunately, Boyd does not spell out just what it is in the text or elsewhere that does identify the others as rhetorical. It is difficult to see why the rhetorical question principle should be applied to the one but not to the other. One hint is found in Boyd's statement, "in the whole of Scripture," a lead that we will follow up later in this chapter.

He summarizes two of these: "First, there are certainly passages in the Bible that are figurative and portray God in human terms. You can recognize them because what is said about God is either ridiculous if taken literally (e.g., God has an 'outstretched arm,' Deut. 4:34; God as 'our husband,' Hosea 2:2), or because the genre of the passage is poetic (e.g., God has 'protecting wings,' Ps. 17:8)."[13] Again, Boyd does not elaborate on

---

[12]Boyd, *God of the Possible*, 59.
[13]Ibid., 118.

what he means by "ridiculous" or "poetic," or the criteria for recognizing these as such. He goes on to assert that "there is nothing ridiculous or poetic about the way the Bible repeatedly speaks about God changing his mind, regretting decisions, or thinking and speaking about the future in terms of possibilities. These passages usually occur within the historical narrative sections of Scripture."[14] Why, then, is it that some treat this latter type of Scripture as less than literal? Boyd says of these passages, "These only strike some as ridiculous because these readers bring to the text a preconception of what God *must* be like."[15]

In the absence of Boyd's giving us criteria for identifying what are definitely literal situations, one must ask why he sees the former type of text as ridiculous but not the latter. What makes them ridiculous? Could it be that he fails to carry through his hermeneutic to these texts because he is bringing to the text a preconception of what God must be like? Perhaps the idea of God's having an arm or making sounds when he "walks" in the garden seems ridiculous to Boyd because he has been influenced by Greek (or some other) philosophy to think that God cannot have a body.

One open theist has carried this hermeneutic through more consistently on this very point. Clark Pinnock observes that one issue that has not really been dealt with in the discussions of the open view is whether God has a body. He then comments, "If he is with us in the world, if we are to take biblical metaphors seriously, is God in some way embodied? Critics will be quick to say that, although there are expressions of this idea in the Bible, they are not to be taken literally. But I do not believe that the idea is as foreign to the Bible's view of God as we have assumed. In tradition, God is thought to function primarily as a disembodied spirit but this is scarcely a biblical idea."[16] He cites the references in Scripture to parts of God's body; to the fact that humans, who have bodies, are made in the image of God; to the theophanies of God; and to the fact that Jesus in his incarnation took on a body, which he took back to heaven with him. He concludes, "It seems to me that the Bible does not think of God as formless. Rather, it thinks of him as possessing a form that these divine appearances reflect. At the very

---

[14]Ibid.

[15]Ibid.

[16]Clark H. Pinnock, *Most Moved Mover: A Theology of God's Openness* (Grand Rapids: Baker, 1991), 33.

WHAT DOES GOD KNOW AND WHEN DOES HE KNOW IT?

least, God chooses to share in the human condition, participate in human history; an intensely and remarkably involved participant."[17] Pinnock sees the possible influence of philosophy on the customary denial of God's embodiment: "I do not feel obliged to assume that God is a purely spiritual being when his self-revelation does not suggest it. It is true that from a Platonic standpoint, the idea is absurd, but this is not a biblical standpoint. And how unreasonable is it, anyway? The only persons we encounter are embodied persons and, if God is not embodied, it may prove difficult to understand how God is a person. What kind of actions would a disembodied God perform?"[18]

This possibility that Pinnock poses (and he does not affirm it to be the case) seems to separate him quite clearly from Boyd. It appears that he has been more consistent in his application of the hermeneutical principle. Some, however, would object that the Bible does assert or at least imply that God is purely spiritual in such texts as John 4:24,"God is spirit, and his worshipers must worship in spirit and in truth," and Acts 17:24, "The God who made the world and everything in it is the Lord of heaven and earth and does not live in temples built by hands." It could be argued that the texts for God's transcendence of the physical universe also imply this spirituality. Presumably, it is such texts that lead Boyd to reject as "ridiculous" the reference to God's body parts. If this is the case, however, we must diligently ask whether there are other texts in Scripture that bear upon the way we interpret some of the texts cited by the open theists like Boyd.

The Analogy of Scripture. One principle that should be applied here is the principle sometimes termed "analogia Scriptura," or the analogy of Scripture, the idea that it supplies its own interpretation. The question is the extent to which the understanding of a given portion of Scripture can be given us by examining other parts of Scripture. Ostensibly, open theists subscribe to this position. Basinger, for example, says, "If there is one hermeneutical issue on which most conservative Christians agree, it is that the interpretation of any given verse (or passage) must ultimately be determined by the overall teaching of Scripture on the issue at hand."[19] Pinnock

---

[17]Ibid., 34.

[18]Ibid.

[19]David Basinger, *The Case for Freewill Theism: A Philosophical Assessment* (Downers Grove, Ill.: InterVarsity, 1996), 51.

also says of the Gen. 18 passage: "In this case, there are other texts which tell us that God did not need to travel to Sodom to find out about it (Jer. 23:24), but none that tell us that God knows everything before it happens (Amos 5:15)."[20] Yet he does not carry this method to other texts that the open theists appeal to, as Ware has done.

One of these can be found in terms of three references in Jeremiah in which God says that what the Israelites had done had not "entered his mind." The three are:

> They have built the high places of Topheth in the Valley of Ben Hinnom to burn their sons and daughters in the fire—something I did not command, nor did it enter my mind. (Jer. 7:31)

> They have built the high places of Baal to burn their sons in the fire as offerings to Baal—something I did not command or mention, nor did it enter my mind.(Jer. 19:5)

> They built high places for Baal in the Valley of Ben Hinnom to sacrifice their sons and daughters to Molech, though I never commanded, nor did it enter my mind, that they should do such a detestable thing and so make Judah sin. (Jer. 32:35)

These three references can be seen to be almost identical. Boyd's interpretation of these is literal, that God did not in any sense anticipate that the Israelites would do such things until they actually did them. One question to ask, however, is whether there are any other references in earlier Scriptures that indicate that God did already know this. Three references in Deuteronomy and Leviticus may be suggested:

> You must not worship the LORD your God in their way, because in worshiping their gods, they do all kinds of detestable things the LORD hates. They even burn their sons and daughters in the fire as sacrifices to their gods. (Deut. 12:31)

> When you enter the land the LORD your God is giving you, do not learn to imitate the detestable ways of the nations there. Let no one be found among you who sacrifices his son or daughter in the fire, who practices

---

[20]Pinnock, *Most Moved Mover,* 61, n.86.

divination or sorcery, interprets omens, engages in witchcraft . . . (Deut. 18:9–10)

'Do not give any of your children to be sacrificed to Molech, for you must not profane the name of your God. I am the LORD.' (Lev. 18:21)

These passages, if taken at face value, indicate that God had indeed anticipated that the people might do these things and had warned them against it. In fact, the Leviticus passage seems to relate explicitly to the statement in Jer. 32:35. It could, of course, be responded that these were simply general warnings against doing what the nations about them were doing, that they are found in lists of such activities, and that they do indicate that Jehovah thought that the people of Israel might do them. Then, however, we must ask just what was the point of these warnings. It appears that, contrary to Boyd, these things did enter God's mind, at least enough to evoke such a response. Here is a case, then, where other portions of Scripture cannot really be reconciled with the open theist interpretation of those "did not enter my mind" texts. A better solution, one that enables us to retain the concept of the unity of the Bible, would be to seek for other interpretations of these three texts.

One such solution would be on the basis of a form of biblical criticism. If, for example, one were to contend that the Bible is not necessarily a unity, that different books reflect the perspective of varying authors, and that there is not a single divine author (or coauthor) behind the several books, then the apparent conflict need not be resolved. It should be noted that some of the biblical commentators whom the open theists cite may be of such a persuasion regarding Scripture. This would certainly be true of Walter Brueggemann, and possibly of Terence Fretheim. Without trying to draw the limits of evangelicalism too tightly, this would seem to represent a different view of Scripture than has previously ordinarily been identified as evangelical.

Consistency of Principle. Another issue of consistency with respect to open theist hermeneutics is the question of whether similar passages are interpreted according to the same theological principle. One example of this is the passages pertaining to the testing of Abraham, the granting of Hezekiah's prayer for extended life, and the prediction of Peter's denial. In the first two of these cases, Jehovah did not know what they would do because he did not know the heart of the person. Only the man's action made clear the contents and attitudes of the heart. In the case of Peter, however, God knew his heart so well that he could predict that Peter would deny Jesus, not once, but three times. This, however, seems to be an inconsistency. If God knew Peter's heart well enough to make such a detailed prediction, could he not have known the heart of Abraham well enough to at least know that Abraham feared him? Bear in mind that the open theists say that God knows the present, including the contents of human hearts, perfectly. What God declares that he now knows is the present condition of the heart, not the future action. Yet God comes to know that present heart condition only as an inference from the action. Thus, at least some of God's knowledge is inferential, just as is his knowledge of the future.

It may, of course, be asserted that God knew the intents of Peter's heart better than he did Abraham's heart. This might be because the incarnate second person of the Trinity had actually lived with Peter, which was not the case with Abraham. It is significant, however, that Boyd does not say that Jesus knew Peter so well that he knew what Peter would do. Rather, it was the Father who had this outstanding knowledge of Peter and revealed it to Jesus. As we pointed out earlier, Abraham had demonstrated his character for a longer time than had Peter.

It should be possible to offer some rationale for this different treatment of the cases of the two men, but strangely, Boyd does not even raise the issue. He simply treats them differently and proceeds. In the absence of some explanation, it must be concluded that he is simply engaged in ad hoc interpretation.

Criteria of Verification. The question of consistency arises not just with respect to the application of theological principles but even in relation to criteria of verification. One of these problems can be seen in Boyd's discussion of whether God's foreknowledge is exhaustive of all of the events of Scripture. He says of Isa. 46:9–11, "Neither this nor any other passage in Scripture says that God foreknows or declares *everything* that is going to occur."[21] In light of this fact and the presence of elements that seem to

---

[21]Gregory A. Boyd, "The Open-Theism View," in *Divine Foreknowledge: Four Views*, ed. James K. Beilby and Paul R. Eddy (Downers Grove, Ill.: InterVarsity, 2001), 16.

teach that God does not know some things, Boyd concludes that God's foreknowledge is not exhaustive.

It is interesting to note, however, that Boyd holds that God's knowledge of the past and of the present are exhaustive. He says of Jesus' prediction of Peter's threefold denial of him: "The only conclusions justified by this episode are that *God possesses perfect knowledge of the past and present* and that some of the future is settled, either by present circumstances (Peter's character) or by God's sovereign design."[22] What is interesting about this statement, however, is that the text does not teach that God has perfect knowledge of the past and present. In fact, no text in Scripture affirms God's exhaustive knowledge of the past and present, any more than it does his exhaustive knowledge of the future. As Hunt points out, this shows that Boyd's proposal that exegesis should always drive one's philosophy, not vice versa, is an oversimplification with respect to Boyd's own practice.[23] In other words, Boyd's treatment of God's knowledge of the future is not consistent with his treatment of God's knowledge of the past and present.

Narrative and Didactic Passages. One further question is the relative role of narrative and didactic passages in hermeneutics. In the context of our present discussion, the question is one of whether the descriptions of what God does are to interpret the teachings about what God is like or vice versa. It is clear that the open theists give primacy to the narrative descriptions, an example being the 1 Sam. 15 passage, where the statements that God repented are used to interpret the statement that he is not a man, and therefore is not one who repents. Pinnock says directly, "In terms of biblical interpretation, I give particular weight to narrative and to the language of personal relationships in it."[24] This approach, to be sure, fits well with the current emphasis on narrative rather than propositional theology. We must ask, however, whether this is preferable to the more traditional approach of giving primacy to the didactic statements of Scripture and interpreting the narratives in light of these.

---

[22]Ibid., 21.

[23]David Hunt, "A Simple-Foreknowledge Response," in *Divine Foreknowledge: Four Views*, ed. James K. Beilby and Paul R. Eddy (Downers Grove, Ill.: InterVarsity, 2001), 50.

[24]Pinnock, *Most Moved Mover*, 20.

I would propose that the general rule to be followed is that the teachings about what God is like should be the explanation of what he appears to be doing in a given situation. This is a general principle in other areas of life as well. How often do we ask someone, "What are you doing?" where that is intended, not as a sort of reprimand, but as a genuine inquiry regarding the actual nature of the actions? What is generally being asked about is the meaning of that act, because physical actions frequently are not self-interpreting or self-evident in their meaning.

Stanley Fish offers us an interesting example.[25] During a class, a student raises his hand and begins to wave it furiously. What is he doing? In one sense, of course, he is simply waving his hand, but the further question asks about the social significance of the action. Some might think this to be a desire to ask a question or make a comment, and therefore this is a request to be recognized. In some settings, however, the student would be thought to be requesting permission to be excused in order to visit the rest room. Other possibilities come to mind. This might indicate an unusual medical condition of the student, so that he cannot control the raising and waving of his hand. It might be an unusual religious practice or form of prayer in the religious group of which this student is a part.

Fish makes the point that it is the social grouping, the community, that gives the action its particular meaning. It is true that there are given actions that are completely opaque to someone who is not familiar with the culture. For example, someone not familiar with the action known as hitchhiking (or "thumbing a ride") might be confused to see a person standing alongside a roadway with his arm extended and his thumb turned upward. "What is he doing?" one might ask. In one sense, it is evident what the person involved is doing. However, what is being requested is an explanation of the *significance* of the act, which in this case is something like, "He is asking for a ride." Additional examples of this type could be suggested. In many cases, we do not even think about the act having an explanation because we are so familiar with it.

---

[25]Stanley Fish, *Is There a Text in This Class? The Authority of Interpretive Communities* (Cambridge, Mass.: Harvard University Press, 1980), 332–33.

It is helpful to observe cases in Scripture of interpretation being given of an action or a narrative. Often the interpretation is simply slipped into the narrative. For instance, in Ruth 4:1–12, Boaz goes to a kinsman, who, because he is a closer relative than is Boaz to Ruth's deceased husband, has the prior right of redemption and thus of marrying Ruth. Boaz proposes this to the other man, who declines the opportunity, then takes off his sandal and gives it to Boaz (v. 8). In itself, this action might not make sense to us, although the context could give us the hint that this was an expression of his statement to Boaz in v. 6. Note, however, the interesting parenthetical statement inserted as v. 7: "(Now in earlier times in Israel, for the redemption and transfer of property to become final, one party took off his sandal and gave it to the other. This was the method of legalizing transactions in Israel.)" Similarly, Jesus' parables were narratives. In themselves, however, they did not bear obvious meaning. So the disciples had to ask for the interpretation, and Jesus offered it, in didactic fashion.

When we come to the passages that have been introduced into this discussion, it is notable that they describe what God did or even how he felt, but in many cases they do not elaborate or explain what is meant by this. For example, God is said to warn the people of Israel that he is going to destroy them. Does this mean that he really expects that he will do this so that when he does not, he has changed his mind? Or does it mean that he has given them this threat as a means of motivating them to change their behavior? There are indeed many things that a person may be doing in asking a question: attempting to determine something one does not know, trying to elicit a particular response from a person, or simply serving notice that this is an important issue. Just as there are "rhetorical questions," there are also "rhetorical assertions." It is only the interpretative or didactic portions of Scripture that enable us to distinguish which of these a given statement may be. Purely narrative passages do not have this capability. Thus, I would contend that the didactic portions, not the narrative passages, should be determinative of the meaning. Where a narrative passage is used to override the "plain meaning" of a didactic passage (as when 1 Sam. 15, verses 11 and 35 are used to reject the meaning of v. 29), it is usually because a different assumed didactic meaning is being used to interpret the narrative.

There is, however, a reciprocal relationship between didactic and narrative passages. The role of narrative is often to illustrate or demonstrate the truth taught in the didactic passages. They are instances shedding light on the didactic truth. Just as illustrations and analogies do not prove what they are illustrating but only show its feasibility, so narratives serve with respect to the "propositional" truth delivered in didactic passages.

WEIGHTING THE MOTIFS OF SCRIPTURE

A further question to be asked concerns the relative importance or emphasis placed on different passages. One of the principles of recent exegetical study has been that not all Scripture is to be treated as if it were "level"; that is, quotations cannot simply be taken from any portion of Scripture and ranged against other references as if all were equally relevant to determining the truth on a particular subject.

Controlling Metaphors. Richard Rice developed the biblical evidence for the open view in *The Openness of God.* He acknowledges that the traditional view can summon an impressive array of biblical texts to support its understanding of God. It is not hard to give biblical support to such an idea, but "the crucial question is whether the idea is faithful to the overall biblical portrait of God—the picture that emerges from the full range of biblical evidence."[26] Most of the biblical material about God is of the nature of metaphors, and these are not all equal in importance. Some are more important because they "bear a stronger resemblance to the divine reality—they are closer, so to speak, to the intended object—and they play a more prominent role within the overall biblical picture of God."[27] Borrowing an expression from Terence Fretheim, Rice labels metaphors that provide a hermeneutical key for interpreting the whole as "controlling metaphors." He seeks "to restore some important biblical metaphors to the prominence they deserve in our thinking about God, in particular metaphors such as divine suffering and divine repentance. Giving such metaphors more weight will enable us to achieve an understanding of God

---

[26]Richard Rice, "Biblical Support for a New Perspective," in Clark Pinnock, Richard Rice, John Sanders, William Hasker, and David Basinger, *The Openness of God: A Biblical Challenge to the Traditional Understanding of God* (Downers Grove, Ill.: InterVarsity, 1994), 15.
[27]Ibid., 17.

that is much more faithful to the Bible than is the familiar alternative."[28] Pinnock also acknowledges the element of arbitrariness in interpretation: "But there is freedom to choose between meanings, both at the macro and micro levels, and one may be influenced by one's own control beliefs and press texts in directions favored by them. For this reason, we cannot expect one model to triumph over the others. A decision will have to be made as to which reading seems more probable and plausible. At the very least, the open view appeals to an impressive array of biblical support."[29] Pinnock does not, however, pursue the question of the origin and validity of these "control beliefs" with anywhere near the intensity with which he contends that the control beliefs of the conventional theists derive from Greek philosophy and distort their reading of Scripture.

The one attribute of God that should be considered most important, according to Rice, is love. In fact, love is more than just an attribute of God: "From a Christian perspective, *love* is the first and last word in the biblical portrait of God. According to 1 John 4:8: 'Whoever does not love does not know God, because God is love.' The statement *God is love* is as close as the Bible comes to giving us a definition of the divine reality. And as Eberhard Jüngel observes, Christian theology has always given this expression pride of place among the many descriptions of God."[30]

Leaving aside for a moment the question of the status of love, whether it is actually this definition of God that Rice contends it is, we need to ask about the logic of this hermeneutic. For in his first introduction of the topic of God's love, Rice indicates its place in the thinking of open theology: "It expresses two basic convictions: love is the most important quality we attribute to God, and love is more than care and commitment; it involves being sensitive and responsive as well. These convictions lead the contributors to this book to think of God's relation to the world in dynamic rather than static terms. This conclusion has important consequences. For one thing, it means that God interacts with his creatures. Not only does he influence them, but they also exert an influence on him."[31]

---

[28]Ibid.
[29]Pinnock, *Most Moved Mover*, 60.
[30]Rice, "Biblical Support," 18.
[31]Ibid., 15.

This love is not merely an attribute of God, even the most prominent attribute of God, "it is more fundamental as well. Love is the essence of the divine reality, the basic source from which *all* of God's attributes arise. This means that the assertion *God is love* incorporates all there is to say about God."[32] This priority of the love of God is found in the other open theists' thoughts as well.

The logic of the argument seems to be this. Not all biblical materials are to be given equal weight in formulating the understanding of God. Rather, certain metaphors which more closely relate to the nature of God and are more prominent in Scripture are to be considered controlling metaphors and allowed to interpret the rest. But the nature of God is that found in the Scripture when the Scripture is interpreted from the perspective of love being the most central dimension of the understanding of God, and love as defined by the open theists. To put it more briefly: the open view is to be adopted because it is supported by the Bible, and in interpreting the Bible we are to emphasize more those elements that support open theism. The circularity here should be apparent. One cannot help but wonder whether the conclusion has already been formed, and the biblical evidence is selected in terms of the extent to which it supports that conclusion.

Sanders attempts to give a rationale for considering repentance a "controlling" metaphor. Following the work of Terence Fretheim, he suggests three lines of evidence for this contention. One is that divine repentance is pervasive within the Old Testament, with only the instances of *niham* appearing some thirty-five times. Second, divine repentance is found within a variety of traditions: Yahwist/Elohist, David-Zion, Deuteronomic history, psalmody, and prophetic works of the seventh and eighth century, both exilic and postexilic. Finally, it appears in a variety of genres, including divine speech (where God says, "I repent") and creedal statements such as Joel 2:13 and Jonah 4:2. On the basis of such evidence, he concurs with Fretheim that repentance should be treated as a controlling metaphor.[33]

This argument also deserves further examination, however. It assumes, for example, that all of the instances of *niham* are to be interpreted as

---

[32]Ibid., 21.
[33]Sanders, *The God Who Risks,* 72–73.

instances of repentance. Yet, as we saw in the semantical study of Parunak,[34] *niham* (the Hiphil stem) may have several possible meanings, of which "repent" is only one, and the other stems have several possible meanings. Thus, the argument appears to beg the meaning of *niham*. As such, it is again a form of circular argument: "These passages should be interpreted as meaning repentance because repentance is a controlling metaphor. We know it to be a controlling metaphor because of its widespread occurrence in passages such as these."

If, however, the approach of openness is not sufficient, what criteria shall we employ in terms of giving priority to certain passages? The open theists are correct that there are, in practice, certain controlling metaphors that are given the "right of way"—or, as they put it, "pride of place," in what we might term the "hermeneutical rules of the road." The question, however, is what these rules of the road should be. I propose several.

Emphasis and Cruciality. One of these is the type of emphasis placed on a given passage or a given concept within a passage. Here it is helpful to observe that in a passage such as Isa. 41–48, God's knowledge of the future, including free human actions, is so strongly emphasized as to be made a distinguishing feature by which one can differentiate between the true God and false claimants to deity. By contrast, those passages where God supposedly does not know or has to ask do not make this essential to the very nature of God. It is true that love is very strongly emphasized in Scripture and is indicated as crucial to the understanding of God, but that this love is of the type described by the open theists is what is in dispute. This argument could be carried further and illustrated at greater length.

Directness and Clarity. A second criterion is the directness and clarity with which something is taught. We may notice that in a passage such as Jesus' prediction of Peter's threefold denial of him. The most straightforward or clear teaching here seems to be that Jesus knew what Peter was going to do and knew the future free action of Peter. To resort to an explanation such as Boyd offers, of Jesus' knowing Peter's character and tendencies and then God three times "squeezing Peter's character out of him," seems unduly complicated and even fanciful. It can hardly be taken to be

---

[34]H. Van Dyke Parunak, "A Semantic Survey of NHM," *Biblica* 56, no. 4 (1975): 512–32.

clearly taught. In fact, it is at best a highly inferential interpretation of the passage.

Recurrence and Frequency. Those themes that are most recurrent in Scripture should be given precedence in interpreting the rest. This principle is introduced last because sheer numbers alone should not be allowed to tip the balance if those numbers are in rather obscure and unclear passages, versus those that may appear less frequently but with greater emphasis and clarity. At least one open theist, although affirming the importance of interpreting specific passages in the light of the whole of Scripture, appears to reject the importance of testing the comparative weighting of different themes. David Basinger says,

> To challenge successfully the right of a Christian with a high view of Scripture to affirm PK [present knowledge], what critics must argue is that it is *impossible,* given neutral hermeneutical principles, to deny that specific passages require that God possess exhaustive knowledge and/or to deny that Scripture *as a whole* portrays God as one who possesses such knowledge. I do not believe, however, that any such argument has yet been produced. (Nor do I believe that such an argument will or even can be produced.) Thus, as I see it, proponents of PK retain the right to offer their perspective as a viable alternative for consideration by any sincere Christian.[35]

I would agree with Basinger that it is unlikely that any such argument will or can be produced *on the terms that he has specified.* Note the high bar that he has raised: critics must argue that it is *impossible.* Basinger does not indicate what he means by "impossible," whether logical, psychological, legal, or what. Short of finding a logical contradiction, it is difficult to conceive of how such an absolute negative thesis could be established. This seems to be a case of attempting to secure immunity by definition. Excluding that stipulation, however, it would seem that one of the ways that one determines the teaching of Scripture as a whole is to examine the frequency of references of various types. This is a matter of probabilities.

All things being equal, then, frequency of mention certainly should indicate something of centrality. For example, in his discourse about the

---

[35]David Basinger, *The Case for Freewill Theism,* 52.

WHAT DOES GOD KNOW AND WHEN DOES HE KNOW IT?

relationship between himself and his disciples as being one of friendship rather than slavery, Jesus used the word *love,* either in noun or verb form, nine times in nine verses (John 15:9–17). This should suggest to us that this was very basic to what he was attempting to convey.

Part of this principle means that if there is a considerable disparity of occurrence, it simply is easier to explain the smaller number than the larger number. At one time I had a New Testament colleague whose specialty was the Synoptic Gospels and who tended to emphasize those passages in which the Synoptics appear to contradict one another. When he left the faculty, he was replaced by a person who said, "We try to interpret the 5 percent (or less) of the passages of apparent disagreement in light of the 95 percent (or more) of the passages which are in agreement with one another."

What happens when we examine the relative frequency of passages supporting the idea of exhaustive definite foreknowledge versus those that call that attribute into question? We must go beyond simply saying that the open view has biblical support and ask, How much support? Steven Roy has done extensive research and compiled the biblical texts that bear upon divine omniscience and especially, divine foreknowledge. As categorized, the summary of results is as follows:

1. 164 texts explicitly teach/affirm God's foreknowledge.
2. 271 texts explicitly teach/affirm other aspects of God's omniscience (e.g., knowledge of past or present or possible states of affairs).
3. 128 texts offer predictions of what God will do through nature.
4. 1,893 texts state predictively that God will do something or other in or through human beings.
5. 1,474 texts state predictively what human beings will do, apart from God directly acting in or through them.
6. 622 texts state predictively what unbelievers will do or have happen to them.
7. 143 texts affirm God's sovereign control of human choices.
8. 105 texts of apparent counter evidence.[36]

Thus, of 4,800 instances, only 105, or 2.1875 percent, directly argue for the open theist view—or to put it differently, cannot be easily accounted

---

[36]Cited in Ware, *God's Lesser Glory,* 100, n. 7.

for by the traditional view of God's knowledge of the future. Of the remaining categories, some are clearly problematic for open theism. Certainly, category 5 is a problem, and category 7 seems to be as well. Category 4 appears to be a problem, although not as clearly so. Some of the texts in category 6, those dealing with what unbelievers will do, certainly fall into this classification, although predictions about what will happen to unbelievers may not necessarily fall here. Categories 2 and 3 do not seem to bear directly upon the issue, and the texts in category 1 would have to be examined individually to determine whether they contradicted the open theist interpretation. Thus, on the most generous assessment, 1,617 texts, or 33.6875 percent of the texts, present a problem for the open theist view, and perhaps as high as 89.5 percent represent difficulties for that position, whereas the traditional view has difficulty with only 2.1875 percent.[37]

It may be helpful at this point to observe a comment passed on to us by John Baillie. As an undergraduate he had written a paper criticizing an accepted philosophical doctrine. The teacher wrote on the paper: "Every theory has its difficulties, but you have not considered whether any other theory has less difficulties than the one you have criticized." In Baillie's case, reflection on this remark led him back to the received doctrine, and he remarks that he has observed a similar result in a remarkable number of others who have followed the same procedure and "returned to the full Christian outlook after years of defection from it."[38]

In this case, when we compare the relative amount of difficulty presented to each view by a wide array of biblical texts, it would appear that the open theist position rather than the traditional theory encounters the most problems.

Progressive Revelation. A further consideration is the matter of progressive revelation. On this basis, God gradually revealed more of his truth with the passage of time and the increased ability of his people to understand it. Thus, the later revelation is clearer, more complete, and more direct, so that it interprets but does not contradict the earlier revelation. When we examine the biblical material involved in the discussion, what do we find?

---

[37]This assumes the accuracy of Roy's research and conclusions. I have not checked all of the texts in detail.
[38]John Baillie, *Invitation to Pilgrimage* (New York: Scribner, 1942), 15.

It is interesting to examine the relative weight given to Old Testament and New Testament materials in formulating the open theist theory. Rice, for example, devotes exactly twice as much space (16 pages) to discussing the Old Testament as the New Testament (8 pages). Pinnock's chapter on the biblical basis has 79 references to Old Testament passages but only 18 New Testament references, a ratio of nearly five to one. Boyd cites the Old Testament 96 times, but the New Testament only 32 times, a ratio of three to one. The most nearly balanced treatment is that of Sanders, whose respective chapters on the Old and New Testaments are almost exactly equal in length, although both parties would claim many of the passages in the latter chapter as supporting their view.

What, then, shall we make of these phenomena? One interpretation is that the further the progressive revelation proceeded, the less material can be found to support the open view. In particular, the New Testament materials are drawn primarily from the narrative rather than the didactic materials and relate more to providence than to foreknowledge, so the evidence for an open view of foreknowledge must be arrived at by inference rather than direct reading. We should also notice that the open theists' claim to the right to many of the providence passages assumes that the traditional view, being the Greek philosophical view, must hold to a particular idea of impassibility, so that it cannot accommodate passages that picture God as interacting with humans. However, if this is disputed, as we shall see is the case, then many of the passages will not necessarily favor the open view.

We should not be surprised to find this type of shift from Old Testament to New Testament. In general, the Old Testament puts matters in more concrete form than does the New Testament. The Hebrew language, although not as sharply different from Greek as some have assumed, nonetheless is a more concrete language with fewer adjectives, so that adjectival expressions are frequently constructed from nouns (e.g., "a man of righteousness," rather than "a righteous man"). Consequently, it should not be surprising to find more anthropomorphisms here than in the more abstract discussions of the New Testament, especially in the didactic passages but also in the interpretations or explanations of the narratives.

The Nature of Universal Statements. The open theists argue that while there are many passages that show God's knowledge of specific aspects or elements of the future, there are no texts that state specifically that God knows *everything that is to happen.* It is important to note the nature of the issue, however. What we are dealing with, in the case of the prophecies, is inductive logic. By its very nature, inductive logic proceeds incrementally. Cases are built up so that on that basis one can generalize to an inclusive rule. In order to build a perfect case, of course, there would have to be prophecies regarding every possible future event, a completely cumbersome and unnecessary collection. It is notable, however, that a large number of prophecies did prove to be accurate.

Furthermore, we should observe here the principle of the greater and lesser. If a prophecy demonstrates a correct knowledge of something highly unlikely, then matters less difficult to predict are also thereby established, at least in principle. To use an analogy from another realm: if I demonstrate that I can lift a 100-pound weight, that also demonstrates my ability to lift a weight of 60, 50, or 40 pounds, barring some unusual quality such as the size and shape of the object, or some other factor, such as a very slippery surface. Thus, passages like Jesus' accurate and very detailed prediction of Peter's denial of him, and Isaiah's prophecy including the name of the king (Cyrus), mean that other matters, less complex or difficult to know, are also accurate.

William Craig puts the point somewhat differently. He says, "The problem with Boyd's procedure . . . is that the defender of divine foreknowledge need only show that God knows just *one* future contingent proposition or CCF [counterfactual of creaturely freedom], for in that case (1) there is no logical incompatibility between divine foreknowledge and future contingents, (2) the Principle of Bivalence does not fail for such propositions, and (3) it becomes ad hoc to claim that other such propositions are not also true and known to God."[39]

---

[39]William Lane Craig, "A Middle-Knowledge Response," in *Divine Foreknowledge: Four Views,* ed. James K. Beilby and Paul R. Eddy (Downers Grove, Ill.: InterVarsity, 2001), 57.

We have examined the open theist hermeneutic, as the open theists have practiced it, in contrast to traditional conservative hermeneutical theory, attempting to assess the validity of that hermeneutic in light of some commonly accepted principles of literary interpretation. On the basis of this examination, it appears that the open theist hermeneutic is less adequate, overall, than that of traditional theism.

CHAPTER 4

THE HISTORICAL DEVELOPMENT of THE DOCTRINE of DIVINE foreknowledge

Part 1

It is helpful to examine the history of the Christian church, to attempt to determine what views of foreknowledge have actually been held. There are a number of reasons why such an endeavor is important.

(1) We are trying to determine whether there is any such thing as an established or orthodox view on this matter. By "orthodox" here, we are using the Vincentian rule, named for the fifth-century Vincent of Lerins, who held that orthodoxy is "that which has been believed everywhere, always, by all."[1] That statement was not intended to be taken completely literally, of course. For if that were the case, then any contradictory voice would nullify the entire endeavor, and there would either be no such thing as heterodoxy, or the content of orthodoxy would be reduced to a rather general common denominator. What Vincent was looking for was a predominance of opinion, a broad major stream of belief.

Many have assumed that there simply was agreement on the traditional understanding of God's foreknowledge, but it is important that we examine the actual history of the tradition. We can benefit by seeing what others before us have thought on this

---

[1]Vincent of Lerins, *A Commonitory for the Antiquity and Universality of the Catholic Faith against the Profane Novelties of All Heresies*, 2.6.

subject. If they were working with the same materials and from the same presuppositions, then presumably we should come to the same conclusions they did. If not, then we must ask whether there is some difference of presupposition or some additional premise that deserves examination.

(2) Another dimension to this inquiry has been introduced by some of the open theists. They have likened their theology to a new reformation, the uncovering of a biblical truth that had long been forgotten or obscured. If this is the case, then it should be helpful in assessing their thesis to look at some of the very earliest theologians, for presumably the original tradition should have persisted for at least a time after the closing of the canon. The earliest interpreters of the Scriptures may be a good guide to us in evaluating this new reformation thesis.

In particular, the open theists have contended that the reason the church has held the traditional view of God's exhaustive divine foreknowledge is that Christian theology early came under the influence of Greek philosophy. Thus, it read the Scriptures in light of the idea of a perfect being who was timeless, immutable, and impassible. The study of the views of the earliest Christian thinkers should help us resolve this issue.

(3) One of the notable historical considerations is that no church council ever took a definite stand on this issue. Does that mean that those who are orthodox on the issues that the ecumenical councils did rule on (such as the incarnation and the Trinity) are free to differ on this issue? Does the silence of the councils on this matter mean that it was not deemed important enough to establish an official position, or should it be interpreted as an indication that the church thought it unnecessary because no contrary view was held and expressed among Christians?

THE EARLY CHURCH FATHERS

It is not practical to examine all of the Fathers in detail. Yet because their statements on the subject of foreknowledge are relatively few in number, a major sampling should shed some light on our question.

Clement. Clement's statements on foreknowledge do not come in abstractly doctrinal issues. He was dealing more with the practical matters of the church. Yet the underlying reasons for his practical teachings are doctrinal in nature and can be distilled from his writings. For example, he discusses Num. 17, in which Moses took the rods of the priests, bound them together, and declared that the one whose rod blossomed would be shown to be the one whom God had chosen to minister. Clement then says of the discovery the next morning that Aaron's rod had not only blossomed but had even produced almonds, "What think ye, beloved? Did not Moses know beforehand that this would happen? Undoubtedly he knew; but he acted thus, that there might be no sedition in Israel, and that the name of the true and only God might be glorified; to whom be glory for ever and ever. Amen."[2] Similarly, he discusses the apostles' choice of a successor to Judas: "For this reason, therefore, inasmuch as they had obtained a perfect foreknowledge of this [the conditions that were to come upon the church], they appointed those [ministers] already mentioned, and afterwards gave instructions, that when these should fall asleep, other approved men should succeed them in their ministry."[3] In both of these cases, it is apparent that the human persons' knowledge of what was to come was because God had made it known to them. That, of course, assumes that God had foreknowledge of these matters.

Justin Martyr. As one of the apologists for the faith, Justin made much of fulfilled prophecy in the Bible. In a chapter entitled "Prophecy Using the Past Tense," he says they are spoken of in this fashion because of the certainty of God's knowledge: "The things which He absolutely knows will take place, He predicts as if already they had taken place."[4]

Interestingly, even at this early date, Justin anticipated the freewill objection to foreknowledge. Lest anyone think that those who fulfilled prophecy by their actions were the victims of fate, Justin says,

> So that what we say about future events being foretold, we do not say it as if they came about by a fatal necessity; but God foreknowing all that shall be done by all men, and it being His decree that the future actions of men shall all be recompensed according to their several value, He foretells by the Spirit of prophecy that He will bestow meet rewards according to the

---

[2]Clement, *First Epistle to the Corinthians,* chap. 43.
[3]Ibid., chap. 44.
[4]Justin Martyr, *First Apology,* chap. 42.

merit of the actions done, always urging the human race to effort and recollection, showing that He cares and provides for men.[5]

Again, he writes, "But if the word of God foretells that some angels and men shall be certainly punished, it did so because it foreknew that they would be unchangeably [wicked], but not because God had created them so."[6]

In a quotation reminiscent of Isaiah's argument in chapters 41–46, Justin ties the matter of foreknowledge to divinity: "For if this is not the case, God will be slandered, as having no foreknowledge, and as not teaching all men to know and to do the same acts of righteousness."[7]

Irenaeus. Irenaeus echoes the argument of Isaiah when he challenges the Gnostics, and especially the Barbeliotes or Borborians. He argues that their god is not a real god if he is not prescient.[8] He then uses a similar argument against the Valentinians and Marcion. The God who conceived of what was to be and the God who brought it into being must be the same God:

> If, again, He is prescient, and contemplated mentally that creation which was about to have a being in that place, then He Himself created it who also formed it beforehand [ideally] in Himself.
>
> Let them cease, therefore, to affirm that the world was made by any other; for as soon as God formed a conception in His mind, that was also done which He had thus mentally conceived. For it was not possible that one Being should mentally form the conception, and another actually produce the things which had been conceived by Him in His mind.[9]

This foreknowledge extends all the way back to his act of creation, Irenaeus says: "For after His great kindness He graciously conferred good [upon us], and made men like to Himself, [that is] in their own power; while at the same time by His prescience He knew the infirmity of human beings, and the consequences which would flow from it; but through [His] love and [His] power, He shall overcome the substance of created nature."[10]

---

[5]Ibid., chapter 44.
[6]Justin Martyr, *Dialogue,* chapter 141.
[7]Ibid., chapter 92.
[8]Irenaeus, *Against Heresies,* 1. 29.1.
[9]Ibid. 2.3.1–2.
[10]Ibid., 4.38. 4.

Like Justin, Irenaeus links foreknowledge to the phenomenon of prophecy: "'Many prophets and righteous men have desired to see those things which ye see, and have not seen them; and to hear those things which ye hear, and have not heard them.' In what way, then, did they desire both to hear and to see, unless they had foreknowledge of His future advent? But how could they have foreknown it, unless they had previously received foreknowledge from Himself?"[11] He sees prophecy as given at least in part as an evidence of divine foreknowledge. He says of the Old Testament that it "foreshadowed the images of those things which [now actually] exist in the Church, in order that our faith might be firmly established; and contained a prophecy of things to come, in order that man might learn that God has foreknowledge of all things."[12]

This foreknowledge is entire. So "God, foreknowing all things, prepared fit habitations for both [believers and unbelievers]."[13] Jesus was aware of the Father's foreknowledge of all things and had a sense of the timeliness of certain matters. This is why he said to Mary, when she urged him to perform the miracle of the wine, "Dear woman, why do you involve me? My time has not yet come" (John 2:4). So Irenaeus comments of Jesus, "With Him is nothing incomplete or out of due season, just as with the Father there is nothing incongruous. For all these things were foreknown by the Father; but the Son works them out at the proper time in perfect order and sequence."[14]

Other Second-Century Fathers. This emphasis on the completeness and uniqueness of God's knowledge of the future continued with the second-century Fathers. Tatian, for example, in his account of his conversion, attributes a major influence in his coming to faith to the phenomenon of divine foreknowledge:

And, while I was giving my most earnest attention to the matter, I happened to meet with certain barbaric writings, too old to be compared with the opinions of the Greeks, and too divine to be compared with their errors; and I was led to put faith in these by the unpretending cast of the

---

[11]Ibid., 11. 1.
[12]Ibid., 32. 2.
[13]Ibid., 40.4.
[14]Ibid., 3.16.7.

language, the inartificial character of the writers, the foreknowledge displayed of future events, the excellent quality of the precepts, and the declaration of the government of the universe as centered in one Being.[15]

Theophilus wrote that God knew the unbelief that was to come and the form it would take: "For the divine wisdom foreknew that some would trifle and name a multitude of gods that do not exist,"[16] and "on the fourth day the luminaries were made; because God, who possesses foreknowledge, knew the follies of the vain philosophers, that they were going to say, that the things which grow on the earth are produced from the heavenly bodies, so as to exclude God."[17]

Clement of Alexandria saw foreknowledge as an evidence of divinity. He wrote, "For He shows both things: both His divinity in His foreknowledge of what would take place, and His love in affording an opportunity for repentance to the self-determination of the soul."[18]

The *stromata,* or miscellanies, contain a large number of references to foreknowledge. Here prophecy and foreknowledge are linked: "Again, prophecy is foreknowledge; and knowledge the understanding of prophecy; being the knowledge of those things known before by the Lord who reveals all things."[19] On this basis, God's judgments and actions can be seen to be righteous: "Not only then the believer, but even the heathen, is judged most righteously. For since God knew in virtue of His prescience that he would not believe, He nevertheless, in order that he might receive his own perfection gave him philosophy, but gave it him previous to faith."[20] This foreknowledge is not only the prerogative of the Father but also of the Son, and is entire: "And He is called Wisdom by all the prophets. This is He who is the Teacher of all created beings, the Fellow-counselor of God, who foreknew all things; and He from above, from the first foundation of the world, 'in many ways and many times,' trains and perfects; whence it is rightly said, 'Call no man your teacher on earth.'"[21]

[15]Tatian, *Address to the Greeks,* ch. 29.
[16]Theophilus of Antioch, *To Autolycus,* 2.10.
[17]Ibid., ch. 15.
[18]Clement of Alexandria, *The Instructor,* 1.9.
[19]The *Stromata,* or *Miscellanies,* 2.12.
[20]Ibid., 6.14.
[21]Ibid., chap. 7.

Tertullian. One of the most articulate spokespersons for the Christian message in the late-second to early-third centuries was Tertullian. Part of his task was apologetic and polemical. Some of his most influential writings were produced in response to Marcion's challenges. Here was an early version of the problem of evil, related to the question of divine foreknowledge. According to Tertullian, Marcion presented the dilemma in such a way as to impugn God's knowledge of the future:

> If God is good, and prescient of the future, and able to avert evil, why did He permit man, the very image and likeness of Himself, and, by the origin of his soul, His own substance too, to be deceived by the devil, and fall from obedience of the law into death? For if He had been good, and so unwilling that such a catastrophe should happen, and prescient, so as not to be ignorant of what was to come to pass, and powerful enough to hinder its occurrence, that issue would never have come about, which should be impossible under these three conditions of the divine greatness. Since, however, it has occurred, the contrary proposition is most certainly true, that God must be deemed neither good, nor prescient, nor powerful.[22]

Tertullian declares his intention of formulating a response to this challenge: "In reply, we must first vindicate those attributes in the Creator which are called in question—namely, His goodness and foreknowledge, and power."[23]

Tertullian's response takes an interesting form. He is not willing to compromise at all God's prescience, "which has for its witnesses as many prophets as it inspired."[24] Indeed, Tertullian concedes that God foreknew that man would sin, the evidence being found in the caution that he proclaimed against it, in terms of the penalty of death. If, however, God possesses attributes that should render it impossible that evil should happen to man, how can we account for such evil? Tertullian's suggestion is that we look to man instead for the cause of this evil: "Let us consider man's condition also—whether *it* were not, in fact, rather the cause why that came to pass which could not have happened through God. I find, then,

---

[22]Tertullian, *Five Books Against Marcion,* 2.5.
[23]Ibid.
[24]Ibid.

that man was by God constituted free, master of his own will and power; indicating the presence of God's image and likeness in him by nothing so well as by this constitution of his nature."[25]

Tertullian saw the potential problem here in the conflict between human freedom and divine foreknowledge, and he essentially adopted the freewill solution to the problem. "The necessary consequence, therefore, was, that God must separate from the liberty which He had once for all bestowed upon man (in other words, keep within Himself), both His foreknowledge and power, through which He might have prevented man's falling into danger when attempting wrongly to enjoy his liberty."[26] This meant that God could foreknow man's sin without violating his freedom, but he could not act to preclude its occurrence. Tertullian says, "Now, if He had interposed, He would have rescinded the liberty of man's will, which He had permitted with set purpose, and in goodness."[27] It appears that, although Tertullian does not elaborate a theory of will and freedom, he was working with a type of compatibilist view of the human will in which it was not contradictory to say that God knew just what the human would do but that the action itself was free and caused only by the agent committing it.

Origen. Much of Origen's writing on foreknowledge in the first half of the third century grew out of his dispute with Celsus, although some of it was in his more specifically didactic material. An example of the latter is his *De Principiis,* in which he takes the approach of God's allowing evil. In a chapter on the freedom of the will he says, "God also, who knows the secret things of the heart, and foreknows the future, in much forbearance allows certain events to happen, which, coming from without upon men, cause to come forth into the light the passions and vices which are concealed within."[28] In his dispute with Celsus, he also makes clear his view that God foreknows all things and that this foreknowledge is complete: "For God, comprehending all things by means of His foreknowledge, and foreseeing what consequences would result from both of these, wished to make these known to mankind by his prophets."[29]

---

[25]Ibid.
[26]Ibid., chap. 7.
[27]Ibid.
[28]Origen, *De Principiis,* 3.1.
[29]Origen, *Against Celsus,* 6.45.

While Origen appears to have held that foreknowledge was an indispensable quality for divinity, for him it was not necessarily or infallibly a sign of divinity. There are others than God who know the future. Among these are physicians, who can diagnose and prognose. There are pilots, who can foretell the weather. There are even birds of augury, which are used in foretelling the future. Yet Origen does not hold that one must therefore term them gods, particularly if their character is bad.

Celsus's position, according Origen, was that if God foreknew all things, including human actions, that led to fatalism. What was foreknown as happening would happen, and there was therefore no human freedom. Origen is quick to reject Celsus's position that the announcement of what was to come, such as Peter's denial or Judas's betrayal, would prevent their doing those acts: "Here the learned Celsus did not see the contradiction in his statement: for if Jesus foreknew events as a God, then it was impossible for His foreknowledge to prove untrue; and therefore it was impossible for him who was known to Him as going to betray Him not to execute his purpose, nor for him who was rebuked as going to deny Him not to have been guilty of that crime."[30]

Origen apparently considers Celsus's objection to divine foreknowledge on the basis of human freedom to be scarcely worth replying to, but he does nonetheless.

> Now, since you wish me to answer even those charges of Celsus which seem to me frivolous, the following is our reply to such statements. Celsus imagines that an event, predicted through foreknowledge, comes to pass because it was predicted; but we do not grant this, maintaining that he who foretold it was not the cause of its happening, because he foretold it would happen; but the future event itself, which would have taken place though not predicted, afforded the occasion to him, who was endowed with foreknowledge, of foretelling its occurrence. Now, certainly this result is present to the foreknowledge of him who predicts an event, when it is possible that it may or may not happen, viz., that one or other of these things will take place. For we do not assert that he who foreknows an event, by secretly taking away the possibility of its

---

[30]Ibid., 2.18.

happening or not, makes any such declaration as this: "This shall infallibly happen, and it is impossible that it can be otherwise."[31]

Origen's reply is based on a distinction between the certainty that something will happen, or what he terms "simple futurity," and the necessity that would contradict freedom:

> We have brought forward all these illustrations on account of the assertion of this learned Celsus, that "being a God He predicted these things, and the predictions must by all means come to pass." Now, if by "by all means" he means "necessarily," we cannot admit this. For it was quite possible, also, that they might not come to pass. But if he uses "by all means" in the sense of "simple futurity," which nothing hinders from being true (although it was possible that they might not happen), he does not at all touch my argument; nor did it follow, from Jesus having predicted the acts of the traitor or the perjurer, that it was the same thing with His being the cause of such impious and unholy proceedings.[32]

In terms of the distinctions with respect to theories of foreknowledge, Origen seems to hold to what would today be termed simple foreknowledge. God knows what persons are going to do in advance of their actions.[33]

Later Views. There was a significant decline in discussions of foreknowledge after the time of Origen. One exception is Lactantius, whose response to those who claimed that Jupiter was a god makes clear the indispensability of foreknowledge to divinity: "And first of all there was in him a want of foreknowledge not befitting a God; for had not Themis related to him future events, he would not have known them of his own accord."[34]

Summary of Early Period. It is notable that there were challenges to the traditional view of divine foreknowledge in the early period. In each case, however, these came from outside the stream of orthodoxy, from persons such as Marcion or Celsus. The uniform testimony of the Fathers was that God correctly knows in advance all that will come to pass. The silence of the ecumenical councils and of subsequent Christian theologians may seem

---

[31]Ibid., chap. 20.
[32]Ibid.
[33]Ibid., 7.44.
[34]Lactantius, *The Divine Institutes,* 1.11.

WHAT DOES GOD KNOW AND WHEN DOES HE KNOW IT?

a puzzle to some.[35] In reality, the best explanation is that the issue was not addressed by a council and formulated in a creed for the simple reason that it was not necessary: no significant segment of the Christian church denied the traditional view.

LATER THEOLOGIANS

Augustine. In the late-fourth and early-fifth centuries, Augustine continued and elaborated the position of God's complete foreknowledge. At times this appears in the form of praise of such a God:

> Surely, if there be a mind, so greatly abounding in knowledge and foreknowledge, to which all things past and future are so known as one psalm is well known to me, that mind is exceedingly wonderful, and very astonishing; because whatever is so past, and whatever is to come of after ages, is no more concealed from Him than was it hidden from me when singing that psalm, what and how much of it had been sung from the beginning, what and how much remained unto the end. But far be it that Thou, the Creator of the universe, the Creator of souls and bodies,—far be it that Thou shouldest know all things future and past. Far, far more wonderfully, and far more mysteriously, Thou knowest them.[36]

One of Augustine's clearest statements of foreknowledge and its effects is developed in contrast to the thought of Cicero, who was attempting to refute the Stoics. Augustine says of Cicero that "this he attempts to accomplish by denying that there is any knowledge of future things, and maintains with all his might that there is no such knowledge either in God or man, and that there is no prediction of events."[37] Augustine does not consider this a wise move, however: "Nevertheless, they are far more tolerable who assert the fatal influence of the stars than they who deny the foreknowledge of future events."[38] Interestingly, this discussion of Cicero's argument brings Augustine to grips with a very contemporary issue, the relationship between divine foreknowledge and human free will,

---

[35]Clark Pinnock, for example, says flatly, "What church council has declared it to be impossible?" (*Most Moved Mover: A Theology of God's Openness* [Grand Rapids: Baker, 2001], 110).
[36]Augustine, *Confessions,* 11.31.
[37]Augustine, *The City of God,* 5.9.
[38]Ibid.

for it was this fear, that divine foreknowledge precludes human freedom, that drove Cicero to his denial. Augustine is quite clear, however, in his contention that there is no such conflict: "Now, against the sacrilegious and impious darings of reason, we assert both that God knows all things before they come to pass, and that we do by our free will whatsoever we know and feel to be done by us only because we will it."[39] He recognizes that it is fear of fate that has motivated the rejection of foreknowledge, so he takes considerable pains to distinguish this foreknowledge and certainty from fate:

> We might, then, use the word fate in the sense it bears when derived from *fari,* to speak, had it not already come to be understood in another sense, into which I am unwilling that the hearts of men should unconsciously slide. But it does not follow that, though there is for God a certain order of all causes, there must therefore be nothing depending on the free exercise of our own wills, for our wills themselves are included in that order of causes which is certain to God, and is embraced by His foreknowledge, for human wills are also causes of human actions; and He who foreknew all the causes of things would certainly among those causes not have been ignorant of our wills.[40]

Thomas Aquinas. In Thomas, the greatest thirteenth-century philosopher, we find the first really thorough development of theology using Aristotle's thought as its philosophical basis. Throughout his theology it is apparent that Thomas held without question to the traditional belief in God's complete foreknowledge. For example, in discussing the effects of Adam's initial sin, he writes, "Nevertheless, since God foreknows all future events, Divine providence has so disposed that these penalties are apportioned in different ways to various people."[41] This means that prophecies, being based on the divine foreknowledge, will definitely come to pass: "Since the same truth of prophecy is the same as the truth of Divine foreknowledge, as stated above, the conditional proposition: 'If this was prophesied, it will be,' is true in the same way as the proposition: 'If this was foreknown, it will be': for in both cases it is impossible for the antecedent

---

[39]Ibid.
[40]Ibid.
[41]Thomas Aquinas, *Summa Theologica,* 4.2b.164.1.4.

not to be. Hence the consequent is necessary, considered, not as something future in our regard, but as being present to the Divine foreknowledge, as stated in the P(1), Q(14), A(13), and 2."[42]

Perhaps Thomas's strongest statement about the force of foreknowledge is to be found in his discussion of Christ's death: "For since it is impossible for God's foreknowledge to be deceived and His will or ordinance to be frustrated, then, supposing God's foreknowledge and ordinance regarding Christ's Passion, it was not possible at the same time for Christ not to suffer, and for mankind to be delivered otherwise than by Christ's Passion. And the same holds good of all things foreknown and preordained by God, as was laid down in the P(1), Q(14), A(13)."[43] So we may summarize Thomas's view by saying that he believed God's foreknowledge to be exhaustive and absolutely accurate. What God foreknows will come to pass. He even speaks of "the necessity which arises of the Divine foreknowledge and will."[44]

Duns Scotus. Scotus's view was to a considerable extent developed out of his response to Thomas's view. Thomas had contended that God knew future contingents because he was eternally present to them and they to him. He further held that God did not know these directly or by intuition but by seeing likenesses to them in his own essence. He even knows those things that will never exist because he can see in his own essence the power to make them.[45]

Scotus chose a different approach. When he considers the nature of contingents, he holds that God by his activity sustains every chain of causes and so co-causes all the effects of such causes. His willing, however, is not necessary; therefore, what follows can be called contingent, for God could have willed into existence different things than he has.[46] Scotus's analysis involves a distinction between the divine will and the divine intellect. In eternity, God's intellect presented to his will all possible states of affair, and from

---

[42]Ibid., 4.2b.171.6.3.

[43]Ibid., 4.5.3.46.2.

[44]Ibid., 4.3.46.2.4.

[45]Aquinas, *Commentary on the Sentences,* 1.38.1.5, responsio.

[46]Scotus, *De Primo Principio,* trans. by Allan Wolter as *A Treatise on God as First Principle* (Chicago: Franciscan Herald, 1966), 84–85.

these, God's will chose certain to become actual. The intellect then grasps what the will has chosen so that it then knows definitely what will be.[47]

There has been a considerable amount of debate over whether Scotus held to a libertarian or a determinate view of freedom, since he makes statements that seem to favor both of these interpretations. His thought became the starting point for several philosophers' thinking on foreknowledge and freedom, including that of Molina and Leibnitz.

William of Ockham. William of Ockham was the most influential philosopher of the fourteenth century. He was born sometime between 1280 and 1290, in Surrey, England. He came under suspicion for some of his writings and was excommunicated by Pope John XXII, but took up residence in Munich under the protection of the emperor.

In his treatments of divine foreknowledge, Ockham was wrestling with the apparent contradiction between God knowing the future, and those future actions of moral agents being free actions. He contends that "every true proposition about the present has [corresponding to it] a necessary one about the past." So if it is now the case that A is doing x—for example, that "Socrates is now seated"—then the statement, "God has known that Socrates would be seated," is necessary. It cannot be changed. It is, however, an accidental necessity, since Socrates might not have been seated. While it could have been otherwise, it cannot now. In the case of statements about the future, however, then the statement, "God knows that A will do x," depends upon a contingent action, namely, A actually doing x. So it is not accidentally necessary.[48]

However, what if A does not do x, which, if he is free, he is able not to do? If God knew that A would do x and he did not, would he not be mistaken, which is impossible? In that case, according to Ockham, God's knowledge would have been different than it would otherwise have been, and he would have known that A would not do x. In this fashion, Ockham believes, he has preserved both divine foreknowledge and human freedom.[49] When pressed as to how God knows future contingent events,

---

[47]Ibid. Cf. Scotus, *Ordinatio* (Vatican City: Vatican Press, 1950), 4.415.

[48]William of Ockham, *Predestination, God's Foreknowledge, and Future Contingents,* trans. Marilyn McCord Adams and Norman Kretzmann (New York: Appleton-Century-Crofts, 1969), 46–47.

[49]Thomas V. Morris, *Our Idea of God* (Downers Grove, Ill.: InterVarsity, 1991), 94–95.

however, Ockham professes inability to answer: "It is impossible for any [created] intellect, in this life, to explain or evidently know how God knows all future contingent events."[50]

Martin Luther. As an Augustinian monk, Luther largely followed the approach of Augustine. He had no problem affirming that God had foreordained all that happens, so that God knows what he has decided and what he predetermines. His understanding of divine foreknowledge and its basis is enunciated most clearly in his debate on free will with Erasmus.

We may note initially that Luther is unequivocal about the extent of divine foreknowledge: "It is, then, fundamentally necessary and wholesome for Christians to know that God foreknows nothing contingently, but that He foresees, purposes, and does all things according to his immutable, eternal and infallible will. This bombshell knocks 'free-will' flat and utterly shatters it; so that those who want to assert it must either deny my bombshell, or pretend not to notice it, or find some other way of dodging it."[51] If God wills what he foreknows, then his will is eternal and changeless because his nature is that way. So what happens may appear to us to be contingent and mutable, but it is actually necessary and immutable: "For the will of God is effective and cannot be impeded, since power belongs to God's nature; and His wisdom is such that He cannot be deceived. Since, then His will is not impeded, what is done cannot but be done where, when, how, as far as, and by whom, He foresees and wills."[52]

Luther wishes a better word were available than the word *necessity,* which is too harsh and suggests a kind of compulsion and "something that is against one's will, which is no part of the view under debate. The will, whether it be God's or man's, does what it does, good or bad, under no compulsion, but it just wants or pleases, as if totally free."[53] Thus, it becomes apparent that Luther is working with a compatibilist view of human freedom, not merely with respect to God's foreknowledge but also

[50]Ockham, *Commentary on the Sentences,* 38.1.
[51]Martin Luther, *Martin Luther on the Bondage of the Will: A new translation of De servo arbitrio* (1525), Martin Luther's reply to Erasmus of Rotterdam, by J. I. Packer and O. R. Johnston (Westwood, N.J.: Revell, 1957), 80.
[52]Ibid., 80–81.
[53]Ibid., 81.

to God's foreordination of those acts. Erasmus, on the other hand, held to an incompatibilist or libertarian view of freedom.

Luther does not consider belief either in foreknowledge or predestination to be optional, but rather as essential for salvation: "To lack this knowledge is really to be ignorant of God—and salvation is notoriously incompatible with such ignorance. For if you hesitate to believe, or are too proud to acknowledge, that God foreknows and wills all things, not contingently but necessarily and immutably, how can you believe, trust and rely on his promises? . . . If, then, we are taught and believe that we ought to be ignorant of the necessary foreknowledge of God and the necessity of events, Christian faith is utterly destroyed, and the promises of God and the whole gospel fall to the ground completely."[54]

John Calvin. In Calvin we find the thorough working out of the system of Christian doctrine on the basic framework that Augustine had laid. It is not surprising, therefore, that Calvin articulated clearly the traditional view of foreknowledge. His understanding of foreknowledge or prescience is definite:

> We, indeed, ascribe both prescience and predestination to God; but we say, that it is absurd to make the latter subordinate to the former, (see chap. 22 sec. 1.) When we attribute prescience to God, we mean that all things always were, and ever continue, under his eye; that to his knowledge there is no past or future, but all things are present, and indeed so present, that it is not merely the idea of them that is before him, (as those objects are which we retain in our memory,) but that he truly sees and contemplates them as actually under his immediate inspection. This prescience extends to the whole circuit of the world, and to all creatures.[55]

There are many places in Calvin's writing where he appears to be opposing the idea of foreknowledge. What he is actually doing, however, is objecting to the idea that God simply foreknows without having initiative in the matter. He feels that even Augustine was not utterly free from what Calvin calls "this superstition."[56] In contrast to the definition of prescience given above, he says, "By predestination we mean the eternal decree

---

[54] Ibid., 83–84.
[55] John Calvin, *Institutes of the Christian Religion,* 3.21.5.
[56] Ibid., 2.4.3.

of God, by which he determined with himself whatever he wished to happen with regard to every man."[57] Again, he asserts the certainty and accuracy of God's foreknowledge: "The decree, I admit, is, dreadful; and yet it is impossible to deny that God foreknew what the end of man was to be before he made him, and foreknew, because he had so ordained by his decree."[58]

Luis de Molina. A Spanish Jesuit who lived 1535–1600, Molina wrestled with reconciling God's foreknowledge and human freedom. As strong as was his desire to preserve divine foreknowledge, his determination to avoid falling into determinism was equally strong. In contrast to the standard Thomist view of divine determinism, Molina contended that there is a cooperation of the human will and divine grace.

The key to this effort to preserve foreknowledge while avoiding determinism is found in Molina's conception of different kinds of knowledge. There is what Aquinas had called "vision," a knowledge of what is. There is also a knowledge of "simple understanding," a knowledge of things purely possible, things and events that have not existed, do not now exist, and will not exist. Between these two types of knowledge, however, there is what Molina termed "middle knowledge." This is a knowledge of future contingent events, all the possibilities that may or may not become actual, depending on whether some contingent event occurs. Molina says, "Finally, the third type is *middle* knowledge, by which, in virtue of the most profound and inscrutable comprehension of each free will, He saw in His own essence what each such will would do with its innate freedom were it to be placed in this or that, or indeed, infinitely many orders of things—even though it would really be able, if it so willed, to do the opposite."[59] God, foreknowing the entire realm of possibilities and what will freely happen in each possible circumstance, chooses which individuals to bring into the world and into what set of circumstances. By so doing, God brings about certain actions of persons, but they are free actions because these persons might have done otherwise.

---

[57]Ibid., 3.21.5.
[58]Ibid., 3.23.7.
[59]Luis de Molina, *On Divine Foreknowledge (Part IV of the Concordia),* trans. Alfred J. Freddoso (Ithaca, N.Y.: Cornell University Press, 1988), 52.9.

Arminius. As the sixteenth century drew to a close and the seventeenth century began, James Arminius made a clear break from the received position on some significant points. The most prominent of these was the rejection of the predestination doctrine, according to which God foreknows because he has predetermined. Yet while altering the basis for the foreknowledge, Arminius in no sense altered the strength of belief in that doctrine. This is especially important, since some have mistakenly identified the difference between the traditional view and open theism on the matter of foreknowledge as being a Calvinistic-Arminian dispute.

It is clear that for Arminius, divine foreknowledge was exhaustive and certain. Thus he wrote, "Inclination in God is natural towards His own creature, whether the man believes or not. For that inclination does not depend on faith, and uncertainty can not be attributed to the will of Him who, in His infinite wisdom, has all things present to himself, and certainly foreknows all future events, even those most contingent."[60] He is also equally clear, however, that this foreknowledge does not conflict with human freedom, because it does not make something necessary: "Prediction sometimes follows this prescience, when it pleases God to give intimations to his creatures of the issues of things, before they come to pass. But neither prediction nor any prescience induces a necessity of any thing [*futuræ*] that is afterwards to be, since they are [in the divine mind] posterior in nature and order to the thing that is future. For a thing does not come to pass because it has been foreknown or foretold; but it is foreknown and foretold because it is yet [*futura*] to come to pass."[61] This is in contrast with what God decrees to do himself: "It is an absurd assertion that 'from prescience that necessity follows in the same way.' For what God foreknows, He foreknows because it is to take place in the future. But what He decrees, purposes, and determines in Himself to do, takes place thus because He decrees it."[62]

Friedrich Schleiermacher. As the nineteenth century began, Schleiermacher's theological method, in which doctrines were taken from human

---

[60]James Arminius, *An Examination of the Treatise of William Perkins,* 1.4, "Most of the Human Race are Left without Christ."

[61]James Arminius, *Private Disputations,* disputation 28, "On the Providence of God," 14.

[62]Arminius, *Examination,* 1.3, "The Predestination of the Stoics."

religious consciousness, differed radically from most theologies that had preceded him. Yet with respect to divine foreknowledge as well as a number of other doctrines, his view was consonant with the traditional conceptions.

Schleiermacher noted the usual distinction between God's knowledge of the past, the present, and the future. However, he held to the idea of divine timelessness. In God, the knowledge of a thing in itself is the same as the knowledge of the laws that govern its development. If we understand this, he says, "we have at least an indication as to how to avoid as far as possible too great a humanizing of the divine knowledge."[63] He does not hold to a middle knowledge view, according to which, in Schleiermacher's judgment, there is a whole realm of God's rejected thoughts, which would be knowledge of nothing. Middle knowledge also involves the idea of God deliberating and choosing, which, Schleiermacher says, is "a view which from of old every form of teaching in any degree consistent has repudiated."[64]

This leaves one special issue: "whether the divine knowledge about the free action of men can co-exist with their freedom."[65] If the answer is given in the negative, then "not only could there have been no further question of an eternal decree of God regarding salvation, but that history in general would become something which God only gradually experienced, and consequently the idea of providence must be given up."[66] Schleiermacher's conclusion is interesting:

> If, then, the temptation to answer the question in the negative, and the need to raise it is grounded in the interests of human freedom, it must be considered that one's own foreknowledge of free actions and the foreknowledge of others must destroy freedom still more than divine foreknowledge does. And yet we deem those people least free who cannot in general know their actions beforehand, *i.e.* those who are not conscious of any definite course of action. But in such cases the special foreknowledge is lacking only because foreknowledge is lacking of the special relevant outer conditions and inner conditions produced from without. In the same way we estimate the intimacy of relationship between two persons by the foreknowledge one has of the actions of the other, without supposing that in

[63]Friedrich Schleiermacher, *The Christian Faith* (New York: Harper and Row, 1963), 222–23.
[64]Ibid., 225.
[65]Ibid., 227–28.
[66]Ibid., 228.

either case the one or the other's freedom has thereby been endangered. So even divine foreknowledge cannot endanger freedom.[67]

John Wesley. Wesley, the eighteenth century evangelist and founder of Methodism, was clearly in the Arminian camp as a theologian. He did not write a great deal about foreknowledge, but it is clear that he espoused the traditional view of exhaustive foreknowledge and related it to his view of God's relationship to time: "The sum of all is this: The almighty, all-wise God sees and knows from everlasting to everlasting all that is, that was, and that is to come, through one eternal now. With him nothing is either past or future, but all things equally present. He has, therefore, if we speak according to the truth of things, no foreknowledge, no afterknowledge."[68] Much of what Wesley wrote on the subject was, as with Arminius, concerned with establishing that God's predestination is logically dependent on his foreknowledge, rather than the reverse.[69] He was aware of the potential conflict between human freedom and divine foreknowledge of human acts and was unable to resolve the difficulty, but he affirmed the reality of foreknowledge nonetheless: "And if any one ask, How is God's foreknowledge consistent with our freedom? I plainly answer, 'I cannot tell.'"[70]

Karl Barth. Barth, probably the foremost theologian of the twentieth century, scarcely mentioned divine foreknowledge in his massive *Church Dogmatics.* However, it is apparent that he held to the traditional view and yet held that foreknowledge did not abrogate human freedom:

> We now take a further step and say of the divine knowledge first that it possesses the character of foreknowledge, *praescientia,* in relation to all its objects, with the exception of God Himself in His knowledge of Himself.... Finally it is worth while noting at this point that among the *res creatae* are also the created wills of angels and men. If we say of them that they, too, have their cause in the divine foreknowledge and are its effect, this cannot mean that they are not real as wills (as created wills), that

---

[67]Ibid.

[68]John Wesley, *Sermons on Several Occasions,* series 2. Sermon 58, Romans 8:29–30, "On Predestination," 15.

[69]Wesley, "A Dialogue Between a Predestinarian and his Friend."

[70]Wesley, "Letter to Dr. John Robertson, September 24, 1753."

they do not have freedom of choice and therefore contingency (even if a created freedom and contingency).[71]

Emil Brunner. Brunner, the co-pilot, as it were, of the ship of neo-orthodoxy, differed with Barth on a number of points, but not on this one. Although he was strongly critical of the influence of Greek philosophy on Christian theology, he nonetheless advocated the traditional view of divine foreknowledge:

> He [God] knows of an action of the creature which is not His own action. He knows above all about the free activity of that creature to which He has granted the freedom to decide for himself. . . . The future can only be known by us in so far as it is contained in the present, as it necessarily follows from that which now is. The freedom of the Other is the border-line of our knowledge. For God this limitation does not exist. His knowledge of the future is not a knowledge based upon something that exists already in the present, but it is a knowledge which lies outside the boundaries of temporal limitations. . . . God knows that which takes place in freedom in the future as something which happens in freedom.[72]

Wolfhart Pannenberg. Like Jürgen Moltmann, Pannenberg emphasizes strongly the future dimension of God. His understanding of foreknowledge in this context is not always easy to understand. He says of the positive attributes of God, such as omnipotence, omniscience, and omnipresence, that they "are either related to a world that is distinct from God but that he knows, has power over, and is present it [sic], or they are to be understood as a simple negation of any restriction of God's knowledge, power, or presence."[73] It is apparent that he affirms God's knowledge of all, including the future: "What is meant by the idea of God's knowledge and the related idea of his omniscience? Sirach (Ecclesiasticus) tells us that the Lord knows all things and at what time everything occurs (Sir. 42:18–19). What is hidden from us is open to God. This applies not only to the future but to other dimensions of what is hidden from us, not least that which we would prefer to remain hidden (Prov. 24:12)."[74] Pannenberg affirms this concept even more definitely:

---

[71]Karl Barth, *Church Dogmatics* (Edinburgh: T. & T. Clark, 1957), 2.1, 558, 560.
[72]Emil Brunner, *The Christian Doctrine of God* (London: Lutterworth, 1949), 262.
[73]Wolfhart Pannenberg, *Systematic Theology,* vol. 1 (Grand Rapids: Eerdmans, 1991), 364.
[74]Ibid., 379.

"When we speak of God's knowledge we mean that nothing in all his creation escapes him. All things are present to him and are kept by him in his presence. This is not necessarily knowledge in the sense of what is meant by human knowledge and awareness."[75]

In the second volume of his systematic theology, Pannenberg wrestles with the meaning of this knowledge in relation to the creation. Part of his concern is how an eternal God relates to time. He states that "the unity of the divine act of creation precedes time and therefore also the distinction of beginning and end in the sense of logical precedence. For this reason God is said to be the First and the Last (Isa. 44:6; 48:12; Rev. 1:8; cf. 21:6; 22:13). He is not restricted to being the First, nor is he only the Last (i.e., as a result of the cosmic process). He stands above the alternative of beginning and end and is Lord of both."[76] He examines Augustine's view, which included two key ideas: that creation, being an eternal act, is simultaneous with the whole process of time, and that the creation was completed on the sixth day. This raises the problem of creaturely freedom:

> This would subject all following events to an ineluctable necessity either of natural causes or of divine foreknowledge. If all creaturely conduct is fixed by the past, there can be no true contingency or creaturely freedom in the course of events. This does not have to be so if divine knowledge, as in Augustine, is thought to be eternally simultaneous with all times. It is unavoidable, however, if this knowledge, as an ordaining foreknowledge, is linked to the idea of a creation that was completed at the beginning of time. For then it is settled at the very beginning what must take place in the future.[77]

Pannenberg is familiar with the problem, having written his dissertation on Duns Scotus's doctrine of predestination. He does not consider two customary answers to be sufficient: "To avoid this conclusion it is not enough to point out that God foreknows what is contingent as contingent, nor to argue that his eternity is simultaneous with everything creaturely, so that linking divine foreknowledge with the completion of the work of

---

[75]Ibid., 379–80.
[76]*Systematic Theology,* vol. 2 (Grand Rapids: Eerdmans, 1994), 140.
[77]Ibid., 141.

creation on the sixth day does not have to have deterministic implications."[78] Furthermore, in considering Barth's view, he rejects another customary conception, simple foreknowledge. Speaking of foreknowledge and
foreordination, he says, "their literal application to the concept of God
leads to an unfittingly anthropomorphic view of God, as though from
some standpoint before the world's beginning God were looking ahead to
a different future. Such a thought is hardly compatible with God's eternity
and infinity."[79]

It appears that the key to Pannenberg's view is in his understanding
that God's being is not simply restricted to the past. While not simply the
common atemporality view, it does mean that God is not restricted by time
and that, while he knows everything that is now future to us, he is dynam-
ically and creatively at work throughout time, so that his knowledge is not
strictly *fore*knowledge.

— —

We have seen that the tradition of belief that God has complete knowledge of the future, including the acts of free moral agents, has been present throughout the history of the church. A large number of variations
arose on the question of *how* God knows this future, but there was strong
agreement that he does.

---

[78]Ibid., 141–42.
[79]Ibid., 143.

the historical development of the doctrine of divine foreknowledge

part 2

We have observed that there is a long tradition of positive affirmation of the view of exhaustive definite foreknowledge. Although deviations from the orthodox view of divine foreknowledge have been rare, there have been some, and these should be examined.

Celsus. Celsus was a second-century philosopher with affinities both for Epicureanism and Platonism. He is alleged to have written a book entitled *A True Discourse,* probably in the latter years of the reign of Marcus Aurelius.[1] While this book has not been preserved, we have considerable knowledge of its contents from extended quotations in Origen's *Against Celsus,* on the basis of which it has been reconstructed.

Celsus engaged in an attack on Christianity and Christians in several areas and on several levels. Part of this attack was moral, criticizing the Christians for quarrelsomeness among the several sects and for lack of patriotism. He then turned to criticism of Christian doctrine. With respect to the issue of foreknowledge, he contends that this must result in a loss of freedom, for "being a God He predicted these things, and the predictions must by all

---

[1]"Celsus," *New Schaff-Herzog Encyclopedia of Religious Knowledge,* ed. Samuel Macauley Jackson (Grand Rapids: Baker, 1958), 2.466.

means come to pass."[2] Celsus seems to have held that the disciples invented the accounts about Jesus, although at other points he appears to have held that they were deceived.[3]

It should be observed that Celsus's rejection of divine foreknowledge was part of a much larger criticism of Christian doctrine and of Christian conduct. For example, he rejected the idea of the divinity of Jesus as inconsistent with the texts indicating his poverty, sufferings, and death.[4] Celsus was in no sense a Christian theologian. He was, rather, a non-Christian philosopher. His rejection of the traditional view of foreknowledge came from outside the Christian faith, not from within it.

Marcion. Just as Celsus's teachings are largely derived from Origen's writings, so those of Marcion are largely to be constructed from Tertullian's work. Marcion lived in the second century, and although the details of his exclusion from the church are disputed, it is apparent that he came under the influence of Gnosticism and appropriated it into his doctrine, especially his doctrine of God.

With respect to divine foreknowledge, Marcion's major concern was in connection with the problem of evil. If God is good, he would wish to prevent evil; and if he is all-powerful, he would be able to prevent evil. If then, he is also prescient, he should have known, when he created humans, that they would fall into evil. Since, however, there is evil in the world, God must be lacking in one of these qualities, and Marcion consequently rejected the teaching of foreknowledge.[5]

Although Marcion considered himself a Christian, his views were unorthodox on other points besides this. His doctrine of God was especially innovative. He distinguished between the Creator, the Old Testament God who was the author of natural evil, not of moral evil, and the New Testament God of love.[6] He also contended that Jesus descended into hell, but to deliver, not the Old Testament saints, but disobedient persons

---

[2]Origen, *Against Celsus,* 2.20.
[3]Ibid., 2.26.
[4]"Celsus," *Cyclopedia of Biblical, Theological and Ecclesiastical History,* ed. John M'Clintock and James Strong (New York: Harper & Brothers, 1841), 2.178.
[5]Tertullian, *Five Books Against Marcion,* 2.5.
[6]"Marcion," *Cyclopedia of Biblical, Theological and Ecclesiastical History,* 5.736.

like Cain, Esau, Korah, Dathan, and Abiram.[7] Thus, he can scarcely be considered part of orthodox Christianity.

Calcidius. One exception to the seeming uniformity of belief in the traditional view is Calcidius, a fifth-century monk who wrote a commentary on Plato's *Timaeus.* In particular, he was concerned about a use made by the Stoics of one particular passage in that dialogue. The Stoics constituted a school of ethics noted for their emphasis on resignation to things as they are. This conception persists to the present in references to persons being "stoical." The philosophy of life derived from a sense of the unchangeability of things. They were willing to accept the traditional view that the future could be known, but they contended that this removed any incentive for trying to affect what would happen. They found support for their conception in Plato. Calcidius summarizes his understanding of the Stoics' position:

> So, if God knows all things from the beginning, before they happen, and not only the phenomena of heaven, which are bound by a fortunate necessity of unbroken blessedness as by a kind of fate, but also those thoughts and desires of ours; if he also knows that, which is contingent by nature, and controls past, present and future and that from the beginning, and if God cannot be mistaken, the conclusion must be that all things are arranged and determined from the beginning, things said to be within our power as well as fortuitous and chance events.[8]

It was necessary for Calcidius to give some response to this stoical view, which appeared incompatible with orthodox theology. He did this by drawing a crucial distinction between knowledge of events as necessary and as contingent. God does know everything, but he knows everything according to its nature. He knows the necessary as necessary and the contingent as contingent. Thus, he knows the things that he himself is going to do as necessary, for he has determined to do them. However, "on the other hand His knowledge of uncertain things is indeed necessary, *viz.,* His knowledge that these things are uncertain and their course contingent—for they cannot be different from their nature—, yet they are themselves possible in

---

[7]Ibid.

[8]Jan Den Booft, *Calcidius on Fate: His Doctrine and Sources* (Leiden: Brill, 1970), 160.47.

both directions rather than subject to necessity."[9] Calcidius does not necessarily draw explicitly the conclusion that for God also the contingent is contingent.

Calcidius's interpretation does not seem to have been propounded by anyone else in his time or in the following centuries. He himself was sufficiently obscure, and his writing done in connection with a comment on a passage of Plato that was not of great concern to the church. Consequently, his view, which may have been proposed simply as a hypothetical solution to the problem, went apparently largely unnoticed by theologians.[10]

The Socinians. Probably the best-known group to oppose the orthodox view was the seventeenth-century Socinians, a late Reformation group that were more radical in their theology than were other reformers. The prime mover in the group, Faustus Socinus, was disturbed by the doctrine of predestination, which was an important part of the theology of both Luther and Calvin. Socinus felt that if predestination was true, then the very foundation of religion was denied or rejected.

One of the important factors in this difficulty is the role of divine foreknowledge. To understand Socinus's approach to the problem, it is necessary to see his understanding of the relationship of God to time. He rejected the atemporalist approach according to which God holds all of time in one simultaneous moment. Instead, said Socinus, God knows all events past, present, and future according to their respective natures. "The future, however," he says, "consists either of what necessarily will occur, or of what only possibly, or under certain conditions and contingently may occur. Under the latter come all acts of human freedom. Since God knows all things as they are, accordingly he knows the necessary future as such and the contingent future also as such. If it were otherwise, God would not know things as they are, for truth is the congruence of knowledge with its object."[11] If, however, God knows the future as determinate, "everything must then be necessary and determined from all eternity, since from all

[9]Ibid., 162.52.

[10]The obscurity of Calcidius can be seen in the fact that he is not mentioned in any standard history of the church or of Christian thought, or any dictionary of theology.

[11]Otto Fock, *Der Socianismus* (Kiel: Carl Schröder, 1847), 438–39.

WHAT DOES GOD KNOW AND WHEN DOES HE KNOW IT?

eternity known by God. But then there is no human freedom. There is also no divine freedom, since from all eternity God could act only as he actually does act."[12]

One major problem for Socinus's view was of course prophecy. Socinus wrote, "One reason by which it is attempted to be proved that man hath no power, but that all things depend on the decree of God, or are certainly necessary, is drawn from the *Foreknowledge* or *Prescience* of God."[13] As common as was the appeal to prophecy as a proof of foreknowledge, Socinus did not think this evidence to be of value, however:

> There are many other sacred testimonies, which seem to establish the notion of the *divine Foreknowledge,* to all which he will be able easily to return an answer who will weigh and consider what we have observed. From which these four rules may be inferred and laid down: First if any passage speak of good works certainly foreseen, God himself hath undoubtedly decreed them. Secondly, Whether it speaks of good or evil actions, the prediction may be founded only on probabilities and on this account not certain, nor arising from that foreknowledge of which we are enquiring. Thirdly, That it may be rather an admonition to do good, or to avoid what is evil. Fourthly, That if it be a certain prediction of an evil work, this work was indeed decreed by God, but not the malignity of heart.[14]

Most who today deny the traditional view of foreknowledge are hesitant to claim the precedent of Socinianism. In his *Trinity and Process,* Gregory Boyd frankly acknowledges that "until the time of the Socinians, the belief that God's omniscience included all future events was not generally questioned."[15] Yet in his *God of the Possible* and his *Satan and the Problem of Evil,* he makes no mention of the Socinians at all, but gives several other persons who did not hold the traditional view.[16] The reason for this reluctance to

[12]Ibid., 439.

[13]Joshua Toulmin, *Memoirs of the Life, Character, Sentiments, and Writings of Faustus Socinus* (London: Printed for the author by J. Brown, 1777), 230.

[14]Ibid., 230–31.

[15]Gregory Boyd, *Trinity and Process: A Critical Evaluation and Reconstruction of Hartshorne's Di-polar Theism Towards a Trinitarian Metaphysics* (New York: Peter Lang, 1992), 296–97.

[16]Gregory Boyd, *God of the Possible: A Biblical Introduction to the Open View of God* (Grand Rapids: Baker, 2000), 115, 172; *Satan and the Problem of Evil: Constructing a Trinitarian Warfare Theology* (Downers Grove, Ill.: InterVarsity, 2001), 91, n. 11.

identify Socinianism as an antecedent may be because the Socinians were unorthodox on a number of other crucial doctrines. For example, they denied the deity of Jesus Christ, and thus modern Unitarians are considered descendents of the Socinians. Pinnock resists this association and claims that the purpose of such association is to "dispose of openness theology by tying it to some known heresy."[17] He says, "To be fair, [R. Strimple] should have noted that open theists are unlike the Socinians trinitarian and orthodox in their Christology."[18] He misses the point: that the denial of the traditional view of divine foreknowledge has, historically, come from those outside, not within, Christian theological orthodoxy.

Jules Lequyer. One whose ideas on free will anticipated much of the current debate is the nineteenth-century Frenchman Jules Lequyer.[19] Persons as widely divergent as William James and Charles Hartshorne have acknowledged that he influenced their thought. Hartshorne and Reese suggest that "about one hundred years ago the reasoning of Socinus concerning omniscience and time reappeared in the French philosopher Lequier."[20] Robert Kane even contends that Lequyer not only anticipated the theological debate over the openness of God but actually made a significant contribution to that debate through his "Dialogue of the Predestinate and the Reprobate."[21] Lequyer was not a theologian or even a philosopher as such. He taught French composition and mathematics and dabbled in politics. His death by drowning in 1854, at the age of 48, may have been a suicide. William James referred to Lequyer as "a French philosopher of genius,"[22] and Charles Hartshorne made frequent references to Lequyer. Viney, however, says that "by 1898 George Séailles accurately called Lequyer 'an

---

[17]Clark H. Pinnock, *Most Moved Mover: A Theology of God's Openness* (Grand Rapids: Baker, 2001), 107. Michael Holmes has verbally expressed a similar complaint (evening service, Trinity Baptist Church, Maplewood, Minnesota, May 2, 1999).

[18]Pinnock, *Most Moved Mover,* 107, n. 122.

[19]The name can be found spelled in various ways. For a discussion of the variant spellings, see Donald Wayne Viney, "Jules Lequyer: Bold Traveler in the Worlds of Thought," in *Translation of the Works of Jules Lequyer,* ed. Donald Wayne Viney (Lewiston, N.Y.: Mellen, 1998), 3–4.

[20]Charles Hartshorne and William L. Reese, *Philosophers Speak of God,* ed. Charles Hartshorne and William L. Reese (Amherst, N.Y.: Humanity, 2000), 227.

[21]Robert Kane, "Foreword," in *Translation of the Works of Jules Lequyer,* xiii.

[22]William James, *The Principles of Psychology* (Cambridge, Mass.: Harvard University Press, 1981), Vol. 2, 1176.

unknown philosopher.' . . . To this day Lequyer is unknown, even among those whose interests most closely parallel Lequyer's."[23] Similarly, Kane says, "Until now, Lequyer's philosophy has been a footnote to history. . . . Had it not been for his friend and admirer, the celebrated French philosopher Charles Renouvier, Lequyer's work may have never been known at all."[24] Yet, Kane contends, "It is now also generally acknowledged that Lequyer anticipated many of the themes of twentieth century process philosophy and process theology, associated with the later work of Alfred North Whitehead and especially with the work of Charles Hartshorne, although there was no direct influence."[25]

Central to Lequyer's thought is his concept of will. Rejecting the compatibilist understanding of freedom as the absence of constraint, he defined freedom as a creative act that brings about a "new mode of being."[26] He illustrates this with an incident from his childhood in which he freely decided to pluck a certain leaf from a hornbeam tree. When he reached for the leaf, however, he startled a bird hidden in the tree, who flew away and was immediately killed by a sparrow hawk.[27] The boy Lequyer had created an event that would not otherwise have occurred. He distinguishes between epistemic possibility (possibility so far as we know) and ontological possibility, or indeterminacy. Freedom requires indeterminacy: "If it is a question of a free action, we know that it is really possible not to do it."[28]

Lequyer's problem with foreknowledge issues from this idea of human freedom: "But it is too clear that freedom taken with this simplicity, and this reality, excludes all prevision of the act that it determines." This is not really a limitation on God's omnipotence, however, for such supposed foreknowledge would be like omnipotence requiring God's ability to make a triangle in which the sum of the three angles was not equal to the sum of

---

[23]Viney, "Jules Lequyer: Bold Traveler," 1.

[24]Kane, "Forward," xi.

[25]Ibid.

[26]Lequyer, "The Hornbeam Leaf," [14], *Translation,* 46. Numbers in brackets refer to the pages in Lequier, Jules, *OEuvres complètes,* édition de Jean Grenier (Neuchatel, Suisse: Éditions de la Baconnière, 1952).

[27]Ibid., 45–46.

[28]Lequyer, "The Dialogue of the Predestinate and the Reprobate," [192], *Works,* 127.

two right angles.[29] Lequyer contends that the principle of excluded middle does not apply to future-tensed propositions: "Between contingent past things and contingent things to come there is this difference: Of two contradictory affirmations concerning contingent past things, one is true, the other false; but of two contradictory affirmations concerning contingent things to come, neither the one nor the other is true, both are false."[30]

This position creates for Lequyer a problem with prophecy. Some, to be sure, are conditional prophecies, such as the destruction of Nineveh.[31] Of the absolute prophecies, however, there are some that pertain to events that are the outworking of causal factors.[32] There are others, however, in which God has a hand in the outworking of prophecies, not only those events that he unilaterally and directly causes but also instances like Peter's denial. God knew that the denials were an inevitable result of Peter's self-determined character, and then God withheld divine help at the crucial moment.[33]

Gustave Theodor Fechner. Fechner, who lived from 1801 to 1887, began his scholarly career as a physicist. As a result of studying psychophysics, he gravitated into what today would be known as experimental psychology and then into philosophical fields such as metaphysics and even esthetics.

In his conception of God's relationship to the world, Fechner drew the analogy of the human soul and body: "For the spirit of God stands not, any more than the human soul, in a dead, external fashion above the bodily world, but manifests itself, rather, as a living essence immanent in it, or else (we shall explain both ways of putting it) nature itself is an expression of God which remains immanent in him."[34] He then elaborates this analogy further in terms of created spirits: "So God may be viewed as a unitary inclusive spirit, as absolute, universal spirit, superior to and contrasted with

---

[29]Lequyer, "Eugene and Theophilus," [404], *Works,* 155.

[30]Lequyer, "Dialogue," [194], 128.

[31]Ibid., [209], 138. Lequyer suggests that "Jonah has in the Church a throng of wrongheaded imitators who know more about the decrees of God, with the example of Jonah, than God has found it good to make known to them, and who, contrary to Jonah, take as absolute prophecies some prophecies perhaps subordinate to conditions of which they are ignorant."

[32]Ibid., [207], 136.

[33]Ibid., [206], 136.

[34]Gustav Theodor Fechner, *Zend-Avesta: Oder über die Dinge des Himmels und des Jenseits, vom Standpunkt der Naturbeschreibung,* 5th ed. (Leipzig: Leopold Voss, 1922), 1:200–202.

the individual created spirits which are its members, in the same way that the spirit of man as a whole is known to include under it separately intelligible and distinguishable ideas as its constituent members."[35]

This God, according to Fechner, is a being who progresses through time, so that Fechner speaks of an old or early God and a new or later God: "While the child learns the old from the old God, the old God learns of the new through the new beings; in and through them he is aware of novelty, and lifts up into the whole every treasure of the new which he collects in and through individuals, brings it to a higher application and a higher development in human intercourse and human affairs than could be possible through the individuals alone, and out of this treasure everyone receives this and that through education and rearing, and develops further by means of the received fund."[36] Yet he does not wish to speak of God as in any sense defective: "Should we say now that because the later God develops beyond the earlier, there was a defect in the earlier? But it was no other defect than that which progress to the higher itself determines, and each earlier time stands in this relation to a later time, and each later time stands in this relation to the one following; in *this* respect the world never advances, because this is the ground of its whole progress, to will something transcending the present; herein lies the impulse of the eternal, progressive development."[37]

Fechner could probably be best classified as a panpsychist, since he believed that plants, planets, and stars had spirits,[38] which Hartshorne and Reese feel rendered his thought a stumbling block for most readers. Whatever the cause, Fechner's direct theological influence has not been extensive: "Of Fechner's pioneer contributions to theism, one may say that they have been not so much forgotten as from the outset unnoticed."[39] Actually, it appears that Fechner's lasting contribution to knowledge was his psychophysics rather than his metaphysics. According to a survey of the history of psychology section of the Fellows of the American Psychological

---

[35]Ibid.
[36]Ibid., 240–42.
[37]Ibid.
[38]Gustav Theodor Fechner, *On Life after Death,* 3rd ed. (Chicago: Open Court, 1914), 16–17.
[39]Hartshorne and Reese, *Philosophers Speak of God,* 254.

Association, Fechner was rated in a tie for eighth in all-time importance, along with Skinner and Binet.[40] Moreover, a twenty-year citation analysis showed that Fechner the psychophysicist was cited 245 times, Fechner the aesthetician was cited 66 times, but Fechner the philosopher and metaphysician was only cited 30 times.[41]

Otto Pfleiderer (1839–1909).[42] Primarily a New Testament specialist, Pfleiderer was influenced by the German idealists who preceded him, but especially by Hegel.[43] He rejected the classical idea of God's omniscience as immediate, eternal, and immutable. Such a conception, he argued, destroys the analogy between the divine consciousness and the human, which necessarily involves succession of states. Furthermore, it "renders questionable either the real relation of God to the temporal process or else the reality of this process (deistic or monistic consequence)."[44] It is necessary, therefore, to understand God as having successive states within his consciousness, but this has a definite effect on our understanding of God's omniscience: "It follows that foresight of the future must be distinguished from knowledge of the present and must be thought to refer not to the accidents of the particular but rather to the essential features of the universal, so that it coincides with the purposive ideas of the world-ordering wisdom."[45]

Omniscience was not the only aspect of Pfleiderer's doctrine of God that underwent modification. He also distinguished his view of creation from the traditional or received view: "For the dogmatic conception of a creation out of nothing, with a temporal beginning, and concluded in six days, we would do well to substitute the generic idea of the beginningless and endless activity of the creative and preservative omnipotence

---

[40]Helmut E. Adler, "William James and Gustav Fechner: From Rejection to Elective Affinity," in *Reinterpreting the Legacy of William James,* ed., Margaret E. Donnelly (Washington, D.C.: American Psychological Association, 1992), 259–60.

[41]Ibid., 260. For a more complete assessment, see E. Scheerer and Z. Hildebrandt, "Was Fechner an Eminent Psychologist?" in *G. T. Fechner und die Psychologie,* ed. J. Brovek and H. Grundlach (Passau, Germany: Passavia Universitätsverlag, 1987).

[42]Boyd refers to "Pfeiderer" (*God of the Possible,* 115), but it is evident that it is Pfleiderer to whom he is referring.

[43]Hartshorne and Reese, *Philosophers Speak of God,* 269.

[44]Otto Pfleiderer, *Grundriss der Christlichen Glaubens und Sittenlehre* (Berlin: Druck & Verlag von Georg Reimer, 1888), 71–72.

[45]Ibid.

and wisdom, which fully satisfies religious faith and leaves to science full freedom to explore the development and laws of the universe and of life on the earth."[46]

It appears, therefore, that Hartshorne and Reese have correctly characterized Pfleiderer by classifying him as an instance of "modern panentheism." They comment that they "regret only that Pfleiderer was not of sufficient stature to produce more than a moderate effect upon the development of religion or philosophy."[47]

It is interesting to note that Charles Hartshorne sees parallels between each of these thinkers and his own process philosophy: "It has been encouraging to discover in recent years that not only Schelling, but also (among others): Fechner and the German theologian, Pfleiderer; in France Jules Lequier and Renouvier; and many writers in England and the United States, have had ideas of God more or less similar to that which I defend. Thus it seems that a new 'natural theology' is growing up, which is about equally distinct from the old naturalism and the old supernaturalism."[48]

Adam Clarke. Boyd claims the late-eighteenth-century theologian and biblical commentator Adam Clarke as another who rejected the traditional view.[49] It is helpful, however, to examine Clarke's comments on some of the crucial biblical passages that come into play in this dispute. His commentary on Gen. 6:7, for example, is instructive: "To complete the whole, God represents himself as repenting because he had made them, and as grieved at the heart because of their iniquities! Had not these been voluntary transgressions, crimes which they might have avoided, had they not grieved and quenched the Spirit of God, could he speak of them in the manner he does here?"[50] Another very relevant passage is 1 Sam. 15. Note his interpretation of two pivotal verses:

> Verse 11. *It repenteth me that I have set up Saul.* That is, I placed him on the throne; I intended, if he had been obedient, to have established his

---

[46]Ibid., 88.
[47]*Philosophers Speak of God,* 270.
[48]Charles Hartshorne, *Reality as Social Process: Studies in Metaphysics and Religion* (New York: Hafner, 1971), 22–23.
[49]Boyd, *God of the Possible,* 115.
[50]Adam Clarke, *The Holy Bible Containing the Old and New Testaments with a Commentary and Notes* (New York and Nashville: Abingdon-Cokesbury, n.d.), 1:69.

kingdom. He has been disobedient; I change my purpose, and the kingdom shall not be established in his family. This is what is meant by God's repenting-changing a purpose according to conditions already laid down or mentally determined.

Verse 29. *The Strength of Israel will not lie.* What God has purposed he will bring to pass, for he has all power in the heavens and in the earth; and he will not repent-change his purpose-concerning thee.[51]

In view of statements such as this, it appears that Clarke cannot be claimed by the openness theologians.

L. C. McCabe. McCabe was a nineteenth-century Methodist who taught philosophy at Ohio Wesleyan University. So far as can be determined, he was orthodox in all major doctrines. His view of foreknowledge, however, in many ways anticipated what was to come in the twentieth-century discussions. He was an Arminian, but his view of the freedom of the will took him quite some ways beyond the usual Arminian position.

In a sense, McCabe's effort grows out of a pastoral concern. The doctrine of foreknowledge creates doubt, and that doubt needs to be removed.[52] He draws a parallel between prophecy and miracle. Miracles are a natural accompaniment of, and testimony to, revelation, since the whole process of revelation must be something out of the ordinary. If, however, God naturally has foreknowledge of all that is to come to pass, then prophecy is not in any sense a departure from God's ordinary way of working.

The key to McCabe's view of foreknowledge is a distinction between situations in which the will is simply influenced and those in which it is constrained. In the latter type of situation, the influences become causal in nature.[53] In fact, he distinguishes between four different kingdoms: the kingdom of nature, of providence, of glory, and of grace. In each of the first three of these, God is sovereign. In the fourth, however, in "the high realms of free grace and human freedom, and accountability for eternal destinies, a new factor is forced upon us, and will not disappear from our vision, however incoherent our reasonings and blinding our prejudices.

---

[51]Ibid., 2.255, 257.
[52]L. D. M'Cabe, *The Foreknowledge of God, and Cognate Themes in Theology and Philosophy* (Cincinnati: Cranston & Stowe, 1887), 20–24.
[53]Ibid., 37.

This new factor, the god-like liberty of the self-moving human will, is capable of thwarting, and in uncounted instances, does thwart the divine will, and compel the great I AM to modify his actions, his purposes, and his plans in the treatment of individuals and of communities."[54] There is a contradiction between true human freedom and God's foreknowledge of those free acts. If God foreknows future actions by knowing the causes of the will, this eliminates the difference between the law of liberty and the law of cause and effect. "The moment a future act is perceived only through the objective, in lieu of the subjective; the moment its securative cause is discovered and located in the objective surroundings, or in the motives addressed to either the reason or the sensibilities, in place of discovering and locating its incipiency in the subjective self, in the free causative will, that moment you inevitably sink human freedom into necessity, and make man a mere creature of circumstances."[55] It is not necessary, however, for God to have "absolute foreknowledge of all the free choices of free beings when acting under the law of liberty," because his plan is flexible.[56]

McCabe recognizes that there are a large number of Scriptures that seem to require the traditional view of foreknowledge, especially the prophecies. Upon closer inspection, however, it will be found that while there were prophecies that came to pass, those prophecies generally did not specify the time of their fulfillment or even the exact form. So he says, for example, that while the death of Jesus was preordained, the instruments were not, and that Jesus could thus have atoned for human sin by some death other than the cross.[57]

If foreknowledge is not required by the teaching of Scripture, we must also observe the problems that arise from it. One of these, of course, is that it is incompatible with human freedom.[58] Beyond that, however, it makes God inconsistent (or more correctly, insincere), for how can he appeal to persons to obey him and live, if he knows that they are to be saved?[59] It also is contrary to divine benevolence to create persons who he already

---

[54]Ibid., 62.
[55]Ibid., 52–53.
[56]Ibid., 64.
[57]Ibid., 102.
[58]Ibid., 310–21.
[59]Ibid., 359.

knows will be lost.[60] Furthermore, foreknowledge prevents certain proper states of feeling in God, for if he already knows what persons are to do, he is not pleased or displeased when they do them.[61] It is inconsistent with certain perfections of the divine. No real explanation can be given of how God knows the contingent future, so there is a defect here. Actually, the better solution is that future events are unknowable in their very nature.[62] Finally, this doctrine has an unfortunate effect on human activities, for if an event is foreknown, there is no motivation either to strive to bring it about or to resist it. If, then, it is unnecessary, impossible, and undesirable to believe in divine foreknowledge as traditionally conceived, we should abandon it gladly.

Edgar Sheffield Brightman. Brightman was a personal idealist or personalist, who held that the key to the universe is personality as the ultimate reality. As the successor to Borden Parker Bowne at Boston University, he followed Bowne in many points but made one major departure from Bowne's view.

Bowne had wrestled with the question of whether divine foreknowledge of human actions is consistent with their being free. Bowne saw the problem but attempted to retain the traditional view. He believed that the difficulty was connected with the nature of time. He felt that if time was real, there was no way out of the difficulty "unless we assume that God has modes of knowing which are inscrutable to us." This was not the solution to which he turned, however, because he held that time was ideal, and consequently, "the problem vanishes in its traditional form, and nothing remains but the general mystery which shrouds for us the epistemology of the Infinite."[63]

Brightman did not find his mentor's response to the problem to be adequate. He said, "We may well inquire whether an hypothesis that leads to such results [either inscrutability or mystery] is worth retaining."[64] A basic principle he works with is that "the expansion of God's knowledge

[60]Ibid., 364.
[61]Ibid., 382.
[62]Ibid., 397.
[63]Borden Parker Bowne, *Theism* (New York: American Book Co., 1902), 189–90.
[64]Edgar Sheffield Brightman, *The Problem of God* (New York: Abingdon, 1930), 101.

and power contracts human freedom and thus the attainment of a divine purpose."[65] This is part of a general principle that the expansion of God actually limits or contracts him. Thus, for example, if we expand the power of God to make him omnipotent, then we are faced with the problem of evil: how an all-powerful and all-loving God can permit evil in the world. This is what Brightman calls a "trilemma," and entails that if God is all powerful, he must not be all good. Since Brightman holds that it is religiously more important that God be good than that he be all-powerful, he formulates a doctrine of God as limited. Similarly, if God is expanded to be thought of as eternal (in the atemporal sense), then that limits his involvement with the world of experience in time. In this case, the tension is between foreknowledge and freedom. "If at any time in advance of an act an absolutely certain knowledge of it is possible, then there must be some present grounds which render that knowledge necessary and nothing that can happen between the moment of knowledge and the moment of the act can in any way alter the nature of the act. Thus, foreknowledge inevitably involves a contraction of freedom."[66] Because God is at work in the world with the goal of developing free human persons, "the expansion of God's knowledge and power results in contraction in the very attainment of a divine purpose."[67] While a God who has absolute foreknowledge may have complete fulfillment of his decrees, he thereby foregoes a world of free, morally self-determining beings. "On the other hand, a God whose purpose it is to develop a society of free persons must forego some knowledge and some power if he is to attain his purpose."[68]

There is, of course, the other alternative, suggested by Bowne, of expanding God above reason so that we believe that he has perfect foreknowledge but that in some inexplicable way this does not contradict human freedom. The cost of such an expansion is great, however, for then we cannot really say anything about him, including that he is good, and consequently there are no grounds either for our worship or devotion to him.[69] Brightman's solution is to define the nature of God in such

[65]Ibid., 100.
[66]Ibid., 101.
[67]Ibid., 102.
[68]Ibid.
[69]Ibid., 102–3.

a way that he is neither omnipotent nor possesses complete and absolute foreknowledge.

Charles Hartshorne. It is the process philosophers and theologians of the twentieth century who have given the greatest impact to the open view. Of these, probably the clearest and most complete statement has been that of Charles Hartshorne. His view of divine foreknowledge and of an indeterminate future must be seen as following from his general metaphysical view.

Like all other process philosophers, Hartshorne holds that the basic unit of reality is not substance but event. Every event has two elements in it, an eternal or abstract element and a temporal or concrete element. Thus, there is both permanence and change in everything that occurs. This general scheme applies to everything, including God, who participates in the same bipolar character of reality. In Hartshorne's terminology, there is both an absolute and a relative pole in God's nature. Hartshorne speaks of God's A-perfection (or absolute perfection) and his R-perfection (or relatedness perfection). The former means "that which in no respect could conceivably be greater, and hence is incapable of increase."[70] The latter means "that individual being . . . than which no *other individual* being could *conceivably* be greater, but which *itself,* in another 'state,' could become greater (perhaps by the creation within itself of new constituents)."[71] Another way of putting it is that perfection is "an excellence such that rivalry or superiority on the part of other individuals is impossible, but self-superiority is not impossible."[72] It is this latter conception of perfection that he is working with when he discusses such attributes as omnipotence and omniscience.

Hartshorne therefore states that it is "perfectly possible to conceive an omniscient being who changes."[73] This may seem strange to someone who is working with the idea of A-perfection, because on this model, God previously did not know something that he now knows. On the model of R-perfection, however, it makes perfectly good sense. "True," says Hartshorne, "a being who changes will know more at one moment than at the preceding

[70]Charles Hartshorne, *The Divine Relativity: A Social Conception of God* (New Haven: Yale University Press, 1941), 19–20.

[71]Ibid., 20.

[72]Ibid.

[73]Charles Hartshorne, *Man's Vision of God and the Logic of Theism* (New York: Harper & Brothers, 1941), 98.

moment; but this implies he was previously 'ignorant' *only* if it be assumed that events are there to be known prior to their happening. For knowledge is true if, and only if, it corresponds to reality, and things that have not happened are, in so far, perhaps, not real. To know them would then be to know falsely, for there is nothing of the sort to know."[74] This, in turn, is related to Hartshorne's conception of the future: "If the future is indeterminate, if there is real freedom between alternatives, any one of which *can* happen, then the true way to know the future is as undetermined, unsettled."[75]

Hartshorne acknowledges the proposal that God is timelessly eternal, and thus sees what we term the future, not as being future, but as simply part of one great eternal present. This cannot be deduced from the idea of omniscience, however, unless "it has been demonstrated that that which to us is future possesses objectively the same reality as that which to us is present or past"; and he contends that this is not self-evident. We experience the future as if it were partly unsettled, indeterminate, and nebulous and assume that this is a consequence of our ignorance; but, he asks, "How do we know that it is not rather, in part at least, the real character of the future?"[76]

Hartshorne notes that we humans are at some points able to predict the future because we have learned the laws that govern these occurrences. This is not the way in which theologians have generally claimed that God knows the future, and if it were, that would assume a type and extent of determinism that theologians generally have not subscribed to. If, however, the future is actually unsettled or indeterminate, knowing it as such rather than as determinate would not be ignorance, but true knowledge.

Hartshorne is also aware that some invoke the law of excluded middle to attempt to establish that future events are determinate. So, for example, he says, "Either I will write the letter tomorrow or I will not write it tomorrow—only one of these can be true."[77] Hartshorne, however, replies that while only one of these statements is true, it may be that both of them are false. Between the two statements is the statement, "I may do it," meaning

---

[74]Ibid.
[75]Ibid.
[76]Ibid., 98–99.
[77]Ibid., 100.

that "the present situation of myself and indeed of the world in its totality is indeterminate with respect to my doing it."[78] Without identifying these terms, he appeals to the distinction between a contradictory and a contrary, so that the contradictory of "it will occur" is not "it will not occur" but "it *may not* occur."[79]

Hartshorne is clear about the intellectual heritage of his approach: "Is God all-knowing? Yes, in the Socinian sense. Never has a great intellectual discovery passed with less notice by the world than the Socinian discovery of the proper meaning of omniscience. To this day works of reference fail to tell us about this."[80]

What of fulfilled prophecies? Do they not indicate that the future that was predicted was determined? No, says Hartshorne, that merely indicates that when the future became the present, it was definite. It may mean that nothing more was involved than coincidence, or that the person making the prophecy knew enough about the pertinent laws, such as the character of the person involved, to be able to predict accurately what would happen. This does not verify the future while it is future. That could only be done by a direct anticipatory intuition. This Hartshorne does not grant, though he does allow the possibility of predicting based upon inference from known present conditions.[81]

Others. Boyd refers to a nineteenth-century Methodist circuit rider named Billy Hibbard, who was known to hold a view of divine foreknowledge similar to that of the open theists. Hibbard, however, was sufficiently obscure that he does not appear in any American church history books, and the work that Boyd cites[82] is not even found in the Library of Congress.

Boyd also cites a statement by Major Jones to the effect that many African-American Christians also hold to a basically open view of God. Boyd's quotation of Jones says, "We [in the African-American Christian

[77]Ibid., 100.
[78]Ibid.
[79]Ibid., 101.
[80]Charles Hartshorne, *Omnipotence and Other Theological Mistakes* (Albany, N.Y.: State University of New York Press, 1984), 27.
[81]*Man's Vision of God*, 103–4.
[82]B. Hibbard, *Memoirs of the Life and Travels of B. Hibbard*, 2nd ed. (New York: Piercy & Reed, 1843).

tradition] believe human actions to be truly free, such that whereas God's knowledge of the past is total and absolute, God's knowledge of future events is not yet complete, particularly so far as acts of human freedom are concerned. The perfection of divine omniscience, then, must be construed to be God's always perfectly increasing knowledge taking in, with the passage of time, all knowable reality it [sic] as it expands."[83] From this citation, one would gain the impression that Jones is speaking of a broad stream of American religious experience. The editorial comment by Boyd makes this quotation somewhat misleading, however. Actually, the first sentence of the paragraph gives us the correct antecedent for the "We" in Jones's statement: "Black Theology upholds that within the inner-personal unity of the trinity of divine beings (God *ad intra*), the responsive relationship in holiness of the Father with the Son and the Holy Spirit was not subject to changes wrought upon God by external events. This does not, however, preclude God's freedom and ability to determine upon self-change. The content of God's consciousness is not so fixed that it cannot—if God will it—be constantly changing to include future events, as yet unknown in their non-being."[84] It is apparent that Jones is referring to a much narrower segment of African-American Christianity than Boyd's citation might have us believe. This is the black theology he has described earlier in the book, a theology that is considerably less conservative and evangelical than much grass-roots black Christianity in the United States.[85]

While no extensive research has been done on belief in divine foreknowledge in popular African-American religion, I have gathered anecdotal evidence from inquiries among evangelical African-American Christians, who though they emphasize God's involvement with the suffering of his people, and his response to their needs, also hold to the traditional view that God knows the future.[86] In fact, the Negro spirituals

---

[83]Major Jones, *The Color of God: The Concept of God in Afro-American Thought* (Macon, Ga.: Mercer University Press, 1987), 95. The quotation is found in *God of the Possible,* 172.

[84]Ibid.

[85]Pinnock also cites this statement by Jones (*Most Moved Mover,* 102), but makes no claim regarding the extent of black Christianity to which this applies.

[86]For example, when the Board of Trustees of Bethel College and Seminary (St. Paul, Minnesota) adopted a resolution approving the right of Gregory Boyd to continue to teach open theism at the school, the lone subsequent dissenter was the sole African-American member of the board.

often referred with confidence to God's working in the future of his people. Bearing in mind that Jones represents a more liberal branch of black Christianity, it seems rather questionable that his statement is representative of African-American lay Christianity.

Other Arminians. A recent symposium of Wesleyan theology gives a somewhat ambiguous answer to the question of divine foreknowledge. Albert Truesdale says, "Debates about the meaning of God's omniscience have been extensive and inconclusive. Speculation about whether God's knowledge includes not only the past and present but also the future, about how extensive is His knowledge of the future, and the bearing God's knowing of the future would have on human freedom has not produced any general theological consensus." He finds Hartshorne's specification that God knows what is knowable to be helpful. From that he goes on to say that "we are wise to leave the dimensions of 'what can be known' up to God. Whatever He knows does not violate His commitment to take finite freedom seriously. This affirmation should be enough to satisfy our understanding of God's omniscience. Nothing is gained by endless wrangling over whether God knows all the details of future events." His next statement indicates, if not an open theistic view, at least something rather similar to it: "It is a mistake to think that God's own being is somehow endangered or diminished unless He knows the future absolutely as though it were the past."[87] Unfortunately, he does not identify those who do hold a similar view.

On the other hand, Leslie Lightner, writing in another symposium of Wesleyan theology, espouses the traditional view: "While it is common to say that God has all knowledge of past, present, and future, one is speaking for human convenience. There is not a past or future with God; all is present, and he knows everything in one simultaneous, all-comprehensive act. All the events of time are known by him as present. The fact of God's omniscience gives the assurance that he is never taken by surprise or shock, nor is he caught off guard."[88]

---

[87]Albert Truesdale, "The Eternal, Personal, Creative God," in *A Contemporary Wesleyan Theology: Biblical, Systematic and Practical,* ed. Charles W. Carter (Grand Rapids: Zondervan, 1983), 1.126.

[88]Leslie L. Lightner, "The Christian Understanding of God," in *Theological Perspectives: Arminian-Wesleyan Reflections on Theology,* ed. Paul R. Fetters (Huntington, Ind.: The Church of the United Brethren in Christ, 1992), 205. Interestingly, each of the contributors was a member of the United Brethren in Christ, the denomination that sponsors Huntington College, where two open theists,

Let us then summarize our findings in this chapter. The preponderance of theology during the history of the church has held to the traditional view of divine foreknowledge. There have been few exceptions, and those have either been from outside the church, were theologians whose views on other major doctrines differ significantly from the orthodox tradition, or were so obscure as not to merit attention by major theologians.[89] There is a tradition of understanding of foreknowledge that is consonant with that of open theism, but it is the tradition of Celsus, Marcion, and Socinus. It is not the tradition of Justin Martyr, Tertullian, Augustine, Thomas Aquinas, Calvin, or Arminius.

This also gives us the answer to the question of whether open theism may be a new reformation similar to that of the sixteenth century. In that case, there was a return to biblical motifs that the church had held from the beginning but had neglected as its history unfolded. In the case of the traditional view of foreknowledge, however, our investigation failed to find a time before which the church held to the idea that God did not have exhaustive definite foreknowledge. The open theist appeal is not a call to return to an earlier, purer version of biblical understanding. It is a call to something new to the mainstream of orthodox Christian thought.

William Hasker and John Sanders, teach, and the editor was dean of the Graduate School of Christian Ministries at Huntington College.

[89]Boyd's reference to "such noteworthy theologians as G. T. Fechner, Otto Pfeiderer [sic] and Jules Lequier" (*God of the Possible,* 115), appears to be a considerable exaggeration.

CHAPTER 6

DIVINE foreknowledge and philosophical influences

part 1

The question of the influence of philosophical conceptions on the foreknowledge debate is an important one. One reason is that many aspects of the discussion involve issues and concepts that are themselves philosophical and have over the years been discussed extensively by philosophers.

There is another major reason why the question of philosophy is important to the debate. It is apparent that for most of its history, Christian theology has held that God does know, and has always known, all that will occur at any point in history. It has read the passages that speak of God discovering something, and changing his mind as being anthropomorphisms and anthropopathisms. Open theism thus faces the prospect that its tenets appear to be something of an innovation. If their view is indeed the correct understanding of Scripture, why has the church not seen this previously?

Here the uniform answer of open theists is that for much of its history, Christian theology has been under the influence of Greek philosophy, which thus distorted its understanding of Scripture. John Sanders, for example, poses the question directly: "Why do we not usually read the Bible in the way suggested [by Richard Rice] in the previous chapter?" How did this come to be? Sanders continues: "The answer, in part, is found in the way Christian thinkers have used certain Greek philosophical ideas. . . . [it] lies in an understanding of the cultural framework within which the early church developed its view of God. The early church fathers lived in the intellectual atmosphere where Greek philosophy (especially middle Platonism) dominated. . . . The classical view is so taken for granted that it functions as a preunderstanding that rules out certain interpretations of Scripture that do not 'fit' with the conception of what is 'appropriate' for God to be like, as derived from Greek metaphysics."[1]

Clark Pinnock seconds this thesis. "Traditional theology has been biased in the direction of transcendence as a result of undue philosophical influences. Greek thinking located the ultimate and the perfect in the realm of the immutable and absolutely transcendent. This led early theologians (given that the biblical God is also transcendent) to experiment with equating the God of revelation with the Greek ideal of deity. However, a price had to be paid in terms of faithfulness to Scripture and relevance to human life."[2] Similarly with the doctrine of immutability: "Some have claimed that God is wholly actual and not at all potential and thus cannot change in any way. They have equated the biblical idea of faithfulness with the Greek idea that requires any changes related to God to occur only on the human side."[3]

Gregory Boyd also addresses this issue and gives the same answer. He acknowledges that not many in church history have held the open view. He explains, "In my estimation this is because almost from the start the church's theology was significantly influenced by Plato's notion that God's perfection must mean that he is in every respect unchanging—including in his knowledge and experience. This philosophical assumption has been losing its grip on Western minds during the last hundred years, which is, in part, why an increasing number of Christians are coming to see the significance of the biblical motif on divine openness."[4]

It is not just professed open theists who view the difference as being a matter of the traditional view deriving from Greek philosophy. Roger

[1]John Sanders, "Historical Considerations," in Clark Pinnock, Richard Rice, John Sanders, William Hasker and David Basinger, *The Openness of God: A Biblical Challenge to the Traditional Understanding of God* (Downers Grove, Ill.: InterVarsity, 1994), 59–60.

[2]Clark Pinnock, "Systematic Theology," *The Openness of God,* 106.

[3]Ibid., 117.

[4]Gregory A. Boyd, *God of the Possible: A Biblical Introduction to the Open View of God* (Grand Rapids: Baker, 2000), 115.

Olson, who claims not to be an open theist himself, raised the question in a review of *The Openness of God* of whether classical theology has been held hostage to philosophy.[5] An editorial in *Christianity Today* seems to lean toward an affirmative answer. While acknowledging that "openness theology ... has been influenced by process philosophy," it gives the definite impression that openness theology is primarily rooted in biblical teaching and that the classical view, at least as presented in the 2000 Evangelical Theological Society annual meeting, draws heavily on philosophy.[6] This thesis therefore needs further exploration and evaluation.

THE TRADITIONAL VIEW AND PHILOSOPHICAL INFLUENCE

A number of considerations must be examined by way of evaluating the open theists' assertion that the traditional view is a synthesis of biblical and philosophical elements. Since this process of synthesizing is thought to have reached its apex in the thought of Thomas Aquinas,[7] it would be instructive to compare the Thomistic and the classical conservative or evangelical views of God.

The Classical View and Thomism. It is important to understand that Thomism is not just a doctrine of one aspect of God's nature, as that he is timelessly eternal. It involves a whole package of interrelated attributes of God. The open theists have acknowledged as much.[8] Thus, one would expect, for example, that contemporary conservative theology, holding to exhaustive definite foreknowledge, would also hold the Thomistic conception of *impassibility*: the doctrine that God is not affected by anything external to himself. Actually, Richard Creel has shown that the word *impassibility*, as applied to God, has numerous possible meanings;[9] however, the usual meaning in these discussions is that God does not feel emotion—specifically, does not feel the emotions that his human creatures are feeling, does not suffer when they suffer. Furthermore, he does not feel emotions occasioned

---

[5]Roger Olson, "Has God Been Held Hostage By Philosophy?" *Christianity Today,* 9 January 1995, 30.
[6]"God vs. God," *Christianity Today,* 7 February 2000, 34–35.
[7]Sanders, "Historical Considerations," 86–87.
[8]E.g., Sanders, "Historical Considerations," 85–87.
[9]Richard E. Creel, *Divine Impassibility: An Essay in Philosophical Theology* (Cambridge: Cambridge University Press, 1986), 9.

by the actions of humans. He does not feel regret over his actions in creating them when he sees them departing from his intentions for them.

It is interesting, in light of this, to examine several recent conservative or evangelical systematic theology textbooks, of which a large number have appeared in the past two decades. For example, Gordon Lewis and Bruce Demarest ask, "Which of the two hypotheses, that God is impassible and that he is passible, coherently fits the data of Scripture? Unquestionably the Scripture speaks of God as passionately involved with sinners and repentant sinners. Even though its language be taken figuratively, it illustrates a nonfigurative point. God really suffers when people sinfully destroy his creation, and God literally rejoices when one sinner repents."[10] Wayne Grudem, a strongly Calvinistic theologian, writes, "The idea that God has no passions or emotions *at all* clearly conflicts with much of the rest of Scripture, and for that reason I have not affirmed God's impassibility in this book. Instead, quite the opposite is true, for God, who is the origin of our emotions and who created our emotions, certainly does feel emotions."[11] Stanley Grenz, while not specifically discussing impassibility, makes much of such divine emotions as compassion.[12] While James Leo Garrett's systematic theology is largely a compilation of one-sentence citations of the views of others, he does say, "Despite the attendant problems and questions, it seems to be necessary to affirm that God has the capacity to suffer, for he has participated in suffering."[13]

A second feature of the Thomistic doctrine of God is his *immutability*. This has usually been understood as God's absolute unalterability, which to open theists seems to mean that God is incapable of making any response to human actions or of altering his actions. Bruce Ware, however, has argued for a view of immutability that does not hold these features of the Greek idea.[14] Similarly, Bruce Demarest clearly distances himself from the idea that immutability means immobility:

[10]Bruce Demarest and Gordon Lewis, *Integrative Theology* (Grand Rapids: Eerdmans, 1987), 1:236.
[11]Wayne Grudem, *Systematic Theology: An Introduction to Biblical Doctrine* (Grand Rapids: Zondervan, 1994), 166.
[12]Stanley Grenz, *Theology for the Community of God* (Nashville: Broadman-Holman, 1994), 122–27.
[13]James Leo Garrett, *Systematic Theology: Biblical, Historical, and Evangelical* (Grand Rapids: Eerdmans, 1990), 1:250–51.
[14]Bruce A. Ware, "An Evangelical Reformulation of the Doctrine of the Immutability of God," *Journal of the Evangelical Theological Society* 29.4 (1986):431–46.

The Christian faith emerged out of the matrix of Judaism with its conception of God as a living, active being relentlessly operative in the ordinary events of nature and the supernatural display of miracles. The God of the Jewish-Christian tradition is changeless in being, attributes and purposes, but in His dealings with the creation God does enter into changing relations. Thus, the divine immutability in no wise implies that God is unconcerned, inactive, or unrelated.... It is wholly irresponsible to replace the God of theism with a finite, evolving Deity in order to affirm relatedness to the world. Biblical faith unhesitatingly affirms that the perfection of God includes creative interaction consistent with His changeless character and purposes.[15]

Finally, the Thomistic view regarded God as *timelessly eternal*. While many who hold the traditional view of foreknowledge are atemporalists, this is by no means universal. Some profess inability to decide between the temporal and atemporal views of God. Ronald Nash says, "Is God a timeless or an everlasting being? At this time, I don't know. Like many theists, there was a time when I simply took the timelessness doctrine for granted.... I then passed through a stage where my confidence in the theory wavered. Some pretty impressive arguments, I thought, had been raised against it. But I no longer find many of those arguments so overpowering.... But the jury is still out and presently I see no reason why theism cannot accommodate itself to either interpretation."[16] Similarly, Thomas Morris declares himself unable to decide between the two views.[17] Some, such as William Lane Craig, while rejecting the traditional atemporalist approach, quite clearly and unequivocally endorse exhaustive divine foreknowledge.[18] Thus it appears that the Thomistic idea of divine timelessness is not an essential feature of the traditional view of foreknowledge.

---

[15]Bruce Demarest, "Process Trinitarianism," in *Perspectives on Evangelical Theology,* ed. Kenneth S. Kantzer and Stanley N. Gundry (Grand Rapids: Baker, 1979), 29.

[16]Ronald Nash, *The Concept of God: An Exploration of Contemporary Difficulties with the Attributes of God* (Grand Rapids: Zondervan, 1983), 83.

[17]Thomas Morris, *Our Idea of God: An Introduction to Philosophical Theology* (Downers Grove, Ill.: InterVarsity, 1991), 138.

[18]William Lane Craig, *The Only Wise God: The Compatibility of Divine Foreknowledge and Human Freedom* (Grand Rapids: Baker, 1987). Craig holds to a modified form, which he terms "relative timelessness," which does not fall into either the classical temporalist or nontemporalist camps.

The attribution of the traditional view's reading of the Scripture to the influence of Greek philosophy seems, at best, an oversimplification, and at worst, an actual inaccuracy. John Sanders observes that some have in recent years modified the classical synthesis, which to some extent he attributes to the influence of process philosophy.[19] In view of the evidence offered above that such "modification" is considerably more widespread than he acknowledges, and the absence of any evidence that these theologians have been influenced by process thought, a more tenable hypothesis may be that the sketch open theists have given of the traditional view is actually a caricature.

Pinnock contends that it is not possible to accept the traditional formulations of some attributes but not others: "The conventional package of attributes is tightly woven. You cannot deny one, such as impassibility, without casting doubt on others, like immutability. It's like pulling on a thread and unraveling a sweater. . . . The conventional package of attributes is tightly drawn. Tinkering with one or two of them will not help much."[20] He cites Nicholas Wolterstorff, who says, "Once you pull the thread of impassibility, a lot of other threads come along with it. Aseity, for example—that is, unconditionedness. . . . One also has to give up immutability (changeableness) and eternity. If God really *responds,* then God is not metaphysically immutable, and if not metaphysically immutable, then not eternal."[21]

Both Pinnock and Wolterstorff seem to assume, without any real argument, that there is a logical connection between these several attributes, so that rejection of one logically entails rejection of the others. Behind this assumption lies the assumption that the origin of this view is actually Greek philosophy. The argument seems to be something like this:

If A, then B. [If one holds the Greek view, one holds all these attributes.]

A. [These theologians hold the Greek view.]

Therefore B. [Therefore they must hold all the attributes, including impassibility.]

---

[19]Sanders, "Historical Considerations," 96.

[20]Clark Pinnock, *Most Moved Mover: A Theology of God's Openness* (Grand Rapids: Baker, 2001), 77–78; cf. 72, p.106, n.120, 108.

[21]N. Wolterstorff, "Does God Suffer?" *Modern Reformation* 8.5 (September/October1999): 47.

This would be, logically, the argument known as affirming the antecedent. There is another way to proceed from the first premise, however, namely, denying the consequent.

If A, then B. [As above]
Not B. [They do not hold all the attributes, specifically, the attribute of impassibility.]
Therefore, not A. [Therefore, they do not hold the Greek view.]

Both Pinnock and Wolterstorff appear to have confused logical consistency with systemic consistency. Logical consistency means that if one holds a given tenet, then one must hold its implications; or if one holds that tenet because of another tenet (in this case, the Greek view) that implies it, then one must hold other implications of that other tenet. Systemic consistency simply means that one holds all the tenets that have traditionally been part of a given set of tenets, whether they are logically entailed by one another or by a common principle or not.

Pinnock sees the potential problem with the argument he has used, namely, that it can be turned against open theism as well: "By the same token, the open view has to consider how far this unraveling can be allowed to go. We have ourselves resisted tossing out creation *ex nihilo,* which plays a major role in the classical package."[22] The open theists frequently claim that because of the relative newness of their movement, not all problems have been resolved and that it is "a research program, not a settled model clearly defined in every way."[23] This cannot be acceptable as an answer indefinitely, however. The question of their limitation of the unraveling deserves attention by open theists.

Actually, the problem is more complex than this. The assumption is that current orthodoxy takes its cue from Thomas Aquinas, who in turn formulated his theology on the basis of Aristotelian philosophy. Even this thesis is not completely accurate, however. For Thomas did not simply slavishly follow Aristotle. For example, there is a passage in Aristotle that indicates that he thought future events were contingent, or not determined, and hence not necessarily knowable.[24] In light of this fact, it is impressive

[22]Pinnock, *Most Moved Mover,* 78.
[23]E.g., ibid., 179.
[24]Aristotle, *On Interpretation,* chap. 9. The passage is discussed on pages 148–49 of this book.

to note that Thomas, who undoubtedly knew of this passage in Aristotle, nonetheless parted on this point from The Philosopher, as Thomas referred to him.

Pinnock also points out that Arius, under the influence of Greek philosophy, rejected the idea of incarnation because it posited change and suffering in God.[25] He does not offer an explanation of why the orthodox party did not have similar difficulties with incarnation if they were so strongly influenced by the same philosophy. One possible answer would be that they were influenced by different strands of Greek thought, but such nuances are not present in the statements about "*the* Greek view."

"Biblical" and "Greek" Thought. It appears that the distinction between the "biblical" and the "Greek" conceptions has been exaggerated at a number of points. For a long time it was customary to draw this distinction, and it even became one of the cardinal points of the so-called biblical theology movement. According to that view, the true biblical mentality is the Hebrew mode of thought. The Hebrews, on this interpretation, were non-theoretical or non-metaphysical in their thinking. They did not ask about the nature of things. Rather, their thinking was concrete and practical. The Greek mentality, on the other hand, was theoretical and speculative. It was concerned about metaphysical issues. It was here that questions about God's nature, his relationship to time, the nature of causation, and other issues came under consideration. The Hebrew view of reality was dynamic, whereas the Greek understanding of things was that reality is static.

The work of Johannes Pedersen, while not primarily theological, laid the foundations for the analysis of the Hebrew mentality.[26] Perhaps the most extensive argument of this type was that of Thorleif Boman, who based his argument on an analysis of the Hebrew language:

> Our analysis of the Hebrew verbs that express standing, sitting, lying, etc., teaches us that motionless and fixed being is for the Hebrews a nonentity; it does not exist for them. Only 'being' which stands in inner relation with something active and moving is a reality to them. This

---

[25]Ibid., 90.

[26]Johannes Pedersen, *Israel: Its Life and Culture*, 4 vols. (London: Oxford University Press, 1926, 1940).

could also be expressed: only movement (motion) has reality. To the extent that it concerned Hebrew thinking at all, static being as a predicate is a motion that has passed over into repose.[27]

Similar arguments can be found in the Christology of Oscar Cullmann,[28] the anthropology of John A. T. Robinson,[29] and numerous other works of the biblical theology movement. We should not simply equate the Hebrew and Greek mentalities with the Old and New Testaments, although ·they were written in these two languages, respectively. The New Testament, in the view of most biblical theologians, reflects the same Hebrew mentality as does the Old, although some of these theologians thought that the influence of Greek thought can already be found in the New Testament, especially in the later writings, which come from a period in which both the Gentile church and the Jewish congregations were under the influence of Hellenism. For the most part, however, the theory rests on the idea that the corrupting influence of Greek thought occurred after the writing of the biblical books, coming into play with the reflection upon them of some of the earliest church fathers. Gregory Dix, for example, says, "S. Paul has by now stood his trial on the charge of 'Hellenising' Christianity to make it acceptable to the Greeks—and the verdict is decisively 'Not Guilty.'"[30] Thus, interpretation of the Bible was done through Greek presuppositions, and theological construction was done using these Greek categories.

This scheme has come under serious attack in recent years, however. One early reaction was that of Leonhard Knothe. In an article entitled "Zur Frage des hebräischen Denkens" ("On the Question of Hebraic Thought"), Knothe disputed Boman's argument, particularly from the prominence of the Hebrew verb. He concluded: "His results and his concepts—such as dynamic, static, subjective, historical—require clarification and correction, and in the preceding I have attempted to indicate a direction for this type of correction."[31]

---

[27]Thorlief Boman, *Hebrew Thought Compared with Greek* (Philadelphia: Westminster, 1960), 31.
[28]Oscar Cullmann, *The Christology of the New Testament* (Philadelphia: Westminster, 1959).
[29]John A. T. Robinson, *The Body: A Study in Pauline Theology* (Chicago: H. Regnery, 1952).
[30]Gregory Dix, *Jew and Greek: A Study of the Primitive Church* (Westminster: Dacre, 1953), 3.
[31]Leonhard Knothe, "Zur Frage des hebräischen Denkens," *Zeitschrift für Alttestamentliche Wissenschaft*, 70 (1958): 175–77, 180–81. Translation mine.

Undoubtedly James Barr, with his *Semantics of Biblical Language,* which took over where Knothe's work had ended, struck the most serious blow. In this study, Barr used the actual languages to examine the supposed theory of the distinctive biblical language. His conclusion was that the theory simply did not conform to the semantical language.[32] For example, Boman had argued for the Hebrew mentality as dynamic by noting that the Hebrew language has only one verb to express the two meanings of "to lie," namely, "to be lying," which is static, and "to lie down," which involves motion. Barr showed, however, that in this respect Hebrew was no different than a number of other languages, including English, Egyptian, and even Greek![33] Similarly, Boman had contended that the Hebrews were not interested in existence, and that consequently their language had no means of expressing existence. Barr agrees that there is no Hebrew verb that expresses the idea "to be." However, he points out that the words *yes* and *ayin,* which are not verbs, are used to indicate existence. A prime example is found in Ps. 14:1, which the biblical theologians must read as "There is no god present." He concludes:

> Our study of *yeš* and *ʾayin* thus brings forward the following points:
> (a) any attempt to emphasize the verb as the basis of Hebrew speech and therefore to asset its peculiar "dynamism" is not only theoretically dubious but must reckon with these important words which are distinctly not verbs of any kind, and (b) there seems to be no linguistic reason why they should not come near the significance of absolute existence and non-existence in certain contexts, and if these concepts were unknown to the Hebrew mind it is hardly because they had no linguistic means of expressing them.[34]

Ironically, the intention of Barr was not to criticize the distinction between Hebrew and Greek thought, but to examine the nature of the evidence and its implications for hermeneutics of the Old Testament. He says early in the book: "The validity of the thought contrast is no part of our

---

[32]James Barr, *Semantics of Biblical Language.* James Leo Garrett Jr., in a review of my *Evangelical Left* (*Southwestern Journal of Theology* 42.1 [Fall 1999]: 91) faults me for citing a nonevangelical, Barr, on this issue. Garrett overlooks the point that the testimony of Barr on this point is more powerful, since he cannot be accused of bias on the basis of holding the traditional evangelical view.

[33]Barr, *Semantics of Biblical Language,* 50–54.

[34]Ibid., 63.

subject; our subject is (a) the way in which the thought contrast has affected the examination of linguistic evidence, and (b) the way in which linguistic evidence has been used to support or illustrate the thought contrast."[35] Nonetheless, Brevard Childs was emphatic and categorical in his assessment of the effect of this book on that scheme of thinking: "Seldom has one book brought down so much superstructure with such effectiveness."[36]

Martin Hengel's approach is somewhat different. He describes the issue in rather similar fashion: "Ever since the beginning of critical investigation of the New Testament in terms of the history of religions it has been customary to distinguish between 'Judaism' and 'Hellenism' (or between 'Jewish' and 'Hellenistic') as two completely different entities, to some degree capable of exact definition. Fundamental importance is often attached to this distinction, in which case it then appears as one of the most important criteria for historical interpretation in New Testament studies."[37] Hengel is primarily concerned with the relationship of the two cultures within the biblical period. His conclusion is a strong one: "*The term 'Hellenistic' as currently used no longer serves to make any meaningful differentiation in terms of the history of religions within the history of earliest Christianity....* We must stop attaching either negative or positive connotations to the question of 'Hellenistic' influence."[38] While Greek thought was used in the expression of certain theological concepts, this does not make them distinct from Hebraic thinking. With respect to Christology, for example, Hengel says, "Even a christology of pre-existence and of the Son of God is intrinsically not 'hellenistic' nor even 'un-Jewish' nor 'un-Palestine.'"[39]

What this says, then, is that the distinction between Greek and Hebrew (or true biblical) mentalities is not nearly as great as had been supposed. If this is the case, then the open theists have probably overestimated the potential for distortion of the biblical understanding of God by interpreters

---

[35]Ibid., 14.

[36]Brevard Childs, *Biblical Theology in Crisis* (Philadelphia: Westminster, 1970), 72.

[37]Martin Hengel, *The 'Hellenization' of Judea in the First Century after Christ* (Philadelphia: Trinity, 1989), 1.

[38]Ibid., 53.

[39]Ibid., 55. See also his *Judaism and Hellenism: Studies in their Encounter in Palestine during the Early Hellenistic Period,* vol. 1 (Philadelphia: Fortress, 1974); and *Jews, Greeks and Barbarian: Aspects of the Hellenization of Judaism in the Pre-Christian Period* (Philadelphia: Fortress, 1980).

influenced by Greek culture. Indeed, one must ask why they have read the Hebrew mentality in the fashion that they have and why most of the biblical support marshaled by open theists for their view is taken from the Old Testament, rather than the New. Perhaps philosophical presuppositions have affected *their* reading of the Scriptures, a possibility that we will consider more extensively later in this chapter.

Similarity of Ideas and the Question of Influence. One additional consideration is whether similarity of ideas indicates influence. Might it not be that the true interpretation of Scripture will at some points resemble some elements of various philosophies? For example, Plato drew a distinction between two realms of reality. There was the realm of unseen realities, the forms or ideas, which were actually qualities. There also was the visible realm, where actual instances of those qualities are to be found. Thus, a circle is a circle because it participates in the idea or form of circularity. Yet the form of circularity is not itself a circle; it is the formula for a circle, that which prescribes a circle. In Plato's thought, however, these actual empirical circles that we perceive are less real than the form or idea of circularity. Physical circles are the reflections or shadows cast by the form of circularity.[40]

Note, now, what Paul says in 2 Cor. 4:18: "So we fix our eyes not on what is seen, but on what is unseen. For what is seen is temporary, but what is unseen is eternal." Here is a parallel thought to Plato's idea of the greater reality of the unseen. Was Paul influenced in this by Plato? Were subsequent interpreters, who read Paul as attributing greater reality to the invisible or spiritual realm reading him through platonic spectacles? Was Plato led to his theory by a working of the Holy Spirit upon him? Or is it simply the case that on this point, Plato and Paul have congruent (although far from identical) concepts? The latter would seem to be the better explanation.

Some who have attributed some of the dimensions of the biblical doctrine of God to the influence of Greek philosophy may have been using a criterion much like the dissimilarity criterion that some form critics, such as Rudolf Bultmann and Norman Perrin, used in assessing the authenticity of sayings attributed to Jesus. On that criterion, a saying can be considered to be an authentic saying by Jesus only if one can find no parallel

---

[40]Plato, *The Republic,* VI-VII.

to it in Judaism or in the early church. That principle required that Jesus be totally original in what he said. It has come under severe criticism, particularly by Morna Hooker.[41] The upshot of that discussion was that dissimilarity should serve as a positive but not a negative tool. While a saying that was markedly different from anything otherwise available would probably only have survived and been incorporated into the text if the church was convinced it had come from Jesus, similarity was not a negative criterion. That principle should be observed here as well: if the conception of God is markedly different from the background culture, that would be a positive indication of the fidelity of the idea to the Bible. That would be true, for example, of Thomas's rejection of Aristotle's idea of the indeterminacy and indeterminability of the future. On the other hand, a similarity between a theologian's concept and that found in an extant philosophy should not necessarily be considered a mark of derivation or influence.

Neo-orthodoxy's Aversion to Philosophy. One other consideration should be noted. In the historical chapter, we noted that neo-orthodox theologians Karl Barth and Emil Brunner also held the traditional view of foreknowledge. Yet each of them, especially Barth, took considerable pains to free his theology from the influence of philosophy. We may note that Brunner went to great lengths to distinguish the biblical view from the philosophical. He says, for example, "There is perhaps an actual contradiction between two ideas of God, which, in point of fact, cannot be combined, two views which may be described as the philosophical and speculative Idea of God on the one hand, and on the other, one which is based upon the thought of God in revelation?"[42] He then engages in an examination of the history of Christian theology in the early centuries in which he draws conclusions about the influence of Greek philosophy on Christian theology. His rejection of any such alliance is strong and clear:

> Anyone who knows the history of the development of the doctrine of God in "Christian" theology, and especially the doctrine of the Attributes of God, will never cease to marvel at the unthinking way in which theologians adopted the postulates of philosophical speculation on the

---

[41]Morna Hooker, "On Using the Wrong Tool," *Theology* 75 (1972): 570–81; and "Christology and Methodology," *New Testament Studies* 17.4 (July 1971): 480–88.

[42]Emil Brunner, *The Christian Doctrine of God* (London: Lutterworth Press, 1949), 241–42.

Absolute, and at the amount of harm this has caused in the sphere of the "Christian" doctrine of God. They were entirely unaware of the fact that this procedure was an attempt to mingle two sets of ideas which were as incompatible as oil and water: in each view the content of the word "God" was entirely different: for each view was based on an entirely different conception of God.[43]

Brunner believes that in the early period of the church, up to about the time of the Nicene fathers, this influence was rather limited. In this regard, his analysis differs somewhat from that of Sanders and other openness theologians. Other than that, however, he follows much the same interpretation of how a certain kind of "orthodox" view arose.

The point of introducing Barth and Brunner is this. They went out of their way to avoid the dangers of corrupting their theology with philosophy, especially Greek philosophy. Yet, having done this, they nonetheless held to the doctrine of divine foreknowledge in the customary or received fashion. According to the principle of difference in inductive logic, the absence of a factor should result in the absence of the second factor if the former is in any sense the cause of the latter, or more correctly, is positively correlated with it. Thus, one must look elsewhere for the cause of belief in the usual doctrine. It is, of course, quite possible that despite their efforts Barth and Brunner have not successfully or completely purged their theology of Greek philosophy, but at least the odds of their having so done are increased by their conscious effort. Interestingly, Clark Pinnock cites Brunner's work in support of his own contention regarding Greek influence, but he makes no mention of Brunner's traditional stance on foreknowledge.[44]

This is not to suggest that the orthodox or classical formulations of the doctrine of God are free from philosophical influence or that they operate without a philosophical basis. All theologies work with some sort of philosophical categories, whether recognized and acknowledged or not. Moreover, all exegesis is done from some philosophical perspective, frequently held unconsciously. In this case, however, the philosophy involved is not really that which has been alleged. While space does not permit arguing

---

[43]Ibid., 242.
[44]Pinnock, *Most Moved Mover,* 65.

the point, I would contend that most contemporary evangelical theology uses what I would term "orthodox realism." In most cases, this has been a commonsense type of realism. More recently, as theologians and exegetes in the evangelical tradition have become more aware of the role of philosophy and the epistemological problems involved, there has been a move toward a critical realism. Even as this has been happening, the commonsense philosophy of Thomas Reid has been undergoing something of a revival of interest.[45]

The Open View and Philosophical Influences

If open theists and others suggest that the traditional view represents a reading of Scripture and construction of theology through the lenses of Greek philosophy, can a similar question be asked about open theism itself? For the most part the open theists have not posed that question. Pinnock, to be sure, acknowledges that "theology never operates without some regard for philosophy and is philosophically influenced to some degree. The question is not so much whether but how it is influenced, not whether but how philosophy plays a role."[46] Yet he does not discuss extensively the relationship of specific philosophies to open theism or the question of whether some contemporary philosophy has colored their reading of Scripture. Moreover, other theologians and commentators have done relatively little with this question. Consequently, the question deserves some careful inquiry.

Interestingly, there are some indications that philosophical factors have been influential in the conclusions of open theists. One of these is Clark Pinnock's acknowledgment that while the initial basis of his break with Calvinism was driven by Scripture, his specific questioning of the traditional view of foreknowledge was that it seemed to lead back into determinism and thus the loss of freedom: "I found I could not shake off the intuition that such omniscience would necessarily mean that everything we will ever choose in the future will have already been spelled out in the divine knowledge register, and consequently the belief that we have truly

---

[45]E.g., Alvin Plantinga, *Warranted Christian Belief* (New York: Oxford University Press, 2000), 218–27.
[46]Pinnock, *Most Moved Mover,* 114.

significant choices to make would seem to be mistaken." This led him to a further step, "Therefore, I had to ask myself if it was biblically possible to hold that God knows everything that can be known, but that free choices would not be something that can be known even by God because they are not yet settled in reality. . . . Can this conjecture be scriptural? When I went to the Scriptures with this question in mind, I found more support than I had expected."[47] Since this process apparently involved philosophical conceptions of the nature of freedom, time, and the future, it is somewhat surprising to find Pinnock reportedly telling the author of a philosophical paper defending the traditional position, "You have just made a very liberal move. You have constructed your belief from philosophy first and only second checked it with Scripture."[48]

Another indication is found in the work of Gregory Boyd, whose *God of the Possible,* published in 2000, makes much of the scriptural basis for the open view. Yet in *Trinity and Process,* published some eight years earlier, the argument had been almost entirely philosophical. There the major basis for the conclusion was philosophical, especially the conflict between divine foreknowledge of an event, requiring that it be definite, and the human freedom of the action in question. To be sure, this was a dissertation, dealing with a philosopher. Nonetheless, since it was a dissertation submitted at a theological seminary, it would not have been inappropriate to consider whether the conceptions involved were biblically supported.

Open Theism and Greek Thought. We have observed that open theists identify the philosophy that they believe has influenced classical theism as being Greek philosophy. We have noted that at several points this analysis did not seem to fit the data. We must also ask the converse, however. Are there points where open theism may itself reflect something of Greek thought? Here the answer may be surprising.

One philosopher whose thought parallels open theism at an important point is Aristotle. In his *On Interpretation* he considers the truth status of various kinds of propositions. A proposition must be either true or false, according to what has been labeled the law of excluded middle. When it

---

[47]Clark H. Pinnock, "From Augustine to Arminius: A Pilgrimage in Theology," in *The Grace of God and the Will of Man,* ed. Clark H. Pinnock (Minneapolis: Bethany, 1995), 25.
[48]"God vs. God," 35.

comes to a discussion of propositions about the future, however, there is a problem. For if it is the case that a certain result will occur or not occur, he says, "There would be no need to deliberate or to take trouble, on the supposition that if we should adopt a certain course, a certain result would follow, while, if we did not, the result would not follow. For a man may predict an event ten thousand years beforehand, and another may predict the reverse; that which was truly predicted at the moment in the past will of necessity take place in the fullness of time."[49] The implications of this are significant: "Wherefore, if through all time the nature of things was so constituted that a prediction about an event was true, then through all time it was necessary that that prediction should find fulfilment; and with regard to all events, circumstances have always been such that their occurrence is a matter of necessity."[50] This, however, leads to an impossible conclusion, for "both deliberation and action are causative with regard to the future, and that, to speak more generally, in those things which are not continuously actual there is a potentiality in either direction. Such things may either be or not be; events also therefore may either take place or not take place.... For in the case of that which exists potentially, but not actually, the rule which applies to that which exists actually does not hold good."[51]

While there have been a variety of interpretations of Aristotle's argument here, most philosophers read this as a *reductio ad absurdum*. Kenny has explained this as follows: "If future-tensed propositions about singulars are already true, then fatalism follows: but fatalism is absurd; therefore, since many future events are not yet determined, statements about such events are not yet true or false, although they later will be."[52] If this is indeed the case, then here is a point at which open theism is closer to the Greek tradition that has been dominant since the thirteenth century than is traditional theism.

There are other elements of open theism that have Greek antecedents. The picture sometimes drawn of ancient Greek philosophy of holding to

---

[49]Aristotle, *On Interpretation,* chap. 9.
[50]Ibid.
[51]Ibid.
[52]Anthony John Patrick Kenny, *The God of the Philosophers* (Oxford: Clarendon; New York: Oxford University Press, 1979), 52.

fixed, immutable realities is at best oversimplified. While it is true that some, such as Zeno, emphasized the fixity of things, that is only one strain of Greek thought. Equally influential was the strain that regarded reality as dynamic and changing. Heraclitus is an obvious example. He believed that everything was in change, so that no one could step into the same stream twice.[53] Cratylus even felt that reality was so dynamic and our ideas so poorly able to match that reality that he declined to make any assertions about reality.[54]

There is no indication of a direct influence of this type of Greek thought on open theism. Because antecedents earlier in the history of Christian thought are few and disconnected, and one of those few, Calcidius, seemed to be dealing with Platonic and Stoic thought, it is unlikely that any heritage of Aristotle or these other Greek philosophers has descended to today's open theists. This is not to say that there may not be indirect influence, and the point is that these are philosophical considerations, nonetheless.

The Problem of Evil. It is interesting to observe the role the problem of evil plays in the open theist argument. John Sanders begins his book on providence with a gripping story of the death of his brother Dick. He found that people attempted to comfort him by assuring him that God had good reasons for ordaining his brother's death. He comments, "Those discussions served to spur my reflection on divine providence for over twenty years."[55]

Similarly, Gregory Boyd tells the story of Suzanne, a Christian woman who came to him in anger after he had preached a sermon on how God directs our paths. She told him her story of how as a teenager she felt called to evangelize Taiwan. In college she met and eventually married a young man who also felt called to Taiwan, which she regarded as a sign of God's leading. During missionary training she discovered that he was involved in an adulterous relationship with another student, a pattern that was repeated.

---

[53]Seymour G. Martin, Gordon H. Clark, Francis Clarke, and Chester T. Ruddick, *A History of Philosophy* (New York: Crofts, 1947), 33–35.

[54]G. B. Kerferd, "Cratylus," *The Encyclopedia of Philosophy,* ed. Paul Edwards (New York: Macmillan, 1967), 2:251–52.

[55]John Sanders, *The God Who Risks: A Theology of Providence* (Downers Grove, Ill.: InterVarsity, 1998), 9.

He also became physically abusive. Two weeks after he left her for his lover, she discovered that she was pregnant. Boyd's comment on the case and on his counseling of Suzanne is, "Without having the open view to offer, I don't know how one could effectively minister to a person in Suzanne's dilemma."[56] This case, which Boyd frequently highlights in his oral presentation of open theism, combines the problem of evil with the question of divine leading.

This use of the problem of evil as an argument for open theism, or more accurately, against classical theism, is found in other open theists as well. David Basinger uses human suffering as a major consideration in his chapter on "practical considerations" in *The Openness of God*.[57] In some cases, it appears as if that is the primary driving consideration, to which, as Pinnock acknowledged, the Scriptures are then found to offer support. The problem of evil is, of course, one of the most difficult problems of Christian theology. Note, however, that this is a *philosophical* problem that is given such a prominent place in the arguments of the open theists.

Process Thought and Its Influence. One disputed issue with respect to open theism is its relationship to process thought. Some open theists have emphatically denied any connection between the two. Perhaps the most vigorous is this from Boyd. When asked, "To what extent do you think this new trend [open theism] in evangelical thinking is indebted to process theology?" he replied, "None. Despite uninformed protests to the contrary, the two movements have next to nothing in common. They both affirm that the future partly consists in possibilities, and that is it. Some open theists (such as myself) find certain arguments of Process theologians for a dynamic view of reality, for a responsive God, and/or for a partly open future persuasive. But I don't know of any who have become open theists for that reason."[58]

Despite this, several open theists declare that their thinking has been influenced by process philosophers. Some seven years earlier, Boyd had

[56]Boyd, *God of the Possible,* 106.
[57]David Basinger, "Practical Considerations," *The Openness of God,* 168–71.
[58]"Is God Dependent On Us? Interview with Gregory Boyd," *Modern Reformation* 8.6 (November/December 1999): 44–45.

indicated Charles Hartshorne's influence on him: "My warmest appreciation must also be expressed to Charles Hartshorne. Though I disagree with him on a great many points, he has influenced my own thinking more than any other single philosopher."[59] Other openness theologians profess a similar influence. Richard Rice, for example, writes autobiographically of his experience in graduate studies at the University of Chicago:

> Process thought did not occupy the position at Chicago in the 1970s that it had in the 1950s (from what I was told), but you could still get a healthy dose of it. I studied the thought of Whitehead in seminars taught by Schubert M. Ogden and Langdon Gilkey. But it was Hartshorne's philosophical theology that particularly attracted me. There were several reasons for this. On the most basic level, I was impressed that a powerful mind, determined to follow reason to the end in matters of religion, found abundant evidence for God and developed impressive arguments for God's existence. I also felt that Hartshorne's particular conception of natural theology could benefit theologians in a number of important ways.[60]

Similarly, William Hasker writes of his own experience with process thought. Speaking of the view that how things are with his creatures really makes a difference with God, Hasker says: "On a personal note, let me state that I first became clearly convinced of this through reading Charles Hartshorne's *Divine Relativity*. Prior to reading Hartshorne, I had puzzled over the medieval doctrine that, while the creatures are really related to God, God has only a 'relation of reason' to the creatures."[61]

We must ask further, however, the extent to which such influence actually shows itself in the thought of the open theists. Are there indications of elements of process thought in the open theist approach to divine foreknowledge? Some of these can be found in statements of points of agreement with process philosophy. We noted above that Boyd emphatically denied any commonality between the two. Similarly, in *God of the Possible*, he said, "Some evangelical authors have wrongly accused open theists of

[59]Gregory A. Boyd, *Trinity and Process: A Critical Evaluation and Reconstruction of Hartshorne's Di-Polar Theism Towards a Trinitarian Metaphysics* (New York: Peter Lang, 1992), preface.
[60]Richard Rice, "Process Theism and the Open View of God: The Crucial Difference," in *Searching for an Adequate God: A Dialogue Between Process and Free Will Theists,* ed. John B. Cobb Jr. and Clark H. Pinnock (Grand Rapids: Eerdmans, 2000), 165–66.
[61]William Hasker, "An Adequate God," in *Searching for an Adequate God,* 216–17.

being close to process thought, but in truth the two views have little in common."[62] He contends that they are different because process theology holds that God needs the world. He could not have existed without it. It also denies God's omnipotence.[63] Yet, in *Trinity and Process,* he seemed to be attempting to work out a conventional Trinitarian view with process categories:

> This work is, in essence, an attempt to work out a trinitarian-*process* metaphysic which overcomes this impasse. It is our conviction that the fundamental vision of the *process* world view, especially as espoused by Charles Hartshorne, is correct. But it is our conviction as well that the scriptural and traditional understanding of God as triune and antecedently actual within Godself is true, and is, in fact, a foundational doctrine of the Christian faith. But, we contend, these two views, when understood within a proper framework, do not conflict.
>
> Indeed, it shall be our contention that Hartshorne's a priori *process* metaphysics, when corrected of certain misconstrued elements, actually requires something like a trinitarian understanding of God to make it consistent and complete! What results, we trust, is the outline of a metaphysical system which establishes, on an a priori basis, a *process* view of the world which requires a trinitarian God for its completion.[64]

Since Boyd has never repudiated this earlier work, his later denial seems puzzling, to say the least.

Clark Pinnock is more forthright:

> Now if we are to be honest, we would have to admit that it has been process thinkers who have called our attention to some of these problems. I have to acknowledge the stimulus I have personally received from them, and how they have made me aware of the need to introduce changes into the received doctrine of God. Hartshorne, for example, has put a lot of effort into exposing the difficulties and suggesting alternatives. I have been helped by his ideas on various things. He has taught me that thinking of God as literally *all*-powerful divests the finite universe of a degree of power. He has pressed the point that God, though unchanging in his character, is certainly able to change in response to a

---

[62]Boyd, *God of the Possible,* 31.
[63]Ibid., 170.
[64]Boyd, *Trinity and Process,* preface; emphasis added.

changing creation. In my theology, at least, God has used process thinkers to compel me to change certain ideas which I had and bring them up to scriptural standards. Without being a process theologian myself, I am certainly indebted to such thinkers for many good insights.[65]

One of the places where Pinnock reflects this influence is in his discussion of metaphysics. He says, "We now think that the universe is composed of dynamic events more than solid things," a statement that is almost the hallmark of process metaphysics.[66]

Hasker notes the similarity between the two views at several points:

> But before I pursue the undeniable differences, I want to speak of some important areas of agreement between the two views. One such agreement is the following: God is really related to his creatures, where "really related" means that it makes a difference to God how things are with the creatures. . . .
>
> A second point of agreement, which builds on the first, is that God is affected by the state of his creatures, and suffers when things go badly for them. . . .
>
> Yet a further area of agreement between process theism and the open view concerns the nature and implications of human freedom. Both of our views reject the compatibilist notion of freedom, which holds that free will is compatible with causal determination. In rejecting this, we also reject the notion of God as all-controlling, as the sole determiner of everything that takes place in the universe. Instead, we affirm the incompatibilist, or libertarian, view according to which one is free only if one would be able, under exactly the same circumstances, to refrain from the act that one has in fact chosen, and to do something else instead. This view, to be sure, is held in common with many of our fellow Christians in various traditions.[67]

In his response to David Ray Griffin, Hasker also calls attention to the similarity between the two types of theism in their method of dealing with the problem of evil: "What strikes me at this juncture (I had not seen this clearly before now) is the *similarity* of the problem of evil as viewed from

---

[65]Pinnock, "Between Classical and Process Theism," in *Process Theology*, ed. Ronald Nash (Grand Rapids: Baker, 1987), 316–17.
[66]Pinnock, *Most Moved Mover*, 130.
[67]Hasker, "An Adequate God," *Searching for an Adequate God*, 216–18.

the perspectives of process theism and free theism. Both views employ versions of the freewill defense, attributing human-caused evil to the undetermined free choices of human beings. Process theists, to be sure, claim that freedom is a necessary part of creation and not the result of a decision on God's part."[68]

Rice also acknowledges several points of similarity between the two theisms. After noting a number of differences, he says,

> Such differences notwithstanding, process theologians and open theists have a good deal in common. I like Howell's eclectic approach to theology; it suggests a way for us to work together. Like her, I feel that process thought provides a significant resource for Christian thinkers today. And like her, I hope that dialogue will continue between process theologians and open theists as we work out the implications of our common conviction that God is deeply involved with the affairs of the world God loves, and that our actions make a profound difference to the world's future and to God's.[69]

In an earlier quotation from Rice, we noted that he found that theologians could benefit from Hartshorne's thought at a number of points. He elaborates what some of those are:

> Most important, I found what growing numbers of conservative Christian thinkers have also discovered in recent years. If we accept a version of Hartshorne's dipolar theism, we can formulate a doctrine of God that is superior by every relevant criterion to the God of classical theism. The notion that a perfect being can change is not only conceptually coherent—a point Hartshorne argues at great length—but it gives us an idea of God that is more faithful to the biblical portrait than is classical theism and more helpful to us on the level of personal religion as well. The idea that God's relation to the world is interactive, or dynamic, makes it possible for us to develop coherent concepts of divine love and creaturely freedom. In so doing it helps us to overcome some of the problems that have perplexed Christian thinkers for centuries, such as the relation of human freedom and divine foreknowledge.[70]

---

[68]Hasker, "In Response to David Ray Griffin," *Searching for an Adequate God,* 42–43.
[69]Richard Rice, "In Response to Nancy Howell," *Searching for an Adequate God,* 94–95.
[70]Rice, "Process Theism and the Open View of God," 166.

In an early writing, which was perhaps the first publication of the open theist movement, Rice had already indicated two points of similarity between open theism and process theism. So he says, "The concept of God proposed here shares the process view that God's relation to the temporal world consists in a succession of concrete experiences, rather than a single timeless perception." Beyond that, however, he says, "It also shares with process theism the two-fold analysis of God, or the 'dipolar theism,' described above. It conceives God as both absolute and relative, necessary and contingent, eternal and temporal, changeless and changing. It attributes one element in each pair of contrasts to the appropriate aspect of God's being—the essential divine character or the concrete divine experience."[71]

John Sanders does not mention any influence of process thought. In fact, he has orally indicated that he has not studied process thought and therefore has not been influenced by it. Yet, strangely, he finds "modifications" in some contemporary evangelical thinking about God, "especially in light of the critique by process theologians," without offering any evidence of such influence.[72] One would think that Sanders would therefore not restrict philosophical influence on his thought to that of which he is consciously aware.

Open theists have been very clear in distinguishing their view from process theism. They especially mention two differences. The first is that process theology believes that God is dependent on the world, which open theism does not. The other is that according to process theology, God never acts unilaterally, whereas open theists hold that God can and does sometimes intervene in the world, even overriding the free wills of humans.[73]

We observed earlier that Pinnock was emphatic that if one rejects some part of the classical or Greek view of God, he must reject all, since it is a tightly knit whole. The parallel argument should be that if one accepts some major elements of process philosophy, he cannot decline to accept others, or that if one rejects some elements of it, he must reject the others. The open theists see the unsoundness of such an argument in the latter case, but not in the former.

---

[71]Rice, *God's Foreknowledge and Man's Free Will* (Minneapolis: Bethany, 1985), 33.
[72]Sanders, "Historical Considerations," in *Openness of God,* 96.
[73]Rice, "Process Theism and the Open View of God," 185–88.

Philosophical Conceptions. It is also important to observe several points at which the open theist argument depends on conceptions that are primarily philosophical rather than biblical in nature. In some cases these philosophical conceptions are identified and argued for; in other cases they are simply assumed.

The first and most obvious and prominent of these elements is the view of human freedom. It is clear that this issue lies at the heart of much of the dispute between open theism and traditional theism. Probably the clearest discussion of the matter is that of Hasker. He states the problem that free will creates for the traditional view of divine foreknowledge as follows:

> By this time it should come as no surprise that there are serious questions concerning the logical compatibility of comprehensive divine foreknowledge and libertarian free will. The idea, roughly, is this: If God knows already what will happen in the future, then God's knowing this is part of the past and is now fixed, impossible to change. And since God is infallible, it is completely impossible that things will turn out differently than God expects them to. But this means that the future event God knows is also fixed and unalterable, and it cannot be true of any human beings that they are both able to perform a certain action and able not to perform that action. If God knows that a person is going to perform it, then it is impossible that the person fail to perform it—so one does not have a free choice whether or not to perform it.[74]

Hasker acknowledges that the view he has sketched and the consequences of it for divine foreknowledge is the libertarian or incompatibilist view. He acknowledges that another view, compatibilism, is held by those who advocate the traditional view of divine foreknowledge. Yet when he discusses the compatibilist conception, he evaluates it through the categories of incompatibilism, simply begging the question. This can be seen quite clearly, for example, in his discussion of Calvinism, in which he contends that the conception of God held by Calvinists undercuts the experience that they claim to have. Notice the imagery Hasker employs: "The Calvinist understanding of the God-human relationship has been compared to a puppetmaster controlling the movements of a puppet, or of a ventriloquist having

---

[74]Hasker, "A Philosophical Perspective," *The Openness of God,* 147.

a 'conversation' with his dummy." He acknowledges that Calvinists would reject these analogies as inappropriate and offers another: "Perhaps a closer comparison would be with a computer wizard who has assembled a lifelike robot and, through a thorough knowledge of the robot's programming, is able to manipulate the robot's responses to an indefinitely large variety of situations."[75] Such analogies, of course, assume the truth of the incompatibilist or libertarian view of freedom. On the compatibilist view, this is by no means such a mechanical or coerced matter.

The other open theists also clearly espouse a libertarian view of human freedom. Clark Pinnock, for example, says flatly, "Philosophically speaking, if choices are real and freedom significant, future decisions cannot be exhaustively foreknown."[76] Earlier he had been even more explicit: "An important implication of this strong definition of freedom is that reality is to an extent open and not closed. It means that genuine novelty can appear in history which cannot be predicted by God. If the creature has been given the ability to decide how some things will turn out, then it cannot be known infallibly ahead of time how they will turn out. . . . It is plain that the biblical doctrine of creaturely freedom requires us to reconsider the conventional view of the omniscience of God."[77] Pinnock believes that Augustine was able to use a belief in human freedom as a solution to the problem of evil without modifying the view of omniscience or omnipotence only because of an element of incoherence in his thought.[78]

Sanders acknowledges that some open theists begin with a libertarian freewill presupposition but argues that for him it is the consequence of his study of the Scriptures, not the presupposition: "It is correct that some proponents of the risk view begin with libertarian freedom as a control belief, using it to reshape the doctrine of God. However, that was not the method used here. I began with an examination of Scripture to see what it says about God and the nature of God's relationship with us. The biblical model of God as a personal being who enters into genuinely reciprocal

---

[75]Ibid., 142–43.

[76]Pinnock, "Systematic Theology," *The Openness of God,* 123.

[77]Pinnock, "God Limits His Knowledge," in *Predestination and Free Will: Four Views of Divine Sovereignty and Human Freedom,* ed. David Basinger and Randall Basinger (Downers Grove, Ill.: InterVarsity, 1986), 150.

[78]Ibid.

relations with us fits nicely with human libertarian freedom."[79] Sanders does not consider the possibility that he interprets the biblical teachings through the conception of the libertarian view.

In his earlier work, *Trinity and Process,* Boyd made much of the freewill argument.[80] In *God of the Possible,* he minimizes this factor, contending that his case has been formed on biblical grounds. He does acknowledge the freewill argument, however. "Freedom is the ability to choose between various possibilities. You are free to cheat on your taxes or not only because it is *possible* for you to cheat on your taxes *or not.* But if the fact that you *will* cheat is written in *God's Book of Known Facts,* and God can't possibly be wrong, then it is not possible for you *not* to cheat on your taxes. Hence you cannot be free to choose between the possibilities of cheating or not cheating. In other words, you can't be free."[81]

All of this documentation should serve to establish that a certain view of human freedom, namely an incompatibilist or libertarian view, plays an important part in the open theist rejection of the traditional view of foreknowledge. This, however, is a philosophical conception, not a biblical conception per se. While it may or may not be supported by biblical considerations, it is a philosophical factor, and its place should be acknowledged.

The Nature of Time. Much of the open theist argument includes the idea that God cannot be atemporal. While the traditional view of complete divine foreknowledge can coexist either with the temporal or the atemporal view of God, open theism must of necessity reject atemporalism. The reason is that if God is outside of time, so that he in effect is contemporaneous with all events at all points in time, then there is no problem with divine foreknowledge and human freedom, because, in a sense, it is not *fore*knowledge at all. God sees it as happening in the eternal present.

What is interesting about Boyd's argument is that it assumes what philosophers call the A-theory of time, or what Alan Padgett terms the "process" view, versus the B-theory, or "stasis" view.[82] These two conceptions of time, as well as the implications of accepting one or the other, are

---

[79]Sanders, *The God Who Risks,* 222.
[80]Boyd, *Trinity and Process,* 296–341.
[81]Boyd, *God of the Possible,* 122.
[82]Alan Padgett, *God, Eternity, and the Nature of Time* (New York: St. Martin's, 1992), 82–121.

much debated among philosophers. Thus, William Craig, for example, adopts the A-theory but still holds to divine foreknowledge, basing it upon a middle knowledge theory.[83] Where one comes down on the issue of which theory, as well as which implications flow from the A-theory, goes a long way toward settling the disputed questions. These are philosophical conceptions, however, and Boyd simply assumes the correctness of one of these without arguing for it or even, in his later writing, acknowledging that such a philosophical conception enters into his view.

The Nature of the Future. Boyd, especially, makes much of the idea that not knowing the future is not a limitation on God's omniscience. The future is not something that is knowable; it has no reality, so inability to know it is not inability to know "something." God's ability to make square circles is not an impingement on his omnipotence because square circles, by their very nature, cannot exist. They are self-contradictory, and hence there is no reality there to be brought into existence. Similarly, God's not knowing the future is not a lack of knowledge because there is no future to be known. Boyd likens this to God's not knowing a false proposition. God does not know the proposition "there is a monkey next to me" because there is no such monkey.[84] His ignorance of that "fact" is not really lack of knowledge because there is no such fact.

Boyd is very clear about the importance of this issue. In fact, he contends that this is the very center of the debate: "It is not really about God's knowledge at all. It is rather a debate about the nature of the future. . . . Open theists, by contrast, hold that the future consists partly of settled realities and partly of unsettled realities. Some things about the future are *possibly* this way and *possibly* that way."[85]

This is the unrealistic view of the future, the idea that it does not have reality that can be known. The various possibilities of what may happen exist, so that God can know the possibilities, but the definite outcomes do not. We have seen above that this view goes all the way back

---

[83]William Lane Craig, "Divine Knowledge and Future Contingency," in *Process Theology,* 98–103.
[84]Boyd, *God of the Possible,* 17.
[85]Ibid., 15–16.

to Aristotle. It has had more recent defenders, such as P. T. Geach.[86] This issue, however, which Boyd admits to be the crucial one, is a philosophical question and should be acknowledged as such.

We have examined the charge of open theists and others that the classical understanding of God rests on philosophical grounds: that the influence of Greek thought, especially of Plato, has caused the church to read the Scriptures through philosophical spectacles and thus to find there a God who is unchanging, timeless, all-knowing, and unaffected by anything external to himself. Yet as we have seen, not only is this interpretation of the classical view not fully accurate, but the open view itself contains considerable philosophical material. That the open theists fail to acknowledge this is, to say the least, infelicitous.

---

[86]P. T. Geach, *Providence and Evil* (Cambridge: Cambridge University Press, 1977), 52–53.

CHAPTER 7

divine foreknowledge and philosophical influences

part 2

In the preceding chapter, we noted that despite the open theists' frequent charges that the traditional view is a result of reading the Bible through the lenses of Greek philosophy, their own view also has significant philosophical content. We must therefore do some evaluation of the philosophical content of open theism. This involves quite a large number of issues.

The Philosophical Basis of Open Theism

While there are some specific variations from one open theist to another, and while many elements must be inferred rather than being openly stated, it is possible to formulate some of the basic tenets of open theism:

1. A strong preference for an incompatibilist view of human freedom, the view that an act cannot be both free and foreknowable. Indeed, this is often simply stated as if any departure from it is a denial of human freedom.
2. An insistence on striving to understand God fully, including an implicit trust in the power of human reason to do so.
3. A belief that one can generally understand divine actions and the divine mind by understanding what

such actions and thoughts would mean if referring to humans. This in turn seems to be based on a belief in an ontological analogy between God and humans.

4. In general, a preference for what is seen as a dynamic understanding of the whole of reality, as contrasted with what they picture as a static view. Growth, change, and development are good. This understanding of the nature of reality extends to humans and even to God himself.

5. A conception that God is in some sense answerable to humans. He must justify his actions and seems to have an obligation to promote their temporal and eternal welfare.

6. A strong preference for the A-theory of time, and for a temporalist understanding of God.[1]

THE CONCEPT OF FREEDOM

It is apparent that the understanding of human freedom plays a very important role in the development of the open theist view of divine foreknowledge. The problem is simply this: if God knows what a human will do in advance of that person's action, then it must be certain what that person will do. If that were not the case, then the person might do something different than what God expected, in which case God would turn out to have been mistaken, which of course he cannot be. The only real alternative to this conclusion would be that a different action now than what God has in the past expected or known would have to alter what God previously knew. Since the past cannot be changed, this is not an acceptable option. If, however, it is certain what the person will do, then he or she cannot do otherwise. In other words, the person is not free. We know, however, that we are free. Our actions presuppose that. If we did not believe that we were free, then we would make no effort.

The definition of freedom is rather simple: it is the capacity to do otherwise than what is ultimately done, or more generally, to be able to choose

---

[1]The A-theory, or process view of time is that events come into being, are, and then pass away. This is contrasted with B-theory or the stasis view of time, or time as untensed. The temporalist view of God is that he is of infinite duration within time ("everlasting"), rather than outside of time ("eternal").

WHAT DOES GOD KNOW AND WHEN DOES HE KNOW IT?

and actually do more than one option. Freedom is a genuine possibility of choosing more than one course of action. It is not to be understood as mere freedom from external constraints. It must include internal freedom and capacity as well.

This is a relatively commonsense view. The answer to the question, "Why did x do that?" is simply, "He chose to do so." The further question, "But why did he choose that?" is not really seriously grappled with. While the open theists may well concede that there are factors that influence a person or incline one in a certain direction, in the final analysis the answer to the question, "Why did he choose?" is "He just did." To introduce more detailed explanation in terms of motives may be acceptable as a sort of final cause, but to offer efficient causes of the person's choice and action would be to posit determinism.

William Hasker has worked this position out in considerable detail. Whereas the issue was often put in terms of whether Henry will mow his lawn on Saturday, Hasker has apparently tired of the sound of Henry's mower. Consequently, he develops the argument along the lines of the choice of breakfast by a fictitious character named Clarence:

(C1) It is now true that Clarence will have a cheese omelet for breakfast tomorrow. (Premise)

(C2) It is impossible that God should at any time believe what is false, or fail to believe any true proposition such that his knowing that proposition at that time is logically possible. (Premise: divine omniscience)

(C3) God has always believed that Clarence will have a cheese omelet tomorrow. (Assumption for indirect proof)

(C4) If God has always believed a certain thing, it is not in anyone's power to bring it about that God has not always believed that thing. (Premise: the unalterability of the past)

(C5) Therefore, it is not in Clarence's power to bring it about that God has not always believed that he would have a cheese omelet for breakfast. (From 3,4)

(C6) It is not possible for it to be true both that God has always believed that Clarence would have a cheese omelet for breakfast, and that he does not in fact have one. (From 2)

(C7) Therefore, it is not in Clarence's power to refrain from having a cheese omelet for breakfast tomorrow. (From 5,6) So Clarence's eating the omelet tomorrow is not an act of free choice.

(C8) Clarence will act freely when he eats the omelet for breakfast tomorrow. (Premise)

(C9) Therefore, it is not the case that God has always believed that Clarence will have a cheese omelet for breakfast tomorrow. (From 3–8, indirect proof)[2]

For C3 to be true, it would be necessary for C8 to be false. Conversely, one may deny C3, leaving C8 intact. Because of their strong commitment to libertarian freedom, however, the open theists have unanimously chosen to reject C3.

Several problems arise for this view of freedom, however. One is the problem of the status of redeemed humans in the life to come. Freedom would seem to require the possibility of following more than one option. Usually, theologians and other Christians assume that these redeemed persons will live a sinless life. If this is the case, however, if it is certain that such persons will never sin, are they free, on openness grounds? It would seem that on these premises, it is not possible for them to do other than the right thing, and they therefore are not free. If this is the case, then the experience of freedom, of spontaneity, of novelty, of growth that is so highly valued will be present in this life but not in the life to come. In other words, a value possessed in this life will be absent in the life to come. Is it then heaven, or is it not less desirable than is this earthly life? Of course, the openness theologians could answer that in heaven we will be free to sin but will without exception choose not to, but then their argument for libertarian freedom in this life has largely lost its effect. Pinnock suggests that the period of libertarian freedom is a period of probation, which will come

---

[2]William Hasker, *God, Time, and Knowledge* (Ithaca, N.Y.: Cornell University Press, 1989), 73–74.

to an end: "It could be that sometime in the future our probation will come to an end and we will be able to love reliably and unchangeably. But, in this present life, we are free to enter into union with God or not. It may be that in heaven, the purpose of our probation having been fulfilled, freedom may be withdrawn. Perhaps we will not sin there because we will have been conformed fully to the image of Christ."[3]

What Pinnock considers hypothetically here, Boyd affirms rather categorically in *Satan and the Problem of Evil*.[4] There he clearly espouses the idea that libertarian freedom of a given human is not perpetual. It is for a period of probation. At some point, however, the character of the individual becomes fixed by his own free choices. From that point on, he acts in conformity with his character and does not have libertarian freedom. This view of Boyd's will be developed more fully in connection with his treatment of the problem of evil, but for our purposes here, it is sufficient to observe that libertarian freedom is not an unreserved good. It is not quite clear just why such a high premium is placed on it in the earlier stages. Given what is said about God wanting freely chosen love, it appears that after the period of probation is ended, and throughout eternity, the love of humans for God is not free, because they cannot do otherwise. Is it therefore virtuous and pleasing to God?

There is another problem of considerable moment for the libertarian view of freedom. Richard Swinburne has suggested that perhaps, on these grounds, God is not free. Swinburne holds that if God is truly free, he cannot even know what actions he is going to take in advance of making those decisions or the results of those actions.[5] This suggestion needs a bit more probing. We could take Hasker's argument and apply it to God as well. The argument would then look something like this:

(D1)   It is now true that God will at time *t* raise Jesus from the dead. (Premise from *God, Time, and Knowledge*, 195)

(D2)   It is impossible that God should at any time believe what is false, or fail to believe any true proposition such that

---

[3]Clark H. Pinnock, *Most Moved Mover: A Theology of God's Openness* (Grand Rapids: Baker, 2001), 31.
[4]Gregory A. Boyd, *Satan and the Problem of Evil* (Downers Grove, Ill.: InterVarsity, 2001), esp. 191.
[5]Richard Swinburne, *The Coherence of Theism* (Oxford: Clarendon, 1977), 176.

his knowing that proposition at that time is logically possible. (Premise: divine omniscience)

(D3) God has always believed that he will at *t* raise Jesus from the dead. (Assumption for indirect proof)

(D4) If God has believed a certain thing, it is not in anyone's power to bring it about that God has not believed that thing. (Premise: the unalterability of the past)

(D5) Therefore, it is not in God's power to bring it about that God has not always believed that he would at *t* raise Jesus from the dead. (From 3,4)

(D6) It is not possible for it to be true both that God has always believed that he would at *t* raise Jesus from the dead, and that he does not in fact raise him. (From 2)

(D7) Therefore, it is not in God's power to refrain from raising Jesus from the dead at *t*. (From 5,6) So God's raising Jesus from the dead at *t* is not an act of free choice.

(D8) God will act freely when he raises Jesus from the dead at *t*. (Premise)

(D9) Therefore, it is not the case that God has always believed that he will at *t* raise Jesus from the dead. (From 3–8, indirect proof)

We must now extend the argument a bit:

(D10) But God has always fully intended that he will at *t* raise Jesus from the dead. (from *God, Time, and Knowledge,* 195)

(D11) What God fully intends to do he believes.

(D12) Therefore God has always believed that he will at *t* raise Jesus from the dead. (from 10–11)

(D13) Therefore it is not the case that God will act freely when he raises Jesus from the dead at *t*.

For Hasker to avoid this conclusion, one of two strategies would seem to be necessary. One would be to reject D11, thus severing the tie between God's intention and his knowledge. This, in turn, either requires a rejection of his truthfulness, since he has declared that he will do what he intends, or his omnipotence in being unable to do it. The other approach would be to say that freedom is not incompatible with one's own knowing what one will do, only with someone else's knowing what one will do, but that would require a major revision of D6. The open theists would presumably claim that this is indeed a case of God not being free at the time he acted, because he had at some point chosen to limit his freedom. It should be noted, however, that this is a belief God has *always* had, so if there was such a self-limitation, it was an eternal one.

Pinnock acknowledges the potential problem when he says, "Nevertheless the future is open for God as well because everything is not yet settled. This is the kind of creation project he freely entered into. Think of what it would mean for God's freedom if everything were settled. God himself would not be free to act except in predetermined ways. He would have to consult his own foreknowledge to know what to do next."[6]

In his response to Bruce Ware's paper, Boyd makes an interesting statement:

> While space restrictions prevent me from fleshing out my own Christology at this point, let me simply go on record as saying that I, for one, hold that Jesus possessed compatibilistic freedom. In my view, Christ was humanity *eschatologically defined.* He was the "already" entering into the "not-yet." He was what we shall be when perfected. The whole purpose of libertarian freedom, in my view, is to become what the God-man was from the start: humans who are defined *in their essence* by openness to God. Being contingent beings who are semi-autonomous from God, we must go through a probationary period, utilizing libertarian free will, to becoming open (or closed) in our essence toward God. But Jesus, being God, was never on probation and hence did not possess libertarian free will (with regard to his openness to God).[7]

There are many issues here that would be interesting to pursue within the area of Christology, such as the peccability/impeccability question. For

---

[6]Pinnock, *Most Moved Mover,* 51. Pinnock's statement that "everything is not yet settled" appears to say that nothing is settled. It is likelier, however, that this is a syntactic error and that what he intended to say is "not everything is yet settled."

[7]Gregory A. Boyd, "Christian Love and Academic Dialogue: A Reply to Bruce Ware," *Journal of the Evangelical Theological Society* 45:2 (June 2002): 242.

our purposes here, however, the last sentence is the most important. If Jesus did not possess libertarian freedom because he was God, then apparently, in Boyd's view, God is not free in the same sense that humans are, at least during the "probationary" period of their lives. It is clear that the reason Boyd does not allow for compatibilistic freedom earlier in human experience is that such is acceptable if it is a result of human choice, of the hardening of one's character through one's own choices, but not if it is externally imposed. Presumably this is why God's lack of compatibilistic free will is acceptable as well. One wonders, then, what becomes of the character of God and of Christ. God, being love, desires humans to be able to love him genuinely, that is, because they could have done the opposite but choose not to. But if God does not have libertarian freedom, he is unable not to love. He is not capable of giving the kind of love, freely chosen, that he desires and expects from his human creatures. Is this love—and Jesus' choice to give his life for the sins of the human race—really virtuous at all? While this makes sense to those who hold that humans have compatibilistic free will, within the framework developed by open theists, it appears that God loves compulsively, not freely.

It appears that the open theists are caught on the horns of not one, but two dilemmas. They must either modify their view of freedom, or confess that we will be less free in heaven than we are now—a serious problem in light of the high value they have placed on libertarian freedom. Similarly, however, they must either modify their view of freedom or conclude that whereas we are free, God is not—a similarly serious, and perhaps more serious, problem.

One of the arguments used repeatedly by open theists is that if one knew the outcome of his actions or knew what he was going to do, this would remove all motivation for action. Since it is already certain what he is going to do, it makes no difference what the person himself does, because the outcome will not be changed. This, however, seems to mistake certainty of outcome with fatalism, or in other words, to conclude that if the end is already set, the means to the end are unimportant. For if the end is certain, it is so because it is the end result of a process that may involve innumerable steps, each of which is essential to the attainment of the end.

It should be noted that for the most part, although one may believe that what will be done is certain, one does not know what it is that will be done. It is the latter knowledge that tends, psychologically, to undercut the urgency of decision and action. Yet having said that, it is interesting to observe that in several significant biblical instances, knowing what was to happen did not seem to remove the sense of responsibility. When Peter heard Jesus' forecast of his (Peter's) denial of him, his immediate response was a sharp disavowal. Either Peter did not believe Jesus, or he thought he was still in control of his decision. Similarly, when Jesus predicted Judas's betrayal of him, this did not remove for Judas the sense of his own responsibility for Jesus' death as is indicated by his remorse (Matt. 27:3–5). One may, of course, object that from the reaction of these two philosophically unsophisticated men, one cannot argue that this does not or should not diminish the sense of inevitability for us today. What is significant, however, is the judgment God made upon their actions. See for example, Jesus' statement addressing this very issue with respect to Judas: "The Son of Man will go just as it is written about him. But woe to that man who betrays the Son of Man! It would be better for him if he had not been born" (Matt. 26:24). Jesus seemed to hold Judas responsible for what he had done.

Notice the concessions that Boyd must make as he seeks to account for such incidents. He suggests that it is possible to understand Jesus' prediction on the basis of his knowledge of Peter's settled character. This seems to be a case of Peter's freedom being limited by past actions, conditioning, and so forth. The question then arises whether this principle could not be extended to other areas as well. In other words, may Boyd's application of the method of explaining prophecy or foreknowledge on a somewhat ad hoc basis conflict with his actual theory of human freedom of the will?

Part of the problem here is that open theists really make no attempt to offer an explanation of why people choose and act as they do. Rather than an explanation, we are offered a label: freedom of the will. To be sure, we should not expect to be able to elucidate the nature of human decision making completely, but the open theists make little effort to explain just what they mean by will. It is as if will has become reified—as some entity that in a sort of free-floating fashion selects among alternatives, perhaps even somewhat randomly or by chance.

There is a problem here with the question of ability and inability or possibility and impossibility of actions. There seems to be no real discussion of the different meanings of "able to." Consider the question of whether John is free to shoot to death Bill, with whom he has had an ongoing disagreement for some time. Is he able to do this, in which case he is free to, or is he unable to, in which case he is not? "Unable" may mean several things. It may mean that he does not have the money to purchase a gun and has no other way of acquiring one. Thus, he cannot shoot Bill. Or he may lack the physical capability of doing so. He may be so weakened physically that he does not have the strength to pull the trigger effectually, or his eyesight is so bad that he cannot see to shoot Bill. He may lack the know-how to be able to load and fire the gun. Perhaps Bill remains constantly behind bulletproof glass, so that John may fire at him repeatedly but never be able to hurt him. All of these are senses of his being unable to shoot Bill. There is another, more important sense of "unable to," however. John may simply not be psychologically able to bring himself to pull the trigger. Murder is not something that is consistent with John's personality, or more correctly, his moral character. It is something he just cannot do. But we must ask ourselves in which of these senses it is appropriate to say that John is not free. If it is the latter sense, of John not being of such a character that he can perform this act, is it appropriate to say that he is unfree? It appears that the open theists have inadequately analyzed the phenomenon of freedom of the will, and their arguments are accordingly defective.

The begging of the question of free will occurs throughout the argument. Boyd does not really raise the question of the compatibilistic or incompatibilistic views of freedom. He simply proceeds by assuming his view of freedom, which is something of the commonsense view of freedom held naively by most persons. Hasker does delineate the difference, but when he discusses the view espoused by the traditional view of foreknowledge, he does so through the presuppositions of incompatibilism. What results is the natural consequence of interpreting a view through the intellectual spectacles of presuppositions foreign to it, namely a contradiction or an absurdity. This can be seen most clearly in the imageries he uses to describe Calvinism and Molinism. His use of expressions like "ventriloquist," "puppet-master," and "computer wizard-robot" reveals this assumption.[8]

One further problem comes from the open theists' conception of freedom of the will. Because God is a God of love, he has limited himself by giving humans freedom rather than coercing them. This raises the problem of how God can be sure that his intention will actually be realized. Here there is virtually unanimous agreement among open theists that when necessary, God can and actually does intervene to act unilaterally. Hasker likens the situation to that of a loving parent who seeks to affect the child's behavior by the use of persuasive power. Then he indicates that in the more extreme problem cases, the parents have resources available to them: "The policy could well be described as the deliberate and intensive application of 'persuasive power'—though to be sure, coercive power is there in reserve, should the child start to run out into a busy roadway. Should not a similar account be given of God's control over us?"[9] In discussing the practical implications of the open theist view, Basinger similarly says, "We who affirm the open view of God deny that God can unilaterally control human decision-making that is truly voluntary but affirm that God can unilaterally intervene in human affairs"[10]

Boyd's view on this matter comes out most clearly in his discussion of the problem of how Jesus could accurately predict Peter's three-fold denial of him. His explanation involves Jesus' thorough knowledge of Peter's character. Added to that, however, Boyd says, "Anyone who knew Peter's character perfectly could have predicted that under certain highly pressured circumstances (that God could easily orchestrate), he would act just the way he did."[11] He then elaborates: "We do not know how much, if any, supernatural intervention was employed by God's orchestration of the events of that evening. But the outcome was just as he anticipated." Boyd sees a parallel

---

[8]William Hasker, "A Philosophical Perspective," in Pinnock, Rice, Sanders, Hasker, and Basinger, *The Openness of God* (Downers Grove, Ill.: InterVarsity, 1994), 142–43.
[9]Ibid., 142.
[10]David Basinger, "Practical Implications," in *The Openness of God,* 160.
[11]Boyd, *God of the Possible,* 35.

between this incident and Jesus' post-resurrection questioning of him: "Three times Peter had his true character squeezed out of him so that, after the resurrection, he might three times have Christ's character squeezed into him."[12]

This is interesting language. It is somewhat different than Basinger's statement, where God does not control decision making but in effect overrides it. What Boyd appears to say is that God sometimes acts unilaterally, manipulating human wills. This would appear to be what open theists identify as coercion. But if this is the case, then the difference between the working of the God of traditional theism and that of open theism is not one of kind. It is simply a matter of degree, of the frequency of God's coercion. So God does not allow quite as much freedom, in the incompatibilist sense, as open theists have suggested. He may not act unilaterally as often as he does in the traditional model, but he does coerce, nonetheless. On either model, whether that of Basinger or that of Boyd, it is not possible to say that Peter could have acted otherwise than he did.

It is also questionable, however, whether Boyd can use this expedient and be consistent with what he has said elsewhere. In *Satan and the Problem of Evil* he argues that God's conferral of libertarian freedom upon humans is irrevocable. He uses an illustration of giving his daughter $200. If he insists that she spend it the way he wants and prevents her doing otherwise, he has not really given her the money. It is still his money, but he has chosen to spend it through her. "If God were to retract our freedom every time we were about to choose something against his will," he says, "then it cannot be said that he really gave us freedom or that we are in fact genuinely *self*-determining. In short, the *genuineness* of the gift of self-determination hinges on its *irrevocability*."[13] Of course, Boyd might insist that the crucial expression is "every time," and that this is the only situation that would constitute a retraction of freedom. This would seem to be a matter of degree, however. It is like saying that Boyd would only object to some of the ways his daughter might choose to spend the money but not to all. This, however, appears to be an intermittent or partial revocation, and as such is also

---

[12]Ibid., 36.
[13]Gregory A. Boyd, *Satan and the Problem of Evil: Constructing a Trinitarian Warfare Theology* (Downers Grove, Ill.: InterVarsity, 2001), 181–82.

a matter of not really having given her the money. Thus, it is hard to see how God's "squeezing Peter's character out of him three times" is not a revocation of the freedom he has given.

Actually, compatibilists would claim that what God does, according to their model, is not coercion. Rather, it is God working in relationship to human will in such a way as to bring it about that they freely choose. John Feinberg, arguing for a strong Calvinist view, uses the following analogy. Suppose that a student in his class is creating a sufficient disturbance that Feinberg decides it is best that he leave the classroom. There are several ways that the professor could accomplish this end. One is, if he is sufficiently larger and stronger than the student, to pick him up and physically carry him out of the room. A second way would be to threaten him at gunpoint, so that he decides to leave. The third way would be to reason with him calmly and quietly, showing how it would be to the student's advantage to leave the room as requested.[14] On which of these three models would we say that the student is not free and that he has been coerced? Certainly that would be the case on the first option, and probably so on the second model. The third, however, is quite different from the other two. Here there is no external compulsion or manipulation; there is simply the influence of reason. Presumably, the student considers the issues and decides that it is in his own interest to comply with the instructor's request. What should be noted, however, is that compatibilists believe that this is how the human will is to be understood and how God works in relationship to it. It is not appropriate to describe this model as if it were either the first or the second. Thus, while "coercion" is an appropriate label for the way the open theist sees God's assuring the result he desires, it is not the way the God of traditional theism accomplishes his purposes. Thus, it appears that while problems apply to both views, the traditional view can practice its theory more consistently than does open theism. It is not, on its own terms, incoherent, in a way that the open view appears to be.

[14]John S. Feinberg, "God Ordains All Things," *Predestination & Free Will: Four Views of Divine Sovereignty and Human Freedom*, ed. David Basinger and Randall Basinger (Downers Grove, Ill.: InterVarsity, 1986), 25–26.

THE CONCEPT OF THE FUTURE

We have observed that part of the open theists' objection to divine foreknowledge is based on a particular conception of the nature of the future. God does not know the future, not because there is something he does not know, but because there is nothing there for him to know. So his lack of knowledge is not a defect because he knows all reality. Since the future is not something that has any existence, any reality, it is not "something" and therefore is not knowable. God's inability to know this is not a defect in his perfection any more than his inability to make square circles is a defect in his omnipotence.

There are several problems with this concept, however. One is the analogy that is sometimes used. Boyd, for example, uses as an analogy the idea of God not knowing that there is a monkey sitting beside him when there is indeed no such monkey. This, he says, is like God not knowing the future free actions of humans, where there also is nothing there. Note, however, the nature of the analogy. In the case of God not knowing that there is a monkey there, it is because "There is a monkey sitting beside me" is a false statement. It has truth value; that is, it can be either true or false. Presumably, what we should say is not that God does not know it, but that he knows that proposition to be false. In the case of propositions about the future, Boyd contends that they have no truth value, thus God cannot know whether they are true or false because they are neither. The traditional view has never denied that God does not know false propositions. Thus, the analogy breaks down.

The usual open theist statement is that the future is partly settled and partly unsettled. Presumably, what this means is that since God has himself decided and determined certain matters, those are settled, whereas those matters that he has left to humans to decide are not settled. Furthermore, based on his knowledge of the present, including the tendencies of humans, God can predict what they are going to do, at least with a sufficient degree of certainty to be able to utter a prophecy. We must ask, however, just how coherent this concept of the future really is. For then it is not really a metaphysical matter, as Boyd seems to have made it. It is not a question of the future not being real because it has not yet happened.

Some parts of it are apparently "real," but some are not. Thus, there is an element of incoherence in the ontological status of the future per se. Those elements of it that are determined (by God, natural laws, or predictable human actions) are real. It is not so much the nature of the future as it is the nature of human freedom.

The problem here is that part of the future is settled, or has ontological reality, but part is not. The difficulty is that these two parts cannot be separated quite so easily. It is like saying that part of a building has been constructed, but part has not. Unfortunately, some of the constructed parts depend on some of the unconstructed parts for support. Similarly, for God to know what he is to do requires in some cases his knowing what humans will do. His predictions about the coming of his Son required knowing that humans would persist in their wicked ways. His prediction of the resurrection of Jesus assumes that he will be rejected and put to death. It is likely that Boyd would reply that God knew the present condition and tendencies of people well enough to know what they would do, but that principle becomes rather vacuous. Perhaps Boyd's language about the ontological status of the future is overstated, but if not, the idea of a future that partly exists and partly does not seems a bit stretched.

If one persists in claiming that it is a matter of the nature of the future, not of God, there is still a problem. For the issue is then whether God is of such a nature that, if the future (or human freedom) is as he has supposedly created it to be, he is then able to know it. That is to say that there might be a way of thinking of God in which he can not only know the possibilities, even all the possibilities that might be but can also tell which of these are inherently likelier to occur than others. In other words, that sort of a God would be capable of knowing what the future will be. Thus, it is not only a question of what the nature of the future is but also of what God is like.

There is another element here that does not seem to have been laid bare in the discussions to this point, namely, the way God knows the future. On the open theists' premises, God does know at least part of the future. He does this, either because it is something that he has personally purposed to do, unilaterally, or because he can calculate or deduce, from his knowledge of the present, what will come to pass. This is true, either in the case of those matters that are caused without involving human free choices, like the weather or various geological events, or those that are caused by humans but can be predicted based on the sufficient knowledge of the persons performing the actions.

Note, however, that on this model, God's knowledge is a mediate rather than an immediate knowledge. He knows what will happen, not by directly knowing it, but by knowing something else that enables him therefore to know it. An example of the difference between the two types of knowing may help our understanding at this point. Imagine a small, closed building with only one door and no windows. If I make the judgment that there are three persons in it, that judgment may be made in two ways. One is to actually look inside the building and count the number of persons therein, concluding that there are three. Or I may at some earlier point make a similar examination and find that there are five persons. I then keep the door under close and continuous observation. I see two people exit the building and none enter. I therefore conclude that it contains three persons. My judgment here is the same as in the first case, but the basis of determination is quite different. It is indirect, or mediated judgment, an inference from other known facts but without direct observation of the current situation. On the open theist understanding, this is how God knows what he does know about the future. It is not that some things are fixed and others are not and that God therefore knows the former directly. Rather, God is able to infer what will be the case. The language about some parts of the future existing and other parts not existing is inaccurate, and the statement about the nature of the future is therefore contradictory.

A further problem is that there is a considerable ambiguity regarding the sense of "does not exist," which works to Boyd's advantage in providing apparent cogency that the argument does not actually have. There is a sense of "does not exist" that means simply "is not currently occurring," or cannot be put in the present tense. In this sense, the past does not exist either, because the events that constitute it are not actually currently occurring. In this sense, it was true to say that my dog Penny did not exist prior to her birth in 1982 or perhaps prior to her conception in 1981. It is also the case that my dog Penny does not now exist and has not since she was euthanized in 1993. Thus, the statement that the future does not exist is clearly true on this reading of it.

What is done, however, is then to make the transition from "does not now exist" to "has no positive ontological status," which is a rather different matter. The past does have a type of existence in that some people remember it, and it can be inferred from certain historical records to have occurred or existed. Thus my dog Penny does exist in my memory as well as in the memories of the other members of my family. We must ask, therefore, whether future events may have some reality or ontological status as well.

In Aristotle's form of the dilemma about the future, what he is basically saying is that future actions cannot be known. That is also what Boyd seems to be saying. That, however, is an epistemological statement. The transition to saying that the unknowability is a question of the nature of the future is a transition from an epistemological to an ontological question. Indeed, there seems to be considerable circularity here: that the future is unsettled or unreal is a conclusion drawn from the fact that it cannot be known. Conversely, however, the reason that it cannot be known is because of its ontological status of unreality. There is a vagueness here that definitely needs correction or at least, clarification.

Part of the problem may be that Boyd and the other open theists are working with a type of epistemology that is so empirical as to preclude the reality of anything non-sensible. This, of course, is selectively applied, because otherwise it would exclude the reality of even God. There is such a strong desire to reject Platonism and anything resembling it that there may have been a rejection of something intimately involved with this question. One might ask, What is the ontological status of mathematical entities or concepts? In fact, whether one refers to them as concepts or entities may reveal something of one's conception. Does the concept of a triangle have any ontological status that it possesses whether or not any empirical triangles exist? In Plato's thought, the ideas or pure concepts were actually more real than the specific objects that resembled or instantiated them. In Augustine and other theologians who employed Plato's philosophy to construct their theology, these concepts were in the mind of God. If this is the case, however, then of course God knows something when he knows his own thoughts, even if they are of things and events that are not yet current. But that means that prehistoric events, events that took place before there were any humans or even angelic beings to know and remember them, nonetheless have a reality somewhere in the whole of reality. But if this is the case, then the future has a type of reality as well. It appears to me that Boyd needs to clarify just what he means when he says that the future is unknowable because it does not exist, and to do so in such a way as to allow for the discipline of mathematics.

Even the rather stringent theory of meaning espoused by logical positivism, namely, the verification principle, allowed for the truth value of "in principle" verifiable propositions. These, even if they could not presently be verified, were deemed meaningful if one knew what the sense data would be if the statement were true and if we had the capability of observing that situation. Thus, statements about the makeup of the other side of the moon were meaningful even before space travel because we knew what the sense data would be if we were able to go there.[15] Similarly, here the fact that we cannot yet observe Clarence either having or not having an omelet for breakfast tomorrow does not mean that it is not a meaningful (i.e., truth-value) statement, for we know what we would observe if we were there at his breakfast table when he has breakfast tomorrow. If the verification principle was deemed too restrictive, then what shall we say about the argument advanced by open theists at this point?

Of course, the question may be raised as to just why meaningfulness is so important. The point here is this: Boyd and others have argued that God's failure to know free future human actions is not a significant consideration of his omniscience, just as his inability to create square circles is not a significant argument against his omnipotence. Note, however, that the latter involves a contradictory or incoherent and therefore meaningless action. The analogy breaks down unless there is something inherently contradictory about the future that prevents its being known, such as that God cannot know that in the future there will be square circles or that the future

---

[15]On this basis, John Hick developed the concept of "eschatological verification," the idea that at some point in the future we would have the opportunity to verify affirmations about God. See John Hick, *Faith and Knowledge* (Ithaca, N.Y.: Cornell University Press, 1957).

WHAT DOES GOD KNOW AND WHEN DOES HE KNOW IT?

shall be other than it is. For this to be the case, however, would require us to resort again to the ontological nature of the future, with all the problems we have already noted with that concept. That a statement about a future event is true and yet unknowable is not a contradiction within the nature of the future but rather a conflict between the nature of free human actions and God's heuristic abilities. The former type of contradiction is a contradiction simply by logical constraints. It depends on nothing outside the concept for its contradictory character. Here, however, whether there is a contradiction depends on the nature of human freedom, which is precisely what is in dispute.

THE DYNAMIC NATURE OF REALITY

One argument advanced especially by Boyd is that current theory in the field of physics supports the open view. Drawing on quantum mechanics, chaos theory, and other similar developments, he contends that unlike the earlier view of a deterministic and completely predictable reality, quantum physics presents a much more open view of reality, even on the subatomic level:

> In the same way, the old Newtonian assumption that the world moves forward in a deterministic fashion has been replaced in quantum theory by an understanding of causation that includes an intrinsic element of indeterminism. The previous universally held assumption that science could, in principle, predict everything about the future has (especially among recent chaos theorists) given way to the understanding that an element of unpredictability is intrinsic to significantly complex systems. In short, the old assumption that the world is a stable, solid, deterministic, thoroughly rational, and utterly predictable system has been replaced by a view of the world as a dynamic process that is to some extent indeterministic and unpredictable.[16]

Boyd adds to this understanding of quantum physics the insights of chaos theory, namely, that "the slightest alterations in the 'initial conditions' of any physical process may result in significant differences in the long-term consequences of that process. . . . This principle suggests that in

---

[16]Boyd, *God of the Possible*, 108.

the actual world initial conditions are never exhaustively knowable. Exhaustive knowledge of the initial conditions of any particular physical process would ultimately require an exhaustive knowledge of the history of the universe leading up to that point."[17]

It appears that for Boyd unpredictability by humans entails that there is not complete determinism. His understanding of quantum mechanics is that we cannot predict with certainty the movement of any particular particle, though we can predict the overall movement of the aggregate of such particles.[18] He adds, "Quantum mechanics has demonstrated that this uncertainty is not due to our limited measuring devices; it is actually rooted in the nature of things."[19] Boyd then draws an interesting conclusion: "This means that even on a quantum level the future is partly open and partly settled. It seems that the balance between openness and settledness permeates reality. The world at every level seems to be constituted as a marvelous dance that exemplifies both form and freedom. There is structure and spontaneity, predictability and unpredictability, everywhere we look."[20]

Boyd does not give further documentation or argumentation for this inference. He appears to equate structure and spontaneity with predictability and unpredictability. John Beckman, a scientist with a Ph.D. in electrical engineering, challenges this equation. It is not possible, from the epistemological fact of human unpredictability of movement of a given particle, to conclude that there is no cause of this seemingly random movement. All this establishes is that there is not a *detectable physical* cause, but that does not mean that there is no *nonphysical* cause. Perhaps God determines by nonphysical causes (fiat or nonphysical secondary causes) which particles will behave in what way. Even if an event looks open at the quantum level, it must have neither a physical nor a nonphysical cause.[21] This is assumed but not proved by Boyd.[22] What is required here for Boyd's conclusion to follow is a metaphysical principle, which he identifies as having

---

[17]Boyd, *Satan and the Problem of Evil*, 217.
[18]*God of the Possible*, 109.
[19]Ibid.
[20]Ibid., 110.
[21]John C. Beckman, "Quantum Mechanics, Chaos Physics and the Open View of God," *Philosophia Christi*, 2.1 (2002): 205. Quoted by Beckman, with Boyd's permission, from a web post by Boyd.
[22]Boyd, *God of the Possible*, 109–10.

derived from Hartshorne: "I would agree with Hartshorne and others who argue that the very notion of one thing exhaustively determining another thing results in a logical contradiction. If X exhaustively determines Y, then there is no distinction between X and Y. There has to be some reality in Y over against X for X to be in any meaningful sense distinct from Y. And this means that Y must have some element of self-determination over and against the determination of X on Y. Hence indeterminacy is not only an empirical category, but a metaphysical category."[23] Beckman, however, questions this nondistinction principle, noting that he may create a software program, but it is certainly distinct from him.[24]

Note, again, that this assumption, derived from Hartshorne, is just that, a metaphysical assumption, made in order to extend from the fact of indeterminability to the idea of indeterminism, but not argued. This is a debatable assumption. There also is the assumption that this additional reality must be a reality in Y, whereas, at least theoretically, there could be additional external causes.

It should be observed that this is a process philosophy assumption. Whereas Boyd has claimed that open theism and process theism have very little in common, this seems to be a clear indication of the extent of the influence of process metaphysics on his thought. We should also observe the circularity of Boyd's reasoning. His interpretation of quantum mechanics is on the basis of a process assumption. In other words, assuming a process view, quantum mechanics is understood as meaning that on the quantum level, there is indeterminacy, or openness. This understanding of quantum mechanics is then used to substantiate the idea of a partly open future: "Science confirms what the Bible declares: The future is partly open as well as partly settled."[25] The circularity is both clear and tight.

A new development has emerged from this argument. Previously, Boyd had contended that part of the future is definite or fixed, and part of it is open. The division had been on the basis that what is open or undetermined

---

[23]Beckman, "Quantum Mechanics," 205.

[24]Ibid., 206, n. 8.

[25]Boyd, *God of the Possible,* 111; Gregory A. Boyd, *Trinity and Process: A Critical Evaluation and Reconstruction of Hartshorne's Di-Polar Theism Towards a Trinitarian Metaphysics* (New York: Peter Lang, 1992), vii.

are free human choices and actions, and that the physical universe is predictable or foreknowable by God. Here, however, what he seems to be saying is that while the particulars of the universe are not foreknown by God, the overall or large collocations are foreknown. Boyd's conclusion that "even on a quantum level the future is partly open and partly settled"[26] is drawn from two statements: "We can predict the range of possible behaviors of a given quantum particle before a quantum measurement, but we cannot predict its exact behavior"; and "We can statistically predict very accurately how large groups of quantum particles will behave, but not precisely how any one of them in particular will behave."[27]

Beckman raises the question of just what Boyd means by saying that "the future is partly open as well as partly settled." He believes there are two possible meanings of this statement: (1) "that God determines some quantum mechanical events by non-physical means and leaves other quantum mechanical events unsettled," and (2) "that the behavior of individual particles is open, whereas the behavior of large groups is settled."[28] This, he thinks, presents Boyd with a dilemma. On the former option, "If the behavior of a large group of quantum particles is predictable only statistically, then it can surprise God, just as the behavior of a large group of humans can surprise Him in the open view, and quantum uncertainty, like human uncertainty, opens the future at all scales instead of leaving it partly settled due to the behavior of large groups."[29] On the latter option, however, "if the future is partly settled at the quantum level because the behavior of a large group of quantum particles is settled, then the link from quantum uncertainty to human uncertainty is undermined, because large groups of humans have multiple possible group behaviors, and hence can surprise God, but large groups of quantum particles would have only one possible group behavior, and hence would be unable to surprise God."[30]

Actually, there is probably another interpretation: that Boyd also holds that individual human actions are unknowable and unpredictable by God,

[26]Boyd, *God of the Possible*, 110.
[27]Ibid., 109.
[28]Beckman, "Quantum Mechanics," 207.
[29]Ibid.
[30]Ibid., 207–8.

but that the behavior of groups of humans is predictable. That, however, requires some linkage or connection between the behavior of quantum particles and individual humans. If this is not the case, then it is difficult to understand why Boyd considers these phenomena to confirm what the Bible teaches. This interpretation fits with Boyd's contention that certain events were predestined, but that it was not determined exactly *who* would perform them: "It was certain that Jesus would be crucified, but it was not certain from eternity that Pilot [sic], Herod, or Caiaphas would play the roles they played in the crucifixion. They participated in Christ's death of their own free will."[31]

There is one basis for such a parallel, assuming that Boyd accepts more of the process metaphysics than he has heretofore acknowledged. In the process understanding of reality, the basic unit of reality is the event, or the "concrete occurrence." This has two components, an eternal pole, or God's initial aim for that event, and the temporal pole, or the event's response of either making God's initial aim its own or rejecting that. This is true of all events, whether of physical particles or human persons. There is an element of spontaneity in everything. It is as if even physical objects had an element of free will, of choosing whether to actualize God's initial aim or not. To most persons unfamiliar with process thought, this seems strange, for they are accustomed to thinking of physical objects as entities rather than as a sequence of occurrences. If this is what underlies Boyd's thinking, then there is justification for finding in the behavior of quantum particles an indication of the spontaneity in all things, including human wills. In so doing, however, the uncertainty or partial unsettledness becomes generalized, not just to free human actions but to all parts of reality. Here is a dilemma that Boyd needs to face and deal with.

Boyd also finds support for the open view in chaos physics. He says that this belief "that an element of unpredictability is intrinsic to significantly complex systems" is similar to open theism because "the old assumption that the world is a stable, solid, deterministic, thoroughly rational, and utterly predictable system has been replaced by a view of the world as a dynamic process that is to some extent indeterministic and unpredictable."[32]

---

[31]Boyd, *God of the Possible*, 45.
[32]Ibid., 108.

Here again, Boyd associates indeterminism with unpredictability, a linkage that Beckman challenges. Beckman says that "chaotic systems are physically deterministic. They are unpredictable to finite creatures, but God can exhaustively calculate their definite future behavior if He has exhaustive, definite knowledge of the inputs and infinite calculating precision."[33] He points out that Coveney and Highfield also state that the problem is epistemological for humans, but it would not be for an omniscient being: *"Determinism can only exist if one enters the realm of religion. For verily, only a being as omniscient as God Himself could hope to handle such a literally limitless amount of* information."[34] Boyd acknowledges as much: "Chaos theory itself has thus far been worked out exclusively on a deterministic basis (so it is sometimes labeled 'deterministic chaos')"[35] He then suggests an additional assumption: "If we add to this the understanding that there is an element of unpredictable spontaneity attending all things, from quantum particles to the animal kingdom to human behavior . . . , the unpredictability of the future grows greater still."[36]

Notice, however, that this assumption plays the same role as does the process metaphysical principle in the discussion of quantum mechanics. If we assume the open view of all of reality, then we have an unpredictability of the movement of quantum particles. This view then supports the open view. Once again, however, we find the same circularity: an assumption drawn from view A enables us to interpret view B in a way that supports view A.

Correlation with a Given Contemporary Philosophy

In an earlier chapter we examined and evaluated at length the contention of the open theists that the traditional view of foreknowledge is based on Christian theology having early formed an alliance with Greek philosophy, resulting in reading the Scriptures through Greek spectacles with a consequent distortion of true biblical thought. What is interesting, however, is

[33]Beckman, "Quantum Mechanics, Chaos Physics and the Open View of God," 208.
[34]Peter Coveney and Roger Highfield, *The Arrow of Time* (New York: Fawcett Columbine, 1990), 272.
[35]Boyd, *Satan and the Problem of Evil*, 218, n. 9.
[36]Ibid.

the extent to which the open theists acknowledge and even claim support for their view from its affinity for certain contemporary conceptions.

Our examination of Boyd's thought in the preceding paragraphs should make clear how much correlation he finds between his open theism and both certain philosophies and scientific theories. A similar correlation can be found in other open theists. Hasker, for example, says, "The doctrine of divine simplicity, so crucial to the classical understanding of God, has been abandoned by a strong majority of Christian philosophers, though it still has a small band of defenders. And the claim that God is timelessly eternal, until recently a majority view among orthodox Christian theists, has suffered massive defections in recent years."[37] Pinnock says, "Modern culture can actually assist us in this task because the contemporary horizon is more congenial to dynamic thinking about God than is the Greek portrait. . . . Modern thinking has more room for a God who is personal (and even tri-personal) than it does for a God as absolute substance. We ought to be grateful for those features of modern culture which make it easier to recover the biblical witness."[38] Similar statements in open theist thought could be multiplied.

While this type of argument could, on closer examination, be seen to display the same circularity that we earlier observed in Boyd's thought, it is not that feature of it that we are concerned about at this point. Rather, the question we must raise is why it is more commendable to correlate one's theology with the philosophies and scientific theories extant in the twentieth and twenty-first centuries than it was for the church to relate and express its theology in categories drawn from the philosophies current in the third and fourth centuries.

One answer to this question, which the open theists do not really address, is that presumably today's philosophies are later in the development of culture than were those earlier philosophies. That, however, assumes that progress has been made in more closely approximating reality. As such, this seems to be the "chronological snobbery" that C. S. Lewis and others have commented on. Beyond that, however, there seems to be

---

[37]William Hasker, "A Philosophical Perspective," 127.
[38]Clark Pinnock, "Systematic Theology," *The Openness of God*, 107.

an element of what I term "chronocentrism"—the idea that our time is superior not only to any that has preceded but to any that will come. Every view up to this point has been displaced by another. So Newtonian physics has been supplanted by Einsteinian physics, quantum mechanics, and chaos theory. There is no reason to believe that these will not also be replaced by succeeding views. It may well turn out to be that the apparent affinity of theology to these philosophies will prove to have been unwise. A looser relationship to culture would seem to be a wise procedure.

In chapter 6 we examined the open theist assertion that the traditional view interpreted Scripture through the spectacles of Greek philosophy. We observed that significant limitations must be placed on this thesis. We also observed that open theism itself contains significant philosophical material. In this chapter we have examined several of these philosophical components of the open theism position and noted that there are significant problems, especially of coherence, in the open theism view.

CHAPTER 8

THe PRACTICAL ImPLICATIONS of DIVINe foReKNOWLeDGe

Underlying the discussion to this point is the assumption that the most important question to be asked about a doctrinal assertion is "Is it true?" By way of assessing that, we have asked both internal questions, such as whether the teaching is internally consistent and coherent, and external questions, such as the degree to which it is supported by objective evidences, especially biblical witness. The pragmatic question of whether it works has been assumed to be secondary to these more objective criteria. On this basis, something will work if it is true, rather than something being considered true because it works.

Yet having said that, the Christian life is generally claimed to be a way of making life more achievable and satisfying. If it is true, then it should enable the believer to cope with some of the major problems and questions of life. We therefore turn now to examine three areas of practical import relating to the doctrine of foreknowledge: the problem of evil, the matter of prayer, and the issue of divine guidance.

THE PROBLEM OF EVIL

Probably the most severe intellectual problem for any theism, Christianity included, is the problem of evil. It can be stated simply: If God is all powerful, he will be able to prevent evil from occurring. If he is all loving, he will certainly want to prevent evil. Yet there is obviously evil in the world. This evil is of two kinds. Natural evil is that which is not directly caused by human wills, including natural disasters and diseases. Moral evil is the evil inflicted by humans, such as war, various kinds of crime, abuse, and discrimination. This is a particular problem for traditional theism. If God knew all that would happen and failed to prevent it, he certainly is culpable. If, beyond that, he actually willed or caused everything to happen, he is especially repugnant.

The open theists have wrestled at some length with the problem of evil. In fact, to some extent, this theology can be seen to exist as a response to this problem. The problem of evil is highlighted in the writings both of Boyd and Sanders. In Boyd's writings, it first surfaces in his correspondence with his father, who was not a Christian at the time. His father raised the question of how God could have allowed someone like Adolf Hitler to wreak all the evil and destruction he did, particularly the slaughter of several million Jews. Boyd's reply is that God did not know what Hitler would do because "God can't foreknow the good or bad decisions of the people He creates until He creates these people and they, in turn, create their decisions."[1] Boyd tells the story of Suzanne, a young woman who believed she was called to mission work in Taiwan, whose story was recounted in a previous chapter. How could God have allowed this? Similarly, Sanders begins his book on divine providence with a story about coming upon an accident and discovering that his brother Dick had been killed. The problem of how a good and powerful God could allow such an occurrence becomes a major thrust of the argument. Open theism claims to be a much superior treatment of the conundrum of evil.

Several elements of the open theist position come together at the point of this problem. One is that God is love, which is not just an attribute of God but a statement of his very essence. God desires his highest creatures to love him in return, however, and to be genuinely love, it must be freely chosen. So when God created humans as well as angels, he made an irrevocable gift of freedom to them. This freedom is what is commonly termed *libertarian* freedom, or as Boyd terms it, "self-determining freedom." This freedom requires the ability to choose the contrary of what one actually does choose.

---

[1]Gregory A. Boyd and Edward K. Boyd, *Letters from a Skeptic* (Wheaton, Ill.: Victor, 1994), 30.

Part of what this means is that there could not be antecedent knowledge by God or anyone else of specific human actions. If this were the case, then of course they would come to pass, since God cannot be in error. Rather, what God knows are events, but not the specific persons who will perform them. Thus, he foreknew that Jesus would be crucified, and it subsequently came to pass. He did not, however, know specifically who would do these things.[2]

One traditional response to the problem of evil is called the *finitist* approach: the idea that there are limitations on God's power. In some ways, open theism is a variation of finitism. God, by giving angels and humans the irrevocable gift of libertarian freedom, has imposed limitations on himself. Another aspect of this open theist variation of the finitist argument is that God does not prevent evil, not because he ultimately lacks the power to do so, but because his limited knowledge qualifies the use of his power. Because he does not know future free human actions exhaustively, he does not know infallibly how to exercise his power.

A fairly serious problem attaches to this solution, and it is one encountered by all finitist solutions. If God cannot, or has chosen not to, overcome evil, what assurance is there that evil will not ultimately be triumphant? The open theist answer, of course, is that God reserves the right to intervene, to act unilaterally, to assure that what he wishes will be accomplished. However, as we observed earlier, this seems to be a case of the coercion that open theists dread so. It is simply a less frequent coercion than is involved in the classical approach. However, as we have pointed out, this appears to constitute an internal contradiction within the open theist position.

There is a further problem, which has already been alluded to. Perhaps God will miscalculate as to what he should do to preclude or negate evil. God knows all the possibilities that will take place, but he does not know which of these will come to pass. He might perfectly accomplish his intentions, even through the use of the unilateral action that the open theists insist he can exercise, but because of his limited knowledge of

---

[2]Gregory A. Boyd, *Satan and the Problem of Evil: Constructing a Trinitarian Warfare Theodicy* (Downers Grove, Ill.: InterVarsity, 2001), 121.

future situations, the result would be evil. Bear in mind that God does not know which of these possibilities will become actuality until they actually occur. By that time, so many factors may be at work that God did not anticipate, that he is unable to prevent the occurrence of evil without overriding human freedom. Thus, there is a dilemma for the open theist. Either acknowledge that God's gift of freedom is not unconditional, or acknowledge that he may be incapable of preventing any given instance of evil.

Here it is helpful to distinguish two senses of the problem of evil. One is the difficulty known as the problem of evil, which is an intellectual issue of attempting to understand how evil can exist. As such, it is a threat to faith because it seems to conflict, on the intellectual level, with belief in a good and powerful God. We may term this *the difficulty of the problem of evil*. The other, however, is what we might call *the difficulty of evil itself*.[3] Here the issue is not whether we can explain the existence of evil, but rather whether there is hope that evil will be eliminated or removed. If the former issue is the *inexplicability* of evil, this is the *irradicability* of evil. It is this irradicability of evil that we have been pointing out to this point, and with which open theism has difficulty coping.[4]

The other issue, the difficulty of the problem of evil, or its inexplicability, also does not succumb easily to the open theist analysis. Boyd and other open theists charge the traditional orthodox view with being unable to resolve the problem. If God is ultimately in control and knows all things, then why does he not prevent the occurrence of evils, such as the atrocities that Hitler and his Nazi subordinates perpetrated? He certainly knew what Hitler would do, and he certainly could have prevented it. The objection that Boyd's father raised applied inescapably to the traditional view. If, however, as he told his father, God did not know what Hitler would do, he cannot be impugned for allowing this to happen. Thus, he claims, open theism gives a satisfactory resolution to the problem. Pinnock also says,

---

[3]I sometimes refer to these two as "the problem of the problem of evil," and "the problem of evil," respectively, but that often proves confusing, given the long-established usage of "the problem of evil."
[4]Pinnock seems to confuse these two when he says, "God can keep his promise even though creatures contribute to history and can resist his will." (*Most Moved Mover: A Theology of God's Openness* [Grand Rapids: Baker, 2001], 139.)

"God did not know all along that [sic] Hitler, or Adam, would do with his freedom. If he did, it would imply that he thought that Hitler's evils could serve a purpose and that it was better that, on balance, they happen rather than they not happen. Surely not! God gave Hitler freedom but it was not settled ahead of time how he would use it. It was always a possibility rather than a certainty what he would do. The future is partially open and partially closed."[5]

This contention requires a bit of additional examination and reflection, however. Boyd contends that God knows all the possibilities that might ever occur. In other words, he has a type of middle knowledge, in which he knows all possibilities, but he does not have actual knowledge of what will occur. He knew that Adolf Hitler might be born, that he might be the type of person he turned out to be, and that he might perpetrate the holocaust against the Jews; but he did not know that this would happen. Each of these events was just one of a huge number of possibilities. Even when Hitler was alive and in power, although God knew what he was likely to do, he could not be absolutely certain until Hitler actually did it, just as he did not know what Abraham would do until he did it.

Does this view get God off the hook then? For if God knew all the possibilities, he would have known that the Holocaust might occur. Because this was such an outrageous atrocity, should he not have acted to prevent it? And as time progressed and Hitler was born and came to adulthood, the possibilities became even more likely. Should not God have allowed young Corporal Hitler to be fatally shot in World War I? This would not have required the cooperation of any human will, just the deflection of the course of a single bullet. And once he became chancellor and began the process of solving "the Jewish problem," it should have become apparent to God that this slaughter of Jews would continue. Should God not have allowed one of the assassination plots against Hitler, such as the bomb placed under the table at the Wolf's Lair, to succeed? Again, this could have been accomplished without overriding human free will. What all of this means is that God's responsibility may be somewhat reduced on this basis, but only to a degree.

---

[5]Ibid., 138.

Boyd says, "If I unleash a mad dog I am certain will bite you, am I not responsible for my dog's behavior? If so, how is God not responsible for the behavior of evil people he 'unleashes' on the world—if, in fact, he is absolutely certain of what they will do once 'unleashed'?"[6] The problem needs to be restated to fit the open theist view. If I unleash a mad dog that I know *may* bite you, am I not also responsible, at least in part? The problem here is that on the analogy of open theism, I do not know what the dog may do. God unleashes people on the world, not knowing what they will do until they do it.

Pinnock suggests, in a strange and indirect way, that Hitler's freedom, which he abused, may have been necessary in order to realize great goods. God may have been limited by certain metaphysical constraints: "How many would advocate that, in order to avoid Hitler and Stalin, God should have precluded Moses, Plato, Aquinas, Leonardo, Beethoven, Picasso, Mother Theresa and more?" Beyond that, however, "the gospel assures us that it has been and will be worth it all. 'The sufferings of this present time are not worthy to be compared with the glory which will be revealed to us' (Rom. 8:18)."[7] So he has recourse to the ancient "greater good" argument.

Combined with the issues we have raised with respect to the difficulty of the irradicability of evil, this far-from-satisfactory solution to the problem of the inexplicability of evil seems to make the open theist position even less satisfactory than the traditional orthodox position with its promise and explanation of how God can and will ultimately eliminate evil. All theological positions have their difficulty with this thorny problem, but open theism may have more than its share.

The dilemma for open theism, then, appears to be that either God must honor his irrevocable gift of freedom, in which case there is no assurance that evil will not be ultimately triumphant, or he must revoke it by intervening or acting unilaterally. This, however, would be coercion, and thus it would conflict with a basic principle of open theism.

Note that presumably on open theist grounds, libertarian freedom must also involve the power of actions to carry to their consequences. If

[6]Gregory A. Boyd, *God of the Possible: A Biblical Introduction to the Open View of God* (Grand Rapids: Baker, 2000), 10.
[7]Pinnock, *Most Moved Mover*, 140.

not, it is a rather spurious form of freedom. Suppose that God permitted persons to exercise their free wills to shoot one another but that whenever this was done in an unjustifiable manner (i.e., not in self-defense, etc.), he would miraculously intervene to deflect the bullet before it could strike the intended target person. Similarly, striking an innocent person with a club would result in the shattering of the club. This would seem to be a denial of freedom, not in the sense of precluding the action, but of negating its intended effect.[8]

Conscious of the problem, Boyd has developed his view further in his major discussion of the problem of evil by introducing the idea of the limitations of influence. This grows out of consideration of the question of why God does not simply destroy rebel creatures so as to prevent their ongoing evil influence. Two answers that have been given are (1) that he tolerates this for a greater good, and (2) that he tolerates this because he hopes that even the evil agents will someday change. Boyd does not find either of these answers to be satisfactory. The first is unacceptable both on a scriptural and on an experiential level. The Bible nowhere says that all evil is for a specific good. It also is difficult to conceive of evils like murders and rapes as increasing the balance of good over evil.[9] The second answer fails for similar reasons. The Bible teaches that there are some spirits that will never change; they are eternally doomed. Furthermore, if love must be chosen, then it is really not possible to guarantee that all will choose love, whether sooner or later.[10]

Boyd presents a third answer, which he believes to be superior to either of the first two. It is found in his sixth thesis: "The power to influence is finite."[11] By this he means that "it is impossible to conceive of contingent beings possessing a quality of freedom that is unlimited in time or scope."[12] This can be seen in the very fact that a given person did not choose to be that being rather than another. One is not free not to be oneself, and this very fact introduces limitations on one's freedom.

---

[8]C. S. Lewis considers such a situation and points out the difficulties with it in *The Problem of Pain* (New York: Macmillan, 1962), 31–34.
[9]Boyd, *Satan and the Problem of Evil*, 179–80.
[10]Ibid., 180–81.
[11]Ibid., 186.
[12]Ibid.

Boyd is clear that while contingent variables do not *determine* the will, they do *condition* the will. One of these variables is the ongoing influence of God. While our self-determination must be free from coercion by God, that does not mean that we must necessarily be free from his influence. Since there is a personal relationship between God and us, we must be open to his influencing us, and this is a reciprocal relationship.[13] Second, there is a conditioning effect from our original constitution. There are limitations on one's freedom imposed by variables such as intelligence, personality type, and physical abilities. Persons are profoundly different, and consequently God may deal with different persons in different ways—ways that seem inexplicable to a casual observer.[14] Freedom's quality is also conditioned by one's own previous decisions, which form a direction and give inclinations to one's will.[15] Other agents, whose actions affect the kind of person we are, condition the quality of freedom. Finally, the quality of freedom is conditioned by prayer—our own, those of others for us, and that by and for all those who would be affected by our actions. Because God has bound himself to the power of prayer, what he does is affected by whether something is prayed for.[16]

What all of this means is that Boyd has apparently adopted a form or degree of the compatibilist view of freedom, in part to avoid the implications of his open view for the problem of evil. This is seen in this thesis of the limitations of influence. In connection with the idea of our own past decisions conditioning our present freedom, Boyd speaks of a probationary period of one's libertarian freedom: "The potential of love or destructiveness . . . needs a probationary period to be decided, but his probationary period is not eternal. Contingent creatures spend their potential one way or the other, and once spent we become what we choose. Libertarian freedom gives way to compatibilist freedom conditioned by the character an agent acquired by the use of their libertarian freedom. So far as we can discern, Satan and his fallen angels have finished their probationary period and are now destined to destruction."[17]

---

[13]Ibid., 192–94.
[14]Ibid., 194–95.
[15]Ibid., 198.
[16]Ibid., 203.
[17]Ibid., 171, n. 43.

This principle becomes an explanation for some of God's actions that otherwise seem inexplicable and also solves what seem to be unresolvable problems. While God does not revoke his gift of freedom, persons can in effect revoke their own freedom: "Those who by God's grace used their irrevocable probational freedom as God intended ultimately become irrevocably aligned with him in love, while those who use their irrevocable probational freedom against God become irrevocably set against him in self-absorbed rebellion. . . . The possibility of going one way or the other does not last forever, though the irreversible consequences of how we actualize this possibility do." This explains "how it is that the possibility of love entails risk without holding that heaven will be eternally risky."[18] In heaven, presumably, our characters will be so fixed that we will always do God's will.

Boyd uses this explanation to avoid the dilemma of failure versus coercion, of which we spoke earlier. We noted that several open theists allow for God's intervening and acting unilaterally, but that sounds like an instance of what they would surely call coercion. However, Boyd, sensitive to this criticism, believes that he has a rationale for God's doing this that does not encroach upon the irrevocable gift of freedom. Although that freedom is irrevocable, it is not without limit: "Appealing to the essential finitude of every agent's quality of freedom in principle explains why God sometimes overrules an agent's decisions, despite his general covenant not to do so. Beyond the parameters of the gift of freedom God has given, God may intervene as he sees fit. . . . after God's irrevocable gift of self-determination to an agent is 'spent,' as it were, God is under no obligation to refrain from intervening on the agent's freedom."[19]

There are two senses in which a person may be responsible for his actions. The first is the common libertarian sense of freedom, according to which one is free if one could have done otherwise than he did. Beyond that, however, one is responsible for actions even when he could not have done otherwise when that inability to do otherwise is a result of the character one has acquired by one's own free choices. Boyd says that "moral responsibility applies to the acquired character of self-determining agents

---

[18]Ibid., 191.
[19]Ibid.

even more fundamentally than it applies to the particular decisions agents make which reflect and reinforce their character."[20] He distinguishes this as what theologians have called *habitus acquirus* from what they have termed *habitus infusus,* which God has given them.

This is Boyd's explanation of how some parts of the future can be open and other parts closed. Whereas he had previously emphasized as the closed portion those occurrences that follow from causes that are not free agency, he now more clearly extends that to involve some choices and acts by humans and angelic beings. The future is open to the extent that moral agents still have self-determining or libertarian freedom. To the extent that they act out of their self-determined characters, however, either of themselves or as influenced by God compatibilistically, their actions are part of a closed future.

Let us see how Boyd applies this principle to the two usually rather difficult cases already referred to. In the more remote past, God foreknew and perhaps even determined that his son, Jesus, would be put to death. This much in general was fixed. He did not, however, know or predestine that Judas would be the specific individual who would betray Jesus. This could not be done insofar as Judas was still a self-determining person. When, however, Judas by his own choices hardened his character as a particular kind of person, "God wove his character into a providential plan. God thus used evil for a higher good (cf. Gen 50:20). Jesus could therefore foreknow that Judas would be the one to betray him. . . . God orchestrated events to the extent that certain wicked people (and certain wicked spirits, Jn 13:27; 1 Cor 2:8) acted out their self-acquired characters and did what they wanted to do in conformity with his plan to have his Son betrayed and crucified." Boyd then makes a crucial additional statement: "But they are still responsible for what they did, for they are responsible for the kind of agents they had freely become. God was simply employing their sinful intentions to his own end."[21]

The point Boyd seems to be making is this: God has given a gift of freedom to humans, which means he cannot overrule their actions, and

---

[20]Ibid., 122.
[21]Ibid., 122–23.

this gift is irrevocable. So God is at work in this world, fighting the war against evil, and in so doing must respect persons' libertarian free will. This freedom is limited, however. Each free act by a person begins to restrict the scope of that free will as the person's character becomes developed. At some point, the person has used up that freedom, so that he or she is no longer able to act contrary to that established character. It is then legitimate for God to orchestrate events so that his intended outcome is realized, but the responsibility of the persons involved is in no sense eliminated thereby. They are responsible for what they are, even though they can perhaps no longer act contrary to that character.

Another instance that has sometimes been thought to be a problem for open theism is the case of Jesus' prediction of Peter's threefold denial. Says Boyd, "It should be clear that this episode poses no significant problem for the open view of the future. God knew and perfectly anticipated (as though it was the only possible outcome) that if the world proceeded exactly as it had up to the point of the Last Supper, Peter's character would be solidified to the extent that he would be the kind of person who would deny Christ in a certain situation." God from all eternity knew all of what Boyd calls "might-counterfactuals," and all the would-counterfactuals that follow from these might-counterfactuals. "On the basis of this knowledge and his sovereign control as Creator, God decides at some point to providentially ensure that just this situation would come about." Based on this middle knowledge, God "knew precisely what it would take to bring Peter to his knees and make him receptive to the teaching he wanted him to receive."[22] Elsewhere Boyd refers to this incident by saying that "God three times squeezed Peter's character out of him."[23]

We must now analyze this argument. It is possible to deal with Judas's case on the basis that his character was irreversibly hardened, although Judas's subsequent remorse (Matt. 27:3–5) seems to cast some doubt on that idea. Peter's situation is quite different, however. It appears that his character was not so solidified, for even in connection with this prediction of Peter's denial, Jesus also spoke of his future turning again and strengthening the brothers

[22]Ibid., 131–32.
[23]Boyd, *God of the Possible*, 33–36.

(Luke 22:32). This seems to indicate that Peter had not gone beyond the point of using up his gift of self-determination. That is the point at which "our individualized probationary periods come to an end as our free choices become crystallized in the form of an irreversible character."[24] If, however, Peter's probationary period had come to an end, it is difficult to understand how he could have reversed course as he did. If, on the other hand, his probationary period had not come to an end, then God seems to have broken his covenant not to work coercively on a self-determining person.

How does this incident relate to Boyd's attempted solution of the problem of evil? Because of the cruciality of the episode of Jesus' prediction of Peter's denial, it deserves some especially intense scrutiny. In particular, we must ask about the status of God's action in "squeezing" Peter's character out of him so that he acted as he did. The specifics of the case would not have come about apart from this divine action. But was not the act of Peter essentially an act of cowardice and self-preservation, a case of sin? If this is the case, then God, by orchestrating the circumstances that would bring about this act of Peter's (which of course was consistent with his character), and by squeezing his character out of him three times, would seem to be at least partially the cause of the sin. This seems to go beyond what most believers in specific sovereignty or meticulous providence would hold. It seems also to breach the principle of differentiation by which this influence is judged acceptable in some cases but not in others. We have argued this at greater length in the chapter on the philosophical issues of open theism, but it bears repeating here. It appears that open theism is able to deal with the problem of evil only by asserting a principle that contradicts its view of will. In other words, it can only succeed by denying one of its major principles, thus making its endeavor appear to be incoherent. Even if Peter's character might have been what Boyd says it was, he would not have committed this act without God's "orchestration" of the circumstances. Boyd's position is that when one finalizes one's character and thus gives up libertarian freedom, it is now legitimate for God to influence that person's actions by what in other contexts some would call manipulation or entrapment.[25]

---

[24]Boyd, *Satan and the Problem of Evil,* 427.
[25]Boyd actually says of the story of Joseph and his brothers: "The passage [Gen. 45:5; 50:20] seems to indicate that God intentionally orchestrated the evil intentions of the brothers in order to get

Secondly, however, if Peter's character was not finally and irreversibly fixed, if he could be influenced in this fashion, could not and should not God do the same with others? If God can override even the will of someone of Peter's type in this situation, why does he abstain from doing so in countless other situations where the influence could be for good, rather than, as in this case, for evil? Since the principle of irrevocable freedom seems to have been revoked here, why should it not be done in other situations as well? Indeed, if God had the capability of doing so and thereby preventing some evil, and he failed to do so, is he not culpable? Failure to avoid an auto accident that was primarily the fault of the other driver but nonetheless was avoidable by us is considered contributory negligence, and an attempt is made to assess the comparative degrees of negligence and hence of each driver's responsibility. One insurance adjuster, for example, told me that the rule of thumb on left turn accidents is 80–20. Even though the driver turning left should have yielded to the oncoming traffic, the other driver should have been able to stop and thus bears 20 percent of the responsibility. Although God works compatibilistically, according to Boyd, he does not receive any responsibility for his actions.

Third, even if persons' characters are irreversibly fixed, is not God at least partially responsible for their being what they are? If one of the factors involved in the formation of a person's character is God's working, should he not have worked more intensely than he did? Should he not have used forces not involving free agency to influence the person? Since he knew all of the possibilities involved, should he not have striven to prevent the most evil from coming to pass?

Fourth, since God can intervene unilaterally in those whose character is irreversibly fixed, should he not do so when he sees what they have become? For example, by the late 1930s it was clear what Adolf Hitler's character was and what he would likely do if left unhindered. Should God not have made sure those worst possibilities did not come to pass? Should he not have caused Hitler to have a fatal heart attack? Or should he not have

Joseph into Egypt" (ibid., 396). He treats this, however, as an extraordinary action in an extraordinary situation and says, "While I agree with compatibilists that this text shows that God *may decide* to orchestrate evil actions according to his sovereign will, I deny that this passage supports the conclusion that *all* evil actions occur in accordance with God's eternal, sovereign will" (ibid., 397).

made certain that one of the attempts to assassinate Hitler succeeded? If God can plead ignorance as an excuse early, it does not seem that he can do so late. It appears that Boyd has not resolved the problem of evil as neatly as he seems to think. He is caught on the horns of a dilemma: either he absolves God of responsibility or he guarantees that God will be triumphant over evil, but it does not appear that he can do both simultaneously.

Fifth, if Boyd is able to accept this limited amount of compatibilism, might it not be possible to expand it? One wonders about this concept of the period of "probation." What biblical basis that does not beg the question does Boyd offer for it, or what argument of any type, other than experiential and anecdotal, does he offer? Without adequate support, this appears to be a sort of ad hoc hypothesis introduced to rescue the view from a more severe version of the dilemma described above. Perhaps the difference between Boyd and some of the versions of the blueprint he rejects so vehemently is simply in the location of the boundary of this period of probation. Admittedly, this is an attempt to preserve freedom by attributing the formation of the person's character to his or her own choices, but is there not a sense in which this is true throughout the process of formation? And, as we have argued in an earlier chapter, perhaps divine working and human working are not so radically opposed as Boyd makes them.

Finally, although it now appears that in Boyd's view God sometimes overrides the irrevocable gift of freedom even when persons are still self-determining persons, rather than having acquired self-determined characters, there is no clear rationale for why he does so sometimes but not others. In the traditional view, God's plan is for the sake of some ultimate good, and those things that come to pass, whether directly ordained by him or simply permitted, are part of that coherent plan, although we may not understand the relationship of the part to the whole. This, however, is what Boyd caricatures and ridicules as the "divine blueprint." Since he rejects that view, it is reasonable to expect him to offer an alternative explanation. None is forthcoming, however. What emerges is a God who appears to be arbitrary.

Boyd would surely object that what seems to us to be arbitrary or confusing is so, not because God *is* that way, but because the world is fragmentary and confusing and opaque. God is acting out of wisdom, and what seems to us to be arbitrariness is so because we do not see all of those variables. We have to trust that God is acting in ways that are infinitely wise. Can we have that sort of trust, however? Can we believe that God is acting wisely when he does not know all that the future will hold? Boyd assures us, for example, that God does not "give away more 'shares' of his power than he could possibly control on a general scale. God is willing to take appropriate risks, as we have seen, but his risks are always wise. It seems that the all-wise Creator would at the very least keep enough 'shares' so that the overall flow of history and the attainment of his ultimate aim in creation would remain within his power."[26] The difficulty, however, is that a God who does not foreknow certain free human future actions may not be capable of calculating the limits of the freedom he should give humans. So open theism cannot have it both ways. God cannot give a gift of freedom to do things he cannot foreknow and still know that he has not given too much freedom. In the final analysis, despite the involved effort by Boyd, the same dilemma remains: either irrevocable freedom or certainty of the outcome, but not both without compromising one or the other in a fashion that results in an internally incoherent system.

There is one other major dimension to Boyd's theodicy that is not found in the other open theists' thought. As the title of his major book on the subject indicates, he places a great deal of emphasis on the role of Satan. This consideration is introduced especially in connection with the presence of natural evil in the world. He maintains that this cannot be explained very well in terms of human sin and misuse of human wills because much of it appears to antedate the presence of humans on the scene. He does discuss Satan's free will in connection with the limitations and abuse of human freedom. Identifying Satan with the reference to Lucifer in Isa. 14, he contends that just like humans, Satan also possessed free will and had the potential for good since he was the highest creation. However, he also had the potential of using this freedom for evil, and he exercised that freedom destructively.[27]

[26]Ibid., 187.
[27]Ibid., 171–77.

Boyd holds that the natural evil in the world can best be explained by understanding that Satan influences nature at a very basic level. This extends even to animals: "This line of thinking has also been applied to the pervasive violence of the animal kingdom. If there is an evil 'prince of matter' able to influence all material things at a structural level, then the supposition that the animal kingdom reflects this influence becomes a rational possibility."[28]

To deal fully with this interesting thesis would require treatment well beyond the scope of this book. It should simply be noted, however, that the same problem attaches to this part of Boyd's theory that attaches to the rest of his theodicy. For presumably, Satan has now reached the point of character fixation where he has a "self-determined character." It should therefore be legitimate for God to intervene unilaterally to bring about his desired end. Why, then, does a good God not so intervene more frequently? And, knowing the possibility of the horrendous evils that might occur, how could he allow such a gigantic misuse of freedom? It would appear that God is either passive or arbitrary with respect to Satan as he is with respect to free humans.

PRAYER

Certainly one of the most crucial practical areas of the Christian's life is prayer. Since Christianity is first and foremost a personal relationship between the believer and God, and prayer is a major way in which communication between the two takes place, this is in many ways at the heart of the Christian life. We must now ask ourselves what happens to the concept and the practice of prayer if the newer view of divine foreknowledge is adopted. It is especially that type of prayer commonly referred to as petitionary prayer that is under discussion.

The open theists are clear about the differences between their view of prayer and the traditional view, or what Basinger calls "specific sovereignty." The major question, as the open theists see it, is whether and when God intervenes in his world, and under what conditions or on what basis. Basinger contends that those who hold to specific sovereignty may

---

[28]Ibid., 298.

justifiably maintain that human petitions affect God's intervening. In such persons' thinking, however, nothing happens that God does not intend, and nothing that God intends fails to happen. Thus, even the praying of these prayers are part of his plan.[29]

The open theists, however, do not believe that God can unilaterally ensure that everything that occurs will be exactly what he intended. This is because, as we have already noted numerous times, they hold that God has granted humans genuine freedom. This means, they say, that together with most Christians they believe that our prayers genuinely make a difference in what happens.[30] In other words, whether something happens or does not happen may depend on whether one or more persons prays, or that "divine activity is at times dependent upon our freely offered prayers."[31] Not only do the open theists believe their view accords with how most people pray or conceive of what they are doing in praying, but they believe "the status of petitionary prayer within this [the open theist] model to be one of its most attractive features."[32]

Here Basinger acknowledges both agreements and differences among various open theists. All would agree that because of God's covenant of human freedom "he will not as a general rule force his created moral agents to perform actions that they do not freely desire to perform or manipulate the natural environment in such a way that their freedom of choice is destroyed."[33] This, of course, means that there are some prayers that God ordinarily will not answer or, in the sense previously defined, cannot answer because of his self-limiting gift of libertarian freedom. He will not ordinarily override the freedom of someone because he was freely asked to do so by someone else.

Might not God, however, simply influence (but not override) the wills of persons in such a way that what is ultimately best for them will occur? Here the difference among open theists appears. Some would say that since

---

[29]David Basinger, "Practical Implications," in Clark Pinnock, Richard Rice, John Sanders, William Hasker, and David Basinger, *The Openness of God: A Biblical Challenge to the Traditional Understanding of God* (Downers Grove, Ill.: InterVarsity, 1994), 158.
[30]Ibid., 156.
[31]Ibid., 160.
[32]Ibid., 162.
[33]Ibid., 160–61.

God loves all persons equally, he is always seeking to do all he can for their good, whether someone prays that he do so or not. "For some of us," Basinger says, "this means that God would never refrain from intervening beneficially in one person's life simply because someone else has failed to request that he do so. And, accordingly, we naturally find prayers requesting even noncoercive divine influence in the lives of others to be very problematic." The other group takes a different approach: "[They] see no necessary incompatibility in affirming both that God always seeks what is best for each of us and that God may at times wait to exert all the noncoercive influence that he can justifiably exert on a given person until requested to do so by another person. And thus they readily acknowledge the potential efficacy of prayers of this type." With respect to prayers for God to intervene on one's own behalf, open theists are more of one mind, believing that God will at times refrain from intervening unless we specifically request him to do so. Even here, however, there are limitations on what God is likely to do. Since one of his major purposes in dealing with his creation is the development of morally mature individuals, it is unlikely that he would grant a request to completely take over a person's life.[34]

What are we to make of this understanding of prayer? Here we are not primarily concerned with whether this view better reflects the biblical teaching on the subject or whether it is the more widely held view, but with what the practical benefits of this view are. To be sure, this belief has a very positive effect in encouraging Christians to pray and in reassuring them that their prayers "make a difference." Yet having said that, we must also observe that some serious problems attach to the understanding of prayer directed to a God who does not know all of the future.

The first problem involves the ability of God to answer prayers. It must always be borne in mind that God has made an irrevocable gift of libertarian freedom to his human as well as his angelic creatures. He will not ordinarily override this freedom, although there are situations, such as in Boyd's concept of persons having used up their probationary freedom, in which he both can and is justified in doing so. This, however, significantly limits the prayers that he can answer. Most importantly, the kinds of

---

[34]Ibid., 160–62.

prayers that God is excluded from answering are really the most important prayers. Here the open theist seems to be faced with the same dilemma described in our discussion of the problem of evil: either God must revoke or at least suspend his gift of freedom, or he may not be able to guarantee that what he wants to do and the person praying wants to see done will happen. On the view of human freedom known as compatibilism, this difficulty does not appear, because God is capable of working to bring it about that a free person wills something without violating that freedom.

There is another problem as well. Even though God is almighty and therefore able to do anything that is not logically contradictory or in violation of his own self-limitation, he also must know what to do. Ordinarily, Christians pray with the assurance that God is able to answer wisely because he knows the future completely. He knows the implications of one event, versus the results of its not occurring. Thus, he is able to do what is ultimately best, not only because he has the power or capability to do it but also because he has the wisdom to know what action will result in the good.

When we examine closely the open theist view of God's answering of prayer, however, something quite different results. Here God does not necessarily know what is needed in the future or how to bring that about. He does not know free human actions in advance of their being performed. Thus, he can hardly project very far ahead what he should do. Perhaps what he grants in response to a human prayer will not, in the long run, turn out to be the good. Bear in mind that God cannot even know who will be born or what their actions will be until their characters become fixed or their probationary period of libertarian freedom is exhausted, to use Boyd's terminology. Thus, the far-reaching consequences of his action cannot be known, although he can know all of the possibilities.

All Christians experience times of perplexity, not knowing how to pray. Two biblical passages offer comfort and reassurance in this setting. One that directly addresses this difficulty is Rom. 8:26–27: "In the same way, the Spirit helps us in our weakness. We do not know what we ought to pray for, but the Spirit himself intercedes for us with groans that words cannot express. And he who searches our hearts knows the mind of the Spirit, because the Spirit intercedes for the saints in accordance with God's will." This promise of the Spirit's intercession presumably is superior to the believer's own unaided prayer, since apparently the Spirit knows, as the human being does not, what should be requested. Note that the basis for this is "in accordance with God's will." Behind the believer's confidence is an implicit trust that God's will is based on all of the information, including what will occur in the future if this request is granted. However, if God does not know the future, then the Holy Spirit's intercession may not be any better informed than is the original prayer.

In the latter part of the Sermon on the Mount, Jesus gave his disciples instructions regarding prayer. He concluded by saying: "Ask and it will be given to you; seek and you will find; knock and the door will be opened to you. For everyone who asks receives; he who seeks finds; and to him who knocks, the door will be opened. Which of you, if his son asks for bread, will give him a stone? Or if he asks for a fish, will give him a snake? If you, then, though you are evil, know how to give good gifts to your children, how much more will your Father in heaven give good gifts to those who ask him!" (Matt. 7:7–11). The problem here seems to be that the person praying might fear that God will give him something evil rather than good. It may strike us as strange that Jesus should even suggest that a person might request bread and the heavenly Father would instead give him a stone, or that he might ask for a fish, and the Father would give him a snake instead. Certainly, Jesus' prior teaching about the goodness of the Father would preclude the very idea of his giving evil rather than good. Note, however, that the emphasis is on the heavenly Father *knowing how* to give good gifts. Wisdom underlies the giving. It may be that Jesus envisioned a situation in which the child, in his immaturity and inexperience, asks for what he thinks is bread but that is actually a stone, or asks for what appears to him to be a fish but is really a snake. The father, however, being wise enough to know that what the child thinks is good is actually evil, does not grant the request.

Such wisdom, however, requires a great deal of knowledge on the part of the father, or in this case, the heavenly Father. If God knows the future, then he is able to distinguish the truly good from the only apparently good.

If he knows the future in all of its entirety, however, he knows how to give good gifts, and the believer can pray confidently.

If this is not the case, then the believer might have to pray with caution. Perhaps I will ask for something that appears good at present but may turn out to have unfortunate long-range consequences, and God will grant it, which he would not have done otherwise. Perhaps it would be better that I not pray, or if I do, I must endeavor to anticipate the future consequences of these prayers.

If this were the case, then we would be in a situation like that described in W. W. Jacobs's short story, "The Monkey's Paw." A couple come into possession of a monkey's paw, which is reputed to be able to grant three wishes, but they are urged not to use it. They decide to wish for just enough money to pay off the mortgage on their home. A few days later they receive a visit from an official of the business where their only son works. He bears the bad news that their son has been killed in an accident at work and that the company, as an expression of sympathy, is giving them a sum of money that happens to be the exact amount they had wished for. Eventually, the wife takes the paw and wishes that their son might come back to life. After a few moments, there is a knocking at the door. Just as the wife reaches the door, her husband takes the paw, makes the third and last wish, and the knocking ceases. It is a powerful reminder to be careful what you wish for, because you may get it.

The point is that Christians need not fear to pray. The first concern will of course be what Jesus emphasized: "Hallowed be your name. Your kingdom come. Your will be done, on earth as it is in heaven." When, however, we pray for our daily bread and similar concerns, we need not fear that an unwise prayer, a prayer for what is ultimately evil, will be granted by the heavenly Father. He knows how to give good gifts.

GUIDANCE

Traditionally, Christians have believed that they could turn to God for guidance for their lives. This practice rested on the belief that God had a plan that included individual humans and that he knew the future in its entirety. Consequently, he would know the future outcome of persons' actions and could make known to believers what course of action would ultimately be best.

Open theists, despite their strong emphasis on God's responsiveness to his human children, have not said much about his guidance of the believer. The most direct discussion of the topic is by Basinger in the closing chapter of *The Openness of God*. He notes that different theologies have different conceptions of the nature and extent of such guidance and that this idea is related to the conception of the nature and extent of God's knowledge. Open theists, he says, do not believe that God has middle knowledge, or knowledge of what would follow from each option open to a person.[35] Nor does God have perfect and complete knowledge of the future, although he has perfect knowledge of the past and present and of those events that will follow deterministically from the past. "But since we believe that God can know only what can be known and that what humans will freely do in the future cannot be known beforehand, we believe that God can never know with certainty what will happen in any given context involving freedom of choice. We believe, for example, that to the extent that freedom of choice would be involved, God would not necessarily know beforehand exactly what would happen if a couple were to marry."

This leads to a certain conclusion regarding the nature of possible divine guidance: "Accordingly we must acknowledge that divine guidance, from our perspective, cannot be considered a means of discovering exactly what will be best in the long run—as a means of discovering the very best long-term option. Divine guidance, rather, must be viewed primarily as a means of determining what is best for us now." God does have a general will for each person, that they might "live in accordance with the principles that he has established." Since, however, [they] "do not believe that God has exhaustive knowledge of the future, it makes no sense for us to think in terms of some perfect, preordained plan for our lives and hence, to worry about whether we are still within it."[36]

What are the implications of such a view versus the more traditional view that God has a plan, based on a perfect knowledge of the future and

[35]Bear in mind, however, Boyd's concept of "neo-molinism."
[36]Ibid., 163–64.

perhaps even on a perfect knowledge of the consequences that would follow upon the choice of one action versus another? To a person who feels that God's having a plan for one's life would be a restriction of that person's freedom, this may bring a great sense of relief. For most Christians, however, this will require some modification of the traditional conduct of their Christian lives.

If God's guidance is in terms of what is the best course of action at the present but is not based on his knowledge of the future, can we even be sure that his guidance in the present is into the best course of action? Perhaps, in retrospect, the believer will see that this was not the best course, since it has resulted in unfortunate circumstances. Basinger says as much: "However, since God does not necessarily know exactly what will happen in the future, it is always possible that even that which God in his unparalleled wisdom believes to be the best course of action at any given time may not produce the anticipated results in the long run."[37] It appears that the corollary of a God who sometimes regrets what he has done is that a Christian who attempts to follow his guidance will sometimes regret his or her action as well, even though it was based on what seemed to be God's direction.

This means that as a Christian I must base my decisions on my own ability to anticipate the future. God knows the past and future more completely and accurately than I do, so my concern should be to ascertain from him as much about the present as I can. If I find myself in a difficult situation, this may indicate that my decision to follow what I thought to be his guidance was mistaken.

The traditional view is quite different. Although there may be differences of opinion regarding whether a believer can miss God's will, there is assurance that God *has* a will, and will watch over and care for those who find and follow it. The promise of God is not for avoidance of difficulty for the believer, but of provision for the believer in that predicament. So, for example, God did not answer Paul's threefold prayer by removing the "thorn in the flesh," but by promising that his grace would be sufficient for Paul—in other words, that Paul would be enabled to endure the

---

[37]Ibid., 165.

trial (2 Cor. 12:1–10). No such assurance is available to the open theist believer.

Note also that the most important decisions of life are not those about the immediate present but rather those that affect the course of one's life for decades to come. These are the decisions regarding which God has the least knowledge. Thus, we are faced with the predicament that God's guidance is of most help to the least important decisions of life and vice versa.

There is another implication of these issues. The believer in the traditional view holds that since God's guidance is based on perfect and exhaustive knowledge of the future, once that guidance is ascertained, it need not be constantly reexamined. The orders are "good until cancelled," as it were. If, however, God's knowledge and guidance are primarily for the present, then I must be continually remaking my decisions. I recall hearing of a group of students in a conservative Bible college who each morning upon arising would pray as to whether they should attend class that day. Ironically, this seems to be the implication of the open theist model. While more traditional believers would seek God's will regarding the specifics of a day that may be part of the means to the more remote end, there will not need to be quite the soul-searching that goes with not having long-range guidance.

the doctrinal structure
of the debate

In a sense, this chapter may appear to be superfluous. Have we not, after all, been examining the doctrinal questions throughout this book? To some extent that is true, for numerous elements of doctrine, especially of the doctrine of God, have gone into our exposition to this point. Yet those doctrinal issues, in the sense of systematic theology, have been interwoven with numerous considerations that would more accurately be labeled historical or philosophical theology. It is time to draw out more fully and systematically the doctrinal issues involved and the doctrinal differences that separate the two opposed systems. Furthermore while the treatment to this point has been largely expository, closer analysis is important.

DOCTRINE OF GOD

Clearly the doctrine of God occupies the central place in the current discussions of foreknowledge by open theists and traditional theists, although it is by no means the only doctrine involved.

Love of God. At the very heart of the open theist view of God is the concept of God's love. In the chapter on the biblical basis of open theism, Richard Rice develops the topic in a somewhat ascending order. He first says, "Love is the most important quality we attribute to God, and love is more than care and commitment; it involves being sensitive and responsive as well."[1] Moving

---

[1]Richard Rice, "Biblical Support for a New Perspective," in Clark Pinnock, Richard Rice, John Sanders, William Hasker and David Basinger, *The Openness of God: A Biblical Challenge to the Traditional Understanding of God.* (Downers Grove, Ill.: InterVarsity, 1994), 15.

a step further, he says that the most important statement in the Bible is in 1 John 4:8, "God is love." Love is the attribute that most fully reveals God. It is the source of all the other attributes. It is as close as the Bible comes to defining God, as contrasted with merely describing him. "Love is the essence of the divine reality," Rice says, "the basic source from which *all* of God's attributes arise."[2]

The other open theists echo this affirmation. Pinnock insists that while some have suggested that a particular view of freedom is the distinctive and driving force behind their view, it should actually be seen as related to love. Of the book *The Openness of God*, he says, "Love and not freedom was our central concern because it was God's desire for loving relationships which required freedom."[3] Boyd says, "The thesis of this book is that the answer [to the question of how we can continue to affirm that God is all-powerful in face of the evil in the world] lies in the nature of love. As Father, Son and Holy Spirit, God's essence is love (1 Jn 4:8, 16). God created the world for the purpose of displaying his triune love and inviting others to share in it (cf. esp. Jn 17:20–25)."[4]

These statements indicate that for the open theists love is not just an attribute of God, not even the central attribute or the most important attribute. It is *the* attribute, the very essence of God. First John 4:8 does not say that God has love or that God is loving; rather, it says that God *is* love.

More traditional conservative theologians have always strongly emphasized the love of God. Some have even made it the most important or most central of God's attributes. Nonetheless, it has been considered one attribute among many. If one uses the grammatical structure of 1 John 4:8 as a cue, then one would have to say, similarly, that based on John 4:24, "God is spirit, and his worshipers must worship in spirit and in truth," God's essence is spirit. However, here the grammatical structure is somewhat different from that in 1 John 4:8, 16. In those verses, there is a copula, "is," whereas in John 4:24 the copula is simply assumed. The following comment does seem to

---

[2]Ibid., 21.
[3]Clark H. Pinnock, *Most Moved Mover: A Theology of God's Openness* (Grand Rapids: Baker, 2001), 3.
[4]Gregory A. Boyd, *Satan and the Problem of Evil: Constructing a Trinitarian Warfare Theodicy* (Downers Grove, Ill.: InterVarsity, 2002), 16.

make clear the meaning of the statement, since the worshipers are to worship in a fashion appropriate to the nature of the one they worship.

Another text that could be introduced is Isa. 6:3, where the seraphs were calling to one another, "Holy, holy, holy is the LORD Almighty; the whole earth is full of his glory." While the statement is not in the grammatical form of an apparent equivalence, it is probably significant that the most prominent quality of God that is mentioned, in fact the only one, is his holiness and that the presence of his glory is also emphasized. A similar passage of encounter with the divine person is found in Ex. 3:5, where, having revealed himself in fire in a bush, God says to Moses, "Do not come any closer. Take off your sandals, for the place where you are standing is holy ground." A somewhat different but similar incident is found in Luke 5. Here Jesus has just led the disciples to cast their nets into an unlikely place at an unlikely time, and the result is a catch of fish so great that it threatens to break their nets. Peter's response is interesting: "When Simon Peter saw this, he fell at Jesus' knees and said, 'Go away from me, Lord; I am a sinful man!'" (v. 8). What apparently happened was that this miracle made clear to Peter that he was not merely in the boat with an outstanding fisherman; this was the Lord, the very son of God. The reaction is an awareness of his own sinfulness and a desire to have this holy one removed from his presence.

One other text is also relevant. In Ex. 3 Moses, fearing that the people of Israel will not believe him or heed his message, asks God his name. The reply is, "I AM WHO I AM. This is what you are to say to the Israelites: 'I AM has sent me to you'" (v. 14). The Hebrew verb here is in the imperfect, signifying uncompleted action, and can also be translated "I will be." This latter rendering is favored by the context, in which God says in the next verse, "Say to the Israelites, 'The LORD, the God of your fathers—the God of Abraham, the God of Isaac and the God of Jacob—has sent me to you.' This is my name forever, the name by which I am to be remembered from generation to generation." One could argue that if this is the name by which God identifies himself, then his existence, or one might say his *aseity*, or self-existence, is his most significant characteristic or is even his very essence. Pinnock comments on the misunderstanding of this verse that transmuted it into a metaphysical principle, whereas Jehovah was simply affirming his faithfulness.[5] Yet he does not consider that perhaps open theists are doing something similar with 1 John 4:8, 16.

The point of introducing these texts is this: one might use them to argue that a different attribute of God, such as his spirituality, his holiness, or his self-existence, was basic or was God's very essence. The open theists, to my knowledge, have not dealt with these texts. It is clear that they make love the supreme truth about God. It is not equally clear that this priority is assigned on the basis of the biblical text alone. It is possible that some other factor is bearing on the elevation of this quality.

It may be helpful here to examine the nature of this love in terms of what it moves God to do. Repeatedly, the open theists argue that this love requires that God create humans with a genuine freedom, with the ability to choose freely whether to love or not to love him in return. Pinnock, for example, comments on the parable of the prodigal son: "The story is about the power of love, not about any love of power. It portrays God as not wanting to control everything, but choosing to give the creature room to exist and freedom to love. It depicts God as personal in his dealings and as one who does not treat persons like puppets." Pinnock believes that this parable sets forth well the open view of God: "He is a loving person who seeks freely chosen relationships of love with his creatures; he is not a pillar around which everything else moves (Thomas Aquinas) or an all-controlling despot who can tolerate no resistance (Calvin)."[6] Pinnock also says flatly, "Love is more than an attribute; it is God's very nature."[7] Similarly, Boyd elaborates his thesis in *Satan and the Problem of Evil:* "God created the world for the purpose of displaying his triune love and inviting others to share in it (cf. esp. Jn 17:20–25). I shall argue that it was not logically possible for God to have this objective without risking the possibility of war breaking out in his creation."[8]

The open theists frequently assert that God's love can only be expressed if the humans he creates are genuinely free, in the sense of libertarian

---

[5]Clark H. Pinnock, "Systematic Theology," in *The Openness of God,* 106.
[6]Pinnock, *Most Moved Mover,* 4.
[7]Ibid., 81.
[8]Boyd, *Satan and the Problem of Evil,* 16.

freedom. Anything less than this would not be genuine love. But if this is the structure of the argument, then it would appear that a particular conception of freedom colors and preconditions the nature of divine love. So perhaps while not on the level of conscious tenet, on the level of presupposition, a view of freedom is actually at the heart of the matter or is the unconscious starting point in defining love.

A further question about this quality of love in God is how other attributes of God enter into the discussion. For it is usually understood that love cannot simply be defined abstractly and then applied to God. It must be seen in the context of the whole of who and what he is, so that love is so defined as not excluding these other attributes. As noted above, traditional Christian theism has generally seen other aspects of God's nature—whether termed holiness, justice, or wrath—that must be taken into account in formulating the understanding of love. These are qualities that sometimes might be thought to be in tension with love, as abstractly defined.

In an earlier writing, referring to the book *The Openness of God,* I observed that in that book "much is made of the passages pertaining to the love of God, but little or no notice is taken of the passages that speak of his holiness, wrath, and judgment."[9] Misreading "little or no" as "none at all" and failing to note the context of comparison, Pinnock responds, "Erickson says that openness theologians do not speak of God's wrath, but we do. . . . On wrath and atonement, see Pinnock, *Flame,* 93–111."[10]

We should note first that *The Openness of God* is indeed devoid of such references, and second that the documentation to which Pinnock appeals was in a work on a different topic, the Holy Spirit. Having said that, it is commendable that in their more recent writings, the open theists have included references to divine holiness and wrath as helping to locate the nature of divine love. Pinnock insists that "making love central does not make wrath unreal. . . . wrath signals that God is not indifferent to our human responses. He is a jealous God and cares about what we do with what he gives. This is a 'holy' love, a love that claims us so seriously that it

[9]Millard J. Erickson, *God the Father Almighty: A Contemporary Exploration of the Divine Attributes* (Grand Rapids: Baker, 1998), 85.
[10]Pinnock, *Most Moved Mover,* 83, n. 59.

does not tolerate spiritual adultery. It is a love that wants to change us and not leave us the same."[11]

Boyd also discusses God's wrath in three contexts. One is the description of annihilationism, a position he personally rejects. He also describes how "this very necessity [the metaphysical necessity of giving humans the power of freedom] and love may also be understood as God's judgment. God's love and wrath unite in allowing creatures to go their own way throughout eternity."[12] This is what he refers to using Barth's term, *das Nichtige*, a leaving of persons to their own way, which is a virtual lack of reality. Finally, he describes God's judgment and wrath against Satan and evil.[13]

It is significant that these open theists have incorporated the discussion of God's holiness, wrath, and judgment into their theology. It should be observed, however, that compared to the discussion of divine love, these treatments are relatively brief (less than a page in Pinnock's book) and considerably less emphatic.

Divine Justice. Open theism strongly emphasizes the justice of God, by which is meant his impartiality. This conception of justice is generally implicit in the ideas of divine love and God's gift of human freedom, but at times it is made explicit. This is particularly offered as a criticism of Calvinism. For example, Boyd says, "Scripture uniformly teaches that God loves everyone and thus desires all to be saved. Though God's people have always had trouble accepting it, Scripture consistently portrays God's love as universal and impartial (Acts 10:34; cf. Deut 10:17–19; 2 Chron 19:7; Job 34:19; Is 55:4–5; Mk 12:14; Jn 3:16; Rom 2:10–11; Eph 6:9; 1 Pet 1:17). The Lord explicitly tells us that he is not arbitrary or unfair (Ezek 18:25)."[14]

Similarly, Sanders says,

Strange as it may seem, according to exhaustive sovereignty God specifically intends that certain people hate him. If God specifically did not want anyone to hate him, then God would ensure that no one did. But if God desires that some people hate him, what has become of the divine

---

[11]Ibid., 82.
[12]Boyd, *Satan and the Problem of Evil*, 354.
[13]Ibid., 356–57.
[14]Ibid., 79–80.

love we read about in the Gospels? In the parables of the vineyard (Mt 20:1–16) and the talents (Mt 25:14–30) divine generosity is lavished on all. Judgment comes only after all had been shown divine favor and had been given an opportunity to respond. Such parables bring out the distributive justice of God, whereas proponents of specific sovereignty typically emphasize only the retributive justice of God.[15]

Divine Knowledge. Probably the most controversial and heavily discussed attribute of God is his knowledge. In keeping with most other Christian theologians, open theists believe that God's knowledge of the past and present is exhaustive. It is with respect to the future that their theology diverges from the general tradition. For here open theists hold that God knows some, but not all, of the future. Specifically, there is much about the free actions of moral agents that God cannot know, not because of a lack on his part, but because it has no reality, and therefore there is nothing there to know until those actions are taken.

In understanding how God knows, it is helpful to examine the types of things that open theists believe God does know about the future. One group is those things that he purposes to do on his own. For these he needs no cooperation from humans, and consequently he can know what he will do. The second, however, are those things that he can determine from a perfect knowledge of the present. This, of course, includes natural events that occur because of factors in the physical universe. Beyond that it also includes knowledge of certain human actions, based on his complete knowledge of the human's present state of mind and heart. This is the explanation of Jesus' prediction of Peter's threefold denial, for example. We should notice, however, that this knowledge of future actions is on a different basis than is the traditional view. According to that view, or to the several varieties of it, God knows because he "sees" in some direct fashion what persons will do in the future. The open theist position, however, is that God's knowledge of future human actions is not direct but is indirect, or inferential. It is a matter of his drawing conclusions from what he knows about the present.

---

[15]John Sanders, *The God Who Risks: A Theology of Providence* (Downers Grove, Ill.: InterVarsity, 1998), 243.

There are varying explanations among different open theists of this self-imposed limitation of knowledge. Frequently the assertion is made that this was a consequence of God's decision to create as he did. When he chose to create beings with libertarian freedom, God determined thereby that he would not be able to predict what they would do with that freedom in every case. In Boyd's way of thinking, this is a metaphysical necessity, and it accounts for his contention that the dispute about open theism is less about the nature of God than about the nature of creation.[16] Similarly, Pinnock says, "God knows that whatever he wills and determines will come to pass but, if God is free and creatures are free, he cannot know in advance always exactly what will happen. This is not a limit on God's foreknowledge, but characteristic of the world that God decided to make. I do not see how one can have genuine freedom (human and divine) and exhaustive definite foreknowledge."[17]

Sanders goes to lengths to point out that not all open theists agree on the reason for God's lack of knowledge of the future. He cites Dallas Willard's concept of "dispositional omniscience," corresponding to dispositional omnipotence. By this Willard means that "just as God has all power but chooses whether to utilize it or not, so God could know our future actions but chooses not to know them. Willard believes that, for God to have truly personal relationships with us, God cannot know what we will do."[18] Sanders does not indicate that he himself holds this particular interpretation.

Although not necessarily using the term *kenosis* of his own view, Pinnock suggests that this is not an unknown concept in theology in general. He says of open theism: "It is not alone in positing libertarian freedom or divine self-limitation of power to make room for the creature. It is not unusual for contemporary theologians to speak of the divine self-limitation or kenosis whereby God freely chooses to allow the world to impact him

---

[16]Gregory A. Boyd, "The Open-Theism View," in *Divine Foreknowledge: Four Views,* ed. James K. Beilby and Paul R. Eddy (Downers Grove, Ill.: InterVarsity, 2001), 12.

[17]Clark H. Pinnock, "There Is Room for Us: A Reply to Bruce Ware," *Journal of the Evangelical Theological Society* 45.2 (June 2002): 216.

[18]John Sanders, "Be Wary of Ware," *Journal of the Evangelical Theological Society* 45.2 (June 2002): 223. It is not clear that the analogy is successful, since God presumably wills in each case whether to exercise his power, but on open theist grounds the decision not to know is a one-time matter.

without, however, losing his lordship over it."[19] The term and concept of kenosis, not just of the incarnate Son but of the entire Godhead, may be an apt one to describe open theism's approach to God's knowledge of the world and activity within it. Kenosis theories of the incarnation are based on Phil. 2:7, the Greek of which literally says, "he emptied himself." On some versions of kenosis, the second person of the Trinity did not really give up anything or divest himself of any powers, but rather, by assuming full human nature, he bound himself to exercising those powers under the limitations involved in human nature. The parallel here would be that God, although able to know everything, decided to create the world in such a way that there would be facets of it that, not being real until they occurred, would not be knowable until then. He could, of course, have chosen to create a world that was quite different, in which he would control everything that happened and thus would know all that was to occur. But by choosing to create the world that he did, he removed such events from the realm of knowability.

Especially interesting is Boyd's theory, which he labels "neo-molinism." In conventional Molinism, God knows all possibilities that would occur in any given world. Thus, by selecting which of these worlds to actualize, he knows what each person will do in that world. These possibilities, generally referred to as "counterfactuals of freedom," Boyd refers to as "would-counterfactuals," what would actually occur in each possible situation. He contends that rather than having knowledge of would-counterfactuals, God knows all "might-counterfactuals." He knows all the possibilities that might occur in each of these situations, but he does not know which will actually happen.[20]

It is questionable how helpful this concept is to Boyd's theory. In the conventional version of middle knowledge, God might not know which situation would arise, but at least he knows what would happen in each of these hypothetical situations. For Boyd, however, God only knows what *might* happen in each hypothetical situation. In a sense, God does not really know anything at all. It is difficult to see how God could even formulate probability judgments on such a basis.

[19]Pinnock, *Most Moved Mover,* 12.
[20]Boyd, *Satan and the Problem of Evil,* 126–29.

One unusual statement Boyd makes is that "for a God of infinite intelligence, *there is virtually no distinction between knowing a certainty and knowing a possibility.* God thus gains no providential advantage by knowing future events as certain as opposed to knowing them as possible. He anticipates each with equal perfection."[21] If what Boyd is saying in the second and third sentences is that God is able to deal equally well with a situation whether he knows it will happen or simply knows that it may happen, that is a debatable proposition. As stated in the first sentence quoted, however, even with the qualifier "virtually," it seems quite difficult to accept. Ordinarily, knowing that something *will* occur rather than merely that it *may* occur is something quite different, at least experientially. It is one thing to say that one knows as thoroughly and vividly the possible state of affairs. *That it will occur* is an additional piece of information, however.

This equating of the two should create a problem for the question of whether God holds false beliefs or makes mistakes. Together with Sanders, Boyd contends that God's statements that turned out to be incorrect should not be thought of as statements of what would happen but only as probability statements. If, however, there is virtually no difference between knowing that something may occur and that it will occur, Boyd's distinction between saying something was likely to occur and being mistakenly certain that it would happen appears to fail.

Immutability. Here, as in the other areas of consideration, there are some marked differences between the open theist view and traditional theism. Both views hold that the essence of God does not change; for example, he is loving, and this moral quality does not change. The changes the open theists attribute to God involve his knowledge and his action. On the traditional view, since God knows in advance all that will happen, his knowledge is not changed (enlarged) when such an event takes place. According to open theism, however, God's knowledge actually changes, because when any free action takes place, God then knows something that he did not know previously.

---

[21]Gregory A. Boyd, "Christian Love and Academic Dialogue: A Reply to Bruce Ware," *Journal of the Evangelical Theological Society* 45.2 (June 2002): 235.

The other area of change in God, according to open theism, is that he changes his mind. What he had purposed to do may well be influenced and even altered by human actions, including prayer. This is a change that the traditional view does not attribute to God. Such theists believe that since God already knows what is to occur, he does not amend his actions when a human action occurs.

To open theism, the traditional view is one of absolute immobility. God does nothing, is unresponsive. Contemporary conservative theology largely rejects such a concept of immutability, however. While God may not change his mind, he acts in ways that, to the observer, may seem to change. However, this is simply to say that God's plan is richly variegated. It also involves a distinction between a static condition, stable action, and unstable action. We might think of this in terms of motion. An automobile parked with its engine turned off and its brakes set is static, at rest. An automobile weaving in and out from one lane of traffic to another, accelerating and braking, is certainly dynamic, but it is a varying dynamism. An automobile moving in a straight line at a constant speed on level ground is also in dynamic motion, but with a more stable characteristic. A more dramatic illustration might be taken from bicycle riding. Sitting at rest on one's bicycle is not motion, it is static. Riding one's bicycle straight and at a constant speed is stable motion. Falling off one's bicycle is also motion, but of an unstable type. It appears that open theism sees activity as necessarily involving variation. Any constant action in accord with preset plans or purposes is seen as static—as an instance of "the myth of the blueprint."

Impassibility. That open theism rejects impassibility in all its forms should be evident. Whether in the sense of feeling the suffering of humans or the sense of being affected by them, open theism emphatically affirms divine passibility. This means two things: first, that God actually feels the emotions of his creatures, so that he suffers when they suffer; and second, that he is responsive. He is moved by the actions of his human creatures. This means that God really is affected by our prayers. It also means that his love is genuine emotion. To the open theist, the traditional view of God seems to make him a puppet master or something of the sort. He has planned from all eternity what is to happen, and he brings about those results. Since he knows in advance everything that is to occur, nothing surprises him, so he does not genuinely feel emotions.

We have seen, however, that the major current evangelical theology textbooks do not hold that view of impassibility. Rather, they hold that God genuinely feels emotions. He loves and he feels pain. Were this not the case, the incarnation would have been impossible. God's accomplishing of his will is not in some mechanical fashion that would make his creatures mere automatons. He does, however, know in advance all that will occur, including the free actions of human agents.

It thus appears that the two positions are not as far apart as is sometimes represented. How, then, can we relate these two to one another? What are their actual views, and how do these two relate? Here it may be helpful to bear in mind a principle that I have often found useful. If one examines the views of two parties in a debate in terms of what each says the other one holds, they are often far apart. If, on the other hand, one takes note of what each says he himself holds, they are frequently considerably closer.

It may be that differing conceptions of the nature of passibility, in terms of the kind of experiencing of emotions that God has, are involved here. If the essence of impassibility is not being affected by anything external, then both parties may reject that but have differing ideas of the nature of the effect on God.

One way to conceive of God's relationship to the actions and emotions of his creatures would be *sympathy*. By this is meant that God actually experiences the same emotions as these creatures do. If they feel joy, God does also. If they feel anger, he does as well. Another way of thinking of this relationship is *empathy*. Here God does not necessarily actually experience the same feeling as the human person, but he understands what the person is feeling. He is able to say, in effect, "I know what you are going through." He is affected by the suffering of the person and cannot merely be indifferent to it.

This distinction is crucial in counseling. The counselor who deals with depressed persons all day and actually sympathizes with each one, personally experiencing the counselee's depression, would not survive long as a counselor. He or she would soon have to become a counselee—or enter another profession! It is, however, essential that a counselor be able to empathize, to sincerely assure the counselee that he or she understands what the counselee is going through.

To the traditional view, this seems to be a more suitable fit for understanding God's responsiveness to his creatures. If he actually sympathized, he would feel, simultaneously, the emotions of each of several billion persons. He would simultaneously feel happiness and sadness, anger and forgiveness, agitation and calm. While it may be that God is so much different from us that he could simultaneously experience conflicting emotions without any adverse effects, traditional theists find it more satisfactory to construct a doctrine of God in which God is moved by the suffering of his children, but the emotion to which he is moved may not be the same as that of the creature. For example, the creature's pain may move God to pity or compassion. The human's anger against God may not actually produce anger on God's part, but perhaps a calming reaction instead. The emotions of the creatures evoke a response from God, but they do not merely replicate their own emotion in God.

ANGELIC BEINGS

The open theist who has emphasized angels is clearly Boyd. Angelic beings play a large part in his understanding of the unfolding cosmic drama, or in his language, "the divine warfare." Some of this emphasis is on unfallen angels, which he refers to as "gods," but he makes it clear that he is not speaking of these as being "in any sense coeternal, cocreator[s] or coruler[s] with the one true God."[22] It is plain from Boyd's writings, however, that these "gods" play a very important part in God's plan and working. He interprets the "we" and "let us" passages in Genesis as referring, not to the Trinity or to a plural of majesty, but to this "heavenly council."[23] The conception of freedom of humans is extended to this treatment of angels as well:

> While the supremacy of Yahweh among the gods is never qualified in the Old Testament, this supremacy is not generally interpreted in a strictly

---

[22]Gregory A. Boyd, *God at War: the Bible and Spiritual Conflict* (Downers Grove, Ill.: InterVarsity, 1997), 116.
[23]Ibid., 131–32.

autocratic fashion. That is, the gods are never portrayed as mere puppets of Yahweh. Rather, they appear to be personal beings who not only take orders but also are invited to give input to their sovereign (1 Kings 22:20; Is 6:8)....

These Gods never rival the Creator's authority. Thus, they are never construed as major competing deities. Herein lies the central difference between the Old Testament and pagan conceptions of the heavenly council. But it is important to note that the Old Testament certainly accepts that some such council exists, and that the members of the council have some say in how things are done. In sharp contrast to the later Augustinian monopolizing view of divine sovereignty, the Sovereign One in this concept invites and responds to input from both his divine and human subjects.[24]

It is the evil angels that play the largest role in Boyd's theology. He sees the drama of the divine warfare as central for the biblical writers.[25] We have examined this aspect of Boyd's thought in our consideration of his treatment of the problem of evil (chapter 8), but here we may simply affirm that for Boyd fallen angels, who oppose God's will in this world, play a very important part in the explanation of the evil, both moral and natural, that plagues us.

REVELATION AND SCRIPTURE

In some respects, the doctrine of revelation held by the two groups is quite similar. Both, for example, seem to hold that God does not merely encounter humans on a personal basis without conveying some informational content. While the expression "propositional revelation" may not be the best one to use, both parties seem to hold that God has actually communicated truth to humans. This is not a neo-orthodox conception of revelation as a dynamic person-to-person encounter. Both parties seem to hold that God does not simply communicate information to the recipient of revelation, but presents himself in this process. The Bible is cited by both as if a correct understanding of its teaching yields an understanding of God and his working.

---

[24]Ibid., 129–30.
[25]Ibid., 22.

One issue that distinguishes the two positions from one another is how the language of the Bible and theology relates to that which it purports to represent. Traditionally, there have been three major conceptions of this relationship: that it is univocal, that it is equivocal, and that it is analogical. Both parties to the discussion would agree that the biblical language is in some sense anthropic. That is to say, the language employed is ordinary human language. If this were not the case, the revelation would be unintelligible. So the Bible describes God by using terms also used of humans: love, strength, and so forth. The question, then, is the degree of similarity of meaning between the references to God and those to humans. The univocal conception would say that they mean the same thing in both usages; the equivocal would say that the meanings are entirely dissimilar; the analogical would say that they are similar but not identical: a quality may apply to both humans and God, but to a much greater degree when applied to God.

At times it appears that open theism regards the use of language applied both to humans and to God as univocal. That means that if the Bible says that God grieves, it means just the same as when it speaks of a human grieving. Although not said this directly, this conception appears to underlie much of the discussion of the divine attributes. It accounts for Boyd's statements about taking the biblical references to God's feelings and emotions at "face value" or in "straightforward fashion." The disdain displayed for any sort of interpretation of these passages as involving anthropomorphisms seems to indicate that statements about God are to be understood in just the same sense as one would take them if they were referring to humans.

In general, the traditional view appears to favor the idea that language about God is analogical. Thus, the love of God is like, but not identical to, humans' love. This is implied by the contention that some of the statements about divine emotions should be understood as anthropomorphic in character. The difficulty with this approach is that it is really not possible to determine the exact proportionality of the two referents. In other words, while the love of God is greater than the love of humans, we do not know how much greater. This is the point of the open theist challenge to the traditional view to explain the meaning of the passages about God changing his mind if they are not to be taken literally.[26]

When we examine the doctrine of Scripture as such, there is generally close formal agreement between the two views in terms of any declared definition of inspiration. The words and details of Scripture are given close attention and are treated as authoritative by both parties, implying a verbal theory of inspiration.

It does appear, particularly in Sanders's writing, that he may have accepted certain types of critical Old Testament methodology usually not found in evangelical works. This can be seen in connection with his claim that repentance should be treated as a controlling metaphor in the Old Testament. Here he argues for the presence of this theme in a variety of types of material and genres. As one of the dimensions of this widespread presence, he writes, "'Divine repentance is in fact found within a variety of traditions, northern and southern early and late: Jahwist/Elohist; David/Zion; Deuteronomic History; eighth- and seventh-century prophets, exilic and post-exilic prophecy, psalmody.' The theme cannot be dismissed as belonging to some small band of esoteric teachers."[27] This statement may indicate an acceptance of the now rather dated documentary hypothesis (JEDP) of the origin of the Pentateuch, and allied theories.

Sanders is quoting Terence Fretheim. This raises another issue. Frequently the open theists support their biblical interpretations by appealing to commentators whose assumptions about Scripture are not the usual ones held by evangelicals. This is particularly the case with Walter Brueggemann's scholarship. It is also true, to a lesser extent, as the quotation above indicates, with the use of Fretheim. We may have a case here either of combining nonevangelical presuppositions with an evangelical view of Scripture, which will naturally lead to internal contradictions, or an indication that the open theists themselves hold a different view of inspiration than their opponents. There are, of course, a considerable variety of theories of inspiration, but it does appear that the open theist view is not on the more conservative end of the scale.

---

[26]Gregory A. Boyd, *God of the Possible: A Biblical Introduction to the Open View of God* (Grand Rapids: Baker, 2000), 119.

[27]Sanders, *The God Who Risks*, 73.

What of the issue of biblical inerrancy? Here again, both parties to the current discussion subscribe to that doctrine. One issue that naturally arises, however, is how the view of limited omniscience fits with the doctrine of inerrancy. At points open theists seem to teach that some statement by God may not be accurate or may not prove true when the time referred to becomes current.

Perhaps the most direct of these statements is found in Sanders. He says, "It is commonly overlooked by proponents of foreknowledge that some predictions in Scripture either do not come to pass at all (for example, the account of Jonah; 2 Kings 20) or do not come to pass exactly as they were foretold (for example, Gen. 27:27–40, in which Jacob's blessing is qualified by Esau's blessing; Acts 21:11, in which it is incorrectly predicted that Paul would be bound by the Jewish authorities and handed over to the Gentiles). One would think that a God with foreknowledge would get such details straight."[28] This sounds like a straightforward statement that some affirmations of Scripture are erroneous.

Elsewhere, Sanders denies that this is an attribution to God of erroneous beliefs, pointing out that he has placed several qualifications on his assertions. He says,

> One of the qualifications I made was to say that, for God to be mistaken or to hold a false belief, it would have to be the case that God "declared infallibly that something would come to pass and it did not. God would never be mistaken so long as he said that X (for example, Adam will not sin) would infallibly come to pass and it did not." God will not *definitely believe* that something will occur unless it is *certain* to occur. If an event is not certain to occur, then God knows the degree of probability that something will happen in a particular way. But God will not hold that belief as absolutely certain if human freedom is involved, because our decisions, though somewhat predictable, are not absolutely so.[29]

Boyd takes a similar position in his reply to Ware.[30] As we observed in an earlier chapter, this idea that God is not making infallible predictions but rather simply giving a probability statement appears somewhat artificial.

---

[28]Ibid., 75.
[29]Sanders, "Be Wary of Ware," 224. The quotation is from his *The God Who Risks,* 132.
[30]Boyd, "Christian Love and Academic Dialogue," 237.

It certainly does not sound like a case of taking the biblical text at face value or in its most straightforward fashion. If one grants this somewhat creative type of interpretation, however, then open theists can claim that their view is not inconsistent with a belief in biblical inerrancy.

There is one other expedient that could be employed by the open theists but that to my knowledge they have not utilized. This is a view held by Edward John Carnell at one stage of his career, and for which he believed there was support in the writing of James Orr.[31] According to this view, inspiration merely guaranteed an accurate report of the sources reported but not necessarily the accuracy of those sources. On one level, this theory can be seen to be rather obviously true. There are erroneous statements of ungodly persons reported in the Bible, one of the most striking being the fool's statement, "There is no God" (Ps. 14:1). Conceivably, this principle could then be extended to say that the biblical prophecies are inerrant statements of what God believes will come to pass, but that God may be in error on this matter. The affirmation then would not be "This will happen," but "God believes this will happen." One wonders, however, how a God with these limitations could inspire fallible humans to make infallible or inerrant statements. It suffices to say that the open theists all insist strongly that they hold to the inerrancy of Scripture.

Humanity

The doctrine of humanity does not receive much direct treatment in the discussions on foreknowledge. The one point that does clearly differentiate the two parties in the debate is the question of freedom. Open theism strongly emphasizes incompatibilist or libertarian freedom. This is regarded as central to the discussion because God's love requires that humans be free to respond or not respond.

Some of the later open theist literature, particularly Boyd's *Satan and the Problem of Evil,* discusses the limitations or conditioning factors on this freedom. In some ways, this begins to approximate the position of compatibilism, which suggests that freedom should be understood as freedom

---

[31]Edward John Carnell, *The Case for Orthodox Theology* (Philadelphia: Westminster, 1959), 102–11. The reference to Orr is to his *Revelation and Inspiration* (Grand Rapids: Eerdmans, 1953), 163–65.

to act in accordance with internal inclinations but implies a freedom from external compulsion.

ATONEMENT

Sanders discusses the nature of Christ's atoning work on the cross and speaks of "the variety of metaphors and explanations that New Testament writers use to explain what Jesus did."[32] While not wanting to take a stand on any one particular theory of atonement, he does explain, "I understand sin to primarily be alienation, or a broken relationship, rather than a state of being or guilt. . . . God considers the breach in our relationship a greater evil than the harm we have caused and so desires reconciliation." In such a situation, he says, "The injured party must suffer the pain, forgoing revenge, in order to pursue reconciliation of the broken fellowship. In this sense, forgiveness is not 'unconditional,' since the person forgiving must fulfill this condition."[33] While Sanders's view of atonement embodies the several dimensions that various theories have attributed to Christ's death, he appears to emphasize a strong element of the moral influence theory. The death of Jesus demonstrates the suffering God has endured throughout the time since the creation, and this should move the alienated sinner to be reconciled to such a God.

Somewhat puzzling is Sanders's statement about the crucifixion: "Although Scripture attests that the incarnation was planned from the creation of the world, this is not so with the cross. The path of the cross comes about only through God's interaction with humans in history. Until this moment in history other routes were, perhaps, open."[34] Unfortunately, Sanders does not really elaborate this hint, but it raises some questions about how broad and how prolonged this contingency was.

Boyd does not really offer a clear explanation of the nature of the atonement. He does, however, make at least one statement that enunciates the moral influence element: "But God did not abandon us. Instead, out of his boundless love, he continued his yes toward creation with a yes of salvation: 'While we still were sinners Christ died for us' (Rom 5:8). God

---

[32]Sanders, *The God Who Risks*, 104.
[33]Ibid., 105
[34]Ibid., 100.

freed us from the devil and forgave all our sin. . . . Yet, God continues to be a God of persuasion, not coercion (Irenaeus). Though the Father lovingly influences every human heart to accept his yes toward them . . . we possess the capacity to continue saying no to this gracious yes."[35]

More frequent in Boyd's writing are references that articulate the Christus Victor theme, the idea that Christ's atoning work was primarily a deliverance of us from evil and thus a triumph over Satan. There are a number of such statements: "Through the work of the cross God has sought to defeat his opponents and to restore humans to their original place as guardians of the earth."[36] Again, "The victory over Satan and the freedom for God's children that Christ won through his death and resurrection will someday be fully manifested."[37] Boyd's most complete statement of this motif also involves it with the destiny of humans:

> It is possible that one of God's original agendas in recreating the earth and establishing humanity as stewards over it was ultimately to employ these earthly guardians in a strategy for overthrowing the rival kingdom once and for all. This was accomplished by the God-man Jesus Christ allowing himself to be crucified by the spiritual 'rulers of this world' and by rising victorious on the third day (Col 2:13–15, cf. Jn 12:31f; 1 Pet 3:21–22). Empowered by the Spirit of our conquering Head, the church is now to fulfill the role of original humanity: reclaiming the earth from the kingdom of darkness as the domain in which the Creator is King.[38]

The Christus Victor theme is consistent with Boyd's entire emphasis on divine warfare. In fact, *Christus Victor* is the name of his ministry organization.

SALVATION

The nature of salvation also is not treated extensively in the open theist literature. There is considerable discussion of certain aspects of the doctrine of salvation elsewhere by Pinnock and Sanders. While this discussion is not in the context of the discussions of divine foreknowledge, there is a

---

[35]Boyd, *Satan and the Problem of Evil,* 341.
[36]Ibid., 311–12.
[37]Ibid., 319.
[38]Ibid., 315.

WHAT DOES GOD KNOW AND WHEN DOES HE KNOW IT?

connection between these dimensions of the doctrine of salvation and the open theist doctrine of God.

One of these doctrines concerns the nature of saving faith. While all evangelicals hold that salvation is only on the basis of Jesus Christ's work, there is a difference regarding the knowledge necessary for that work to become effectual. Many traditional evangelicals contend that one must have a conscious faith in Christ and his atoning death and resurrection to be saved. Pinnock and Sanders, however, hold to the efficacy of "implicit faith."[39] This is a faith that may not include knowledge of Jesus but, based on the general revelation, trusts in God and his gracious forgiveness. On the basis of this faith, God applies the redemptive work of Jesus Christ. Pinnock and Sanders believe that there may be large numbers of those who have never had the gospel presented to them who nonetheless will be counted among the saved on the basis of this implicit faith.[40]

The other relevant issue is what has become known as "postmortem evangelism." This teaching, advocated by Pinnock and Sanders, is that those who do not have an opportunity to hear of Christ during this lifetime will have an opportunity to hear and believe after death.[41] They base this belief on the "descent into Hades" passages in 1 Peter 3:18–22 and 4:6. This is not a second-chance type of teaching, but rather an insistence that everyone will have a first chance to hear, believe, and be saved, whether in this life or afterward.

Is this doctrine in some sense related to the doctrine of foreknowledge? If God has foreknowledge, including middle knowledge, or knowledge of all possibilities, then he can know not only who will accept the offer of salvation but also who would accept this offer if it were made. On that basis, God would be just in not enabling those to hear who would not believe even if given the opportunity. On the open theist scheme, however, God does not know what might happen. The only way he can be certain what a given person's response would be is by actually giving the person such an

---

[39]Clark H. Pinnock, *A Wideness in God's Mercy: The Finality of Jesus Christ in a World of Religions* (Grand Rapids: Zondervan, 1992), 95–101; John Sanders, *No Other Name: An Investigation into the Destiny of the Unevangelized* (Grand Rapids: Eerdmans, 1992), 227–67.
[40]Pinnock, *Wideness*, 20–38; Sanders, *No Other Name*, 60–71.
[41]Pinnock, *Wideness*, 168–71; Sanders, *No Other Name*, 205–10.

opportunity; and if there has not been such an occasion within this life, then there must be after death. Thus, there is a connection between the open theistic view of divine foreknowledge and this aspect of the doctrine of salvation.

Last Things

The doctrine of the last things or eschatology does not play a large part in the theology of open theism, but it certainly is an element of the overall view. In terms of cosmic eschatology, although open theism insists that God allows humans and angels free choice and does not directly control everything that happens, there is nonetheless a strong confidence that God's purposes will be fully attained in the end.

One point of individual eschatology comes into play in a rather significant fashion, namely, the question of hell. If some persons will experience eternal suffering, that appears to be such a significant element of evil as to be incompatible with the belief that God is all-loving. How can these things be reconciled?

One direct answer to this question, annihilationism, has been proposed by Pinnock. On this way of thinking, those who have not obtained salvation experience eternal death, but this is not eternal suffering. Rather, they simply cease to be.[42] The belief in an eternal hell, he believes, is a carryover from the Greek idea of the immortality of the soul, on which basis, the person cannot cease to be. Pinnock is joined in this position by a number of noted evangelicals, especially British evangelicals such as John Stott, Michael Green, John Wenham, Philip Edgcumbe Hughes, and Stephen Travis.

Boyd's view is more nuanced. Adopting and adapting Karl Barth's concept of *Das Nichtige* (literally, "the nothingness"), he attempts to combine the traditional idea of endless conscious punishment of the unrepentant and the idea of annihilation. The dignity of freedom that God gave humans in creation remains with them. What has happened, however, is that what

---

[42]Clark H. Pinnock, "The Destruction of the Finally Impenitent," *Criswell Theological Review* 4/2 (1990): 243–59. For a more complete discussion of annihilationism, see Millard J. Erickson, *How Shall They be Saved? The Destiny of Those Who Do Not Hear of Jesus* (Grand Rapids: Baker, 1996), 217–32.

they have chosen has ceased to exist. The entire reality is that of God, and beyond that there is nothing. Thus, these people have chosen and continue to choose that which now has no reality.[43] Because relating by agents requires some neutral objective shared medium, and because there is no such reality apart from heaven, in which they cannot participate, to the redeemed these unredeemed no longer exist.[44] They were, but are no longer. The reality of these people, self-chosen, is reality only to them. They will always be, but only to themselves.

While not all of the open theists have specifically declared themselves on this point of individual eschatology, there is sufficient discussion of this annihilation (in the case of Pinnock and Sanders) and of what we might term "semi-annihilation" (in the case of Boyd), that we might well ask whether there is any connection between this and the open theistic conception of God. I believe there is.

If God's passibility means that he genuinely experiences the emotions of each of his creatures, not simply empathetically but sympathetically, then if there is eternal conscious suffering of the lost, God must also experience that suffering for all eternity. If, however, they cease to be, or cease to be for all others than themselves, then God is spared that eternal pain.

---

[43]Boyd, *Satan and the Problem of Evil,* 342.
[44]Ibid., 347.

evaluation and conclusion

Throughout this examination, we have made evaluative judgments of one or the other of the two major alternative positions at various points. The time has now come, however, to weigh the two in a more formal and inclusive fashion. As we do so, a number of considerations should be borne in mind.

The first regards the criteria of criticism. Two types of criteria are appropriate. The first are universal criteria, which count for or against the cogency of any view. Consistency, or the absence of internal contradiction, and coherence, or the positive connectiveness of the various tenets of a view are examples of such universal criteria. While space does not permit our arguing why any view must hold these, it may suffice simply to note that for any assertion to be understandable and meaningful, such logical factors must be present. There are also certain external criteria that a cogent view must fulfill. It must accurately fit that which it purports to describe. Beyond that, however, it must more completely account for more of the data being dealt with, and with less distortion, than the alternatives. So, for example, if two views claim to be based on the Bible, the one that accounts for a larger sweep of the biblical content and with less distortion is to be preferred.

There also are pragmatic factors that any view that claims to be a life view must meet. Does this view enable the person who adopts it to live, practically and satisfyingly, his or her life? In the case of Christian theological theories, does this one enable the person who holds it to experience and embody the types of qualities or virtues that Christianity, as understood on the basis of the appropriate authority, describes and prescribes? This criterion must not be made the primary one, but it can be an appropriate and useful means of discrimination, especially if applied on a sufficiently long-term basis.

There also are specific criteria that a view must meet—the criteria it sets for itself. These criteria may vary from one scheme to another, but they require simply that the view delivers on its promises or achieves its goals. The attainment of more of these than an alternative view attains of its respective goals is a strength, while falling short of more of these than do the competitors is a weakness. Sometimes, of course, those who advocate a particular view do not make these criteria explicit, but the criteria can usually be identified with a certain amount of effort.

What is not legitimate is to criticize a view using criteria that are not espoused by its advocates or required for all such views. This is, however, a very common procedure. Someone who holds view A criticizes view B because it does not fulfill the objectives of view A. However, this may simply be a contention that B is not a very good example of A, and as such it is actually irrelevant unless one has already established the truth of A. If not, this is simply a case of begging the question.

Having laid down these preliminary qualifications, let us attempt to weigh the relative strengths and weaknesses of each of these two rather contrasting views. The fallibility of human understanding being what it is, we should not expect to find all of the weight on one side. It will not do to make our judgment on the basis of a single source of strong support or of a single or a few problems with a given view. The question must rather be, Which view has the greater support, and which view has the fewer and less significant problems?

Biblical Evidence

Both the traditional view and the open theist view make strong claims to being biblical. This is therefore a legitimate criterion to apply: Which of these two competitive views is better supported by the overall weight of the biblical evidence? We shall examine each in turn. The strengths of each will constitute the problems for the other, and vice versa.

The Traditional View. It is apparent that the traditional view has much support in Scripture. There are didactic passages in which God is said to know what no human could know, including details about the future. There also are large amounts of prophecy. In this latter case, the argument is inferential. The argument is that someone who can predict the future knows the future. Since God predicts the future, the conclusion is that he must know the future.

There are, however, problems for this view. There are statements that, taken in their simplest or plainest sense, seem to indicate that God lacks some knowledge, discovers something, or changes his mind. There also are passages that seem to indicate regret on God's part for some action he has taken, particularly because of the consequences of that action. While those who hold the traditional view are able to offer explanations of these passages, often by taking them as anthropomorphic or anthropopathic, or as describing from a phenomenal point of view, these are not the most natural explanations.

There also are some lacuna in the evidence. While there are numerous statements about the future and about items that God knows about the future, it is not the case that any single statement of Scripture overtly claims that God knows everything that is to happen. At times the advocates of the traditional argument overstate the case or draw unwarranted inferences. For example, Ware claims regarding Ps. 139:4, that the statement, "Before a word is on my tongue you know it completely, O LORD," means that God knows our actions in advance. Actually, this may only entail that God knows our thoughts before we enunciate them in speech. It also does not say how long before the speech God knows the thought. It may be only an instant. The text certainly does not say that God has known from all eternity what the psalmist was going to say. His argument in this connection that we all say things that are surprising, even to ourselves, does not seem very weighty to me. On the open theist grounds, God knows persons presently in infinite fashion, so that what might be surprising to others or even to ourselves need not surprise God. A further weakness of the traditional approach is also illustrated here. The psalmist is describing the intimacy of God's knowledge of him as a person. That is the context of the passage, one of fellowship and its basis. Some would contend that it is not legitimate to extend this to a statement about God's knowledge of all facts, personal and impersonal, or to knowledge of persons with whom he has no particular fellowship or sharing of common values.

Some interpretations offered by the traditional view of certain passages give the impression at times of being somewhat artificial or even forced. For example, the passage about Abraham being tested by God's command to sacrifice Isaac seems to say that it was God who benefited from this because he learned something about Abraham that he did not previously know. Open theists such as Boyd are right in pressing upon traditional theists the question of what the passage really does mean. For the most part, traditional theists have pointed out (correctly) the difficulties with the open theist interpretation of the passage but have not always offered a very satisfactory explanation of what the narrative really is about. Similarly, the passages describing prayer and its benefits present problems for the traditional view.

The Open Theist View. The obvious strength of the open theist view is that it enables one to take seriously and even literally texts that sometimes are interpreted in a somewhat strained fashion, a prime example being the passage just mentioned, Gen. 22. On the face of it, this seems to say just what the open theists say it does, namely, that God did not know what Abraham would do until he actually acted.

There is one rather major point at which Hebrew syntax supports the open theistic argument. This concerns the nature of the conditional statements, such as "they may." Here, as we observed, the structure of the sentences favors the idea of there being a genuine conditionality or unsettledness about the situation described.

The open theists contend that their reading of the Bible is that which most Christians instinctively do, especially where practical matters such as prayer are concerned. The argument here is that they have united the theoretical interpretation and the practical application. In this sense, their reading of Scripture is something of a commonsense one.

There are a number of problems with the open theists' handling of Scripture, however. One rather general one is that while their reading takes the Scripture at its plainest or most obvious meaning, it often does not go beyond that level. Although they refer to their work as exegesis, there is little of the detailed examination of passages that is generally associated with that term. For example, the word *niḥam* is simply interpreted as meaning, "to repent," without sufficient attention to the nuances of the various stems. Nothing of the scope of Parunak's work is found here.

There are also some logical or rhetorical gaps in the open theist case. For example, much of the argument involves an inference that is not always made explicit. It is these additional assumptions or premises that are the weak points in the argument. An example is the common assumption that God's repenting means that he did not know what would happen. If the word rendered "repent" means simply that God feels pain, then it does not necessarily follow that God did not know this would happen. I have pointed out that there are situations one knows in advance will someday happen, such as the death of one's parents, but that does not necessarily lessen the sorrow one feels. The premise that one only feels pain at something one did not anticipate is not adequately argued, or even identified, in some cases.

Sometimes this logical gap is combined with insufficient exegetical attention to the details of the passage. An example is the temptation of Abraham (Gen. 22). Here the conclusion is that God did not know what Abraham would do. The text, "Now I know that you fear God, because you have not withheld from me your son, your only son" (v. 12), does not say that, however. While the conclusion that Abraham feared God is drawn from what he did, the text interpreted in an open theist fashion actually says that God did not know that Abraham feared him; in other words, God not only did not know what he would do, but did not know what was in his heart. This has serious consequences for some of the other dimensions of open theist theology.

At times open theists depart from their expressed hermeneutical method of taking passages at face value. This may be seen most clearly in the discussions of whether God is ever in error or makes mistaken judgments. The answer given by both Sanders and Boyd is that God is making a probability statement, "This is what is most likely to happen," rather than an infallible statement of certainty, "This is what is most definitely going to occur." It is highly questionable, however, whether this interpretation of those statements is accurate. On the plainest or simplest reading of the text, it seems as if God is declaring that he definitely expects these things to come to pass.

This sort of exegetical creativity is also apparent in Boyd's treatment of Jesus' prediction of Peter's threefold denial. Here Boyd argues that God knew the personality of Peter so well that he knew how Peter would react in a certain situation and then "orchestrated" the circumstances in such a way that "Peter's character was squeezed out of him three times." It should be observed that this is a matter of secondary interpretation, or more than just a statement of what happened; it is an explanation of how or why it happened. This may indeed be the correct explanation, but it certainly is not the simplest or the most obvious. Here is a case where, contrary to its professed intention to take Scripture at face value, open theism engages in some rather complex and almost contrived interpretation.

Open theism also does not deal with some of the most crucial passages advanced by the traditional theism. One of the most notable is the extended section of Isaiah in which God distinguishes himself from the false gods on the grounds that, unlike him, they cannot foretell events. This is a very powerful portion of Scripture in terms of support for the traditional view; however, the open theists do not discuss some of the most forceful parts of this section, especially chapter 41. Both Boyd and Sanders limit their discussion to chapters 46 and 48, which are more amenable to their type of interpretation. Another example is Bruce Ware's appeal to Dan. 11 as an example of a prophecy involving an immense number of future free choices and actions.[1] Although Pinnock, Sanders, and Boyd all wrote responses to that article in the same journal issue, not one of them responds to his use of this passage or to the larger argument of which this is a part.

This type of omission is disappointing in light of open theist complaints about traditional theists' failure to treat the Scriptures that open theists appeal to, or to respond to their arguments. Actually, the failure may lie less with the traditional theists and more with open theists' failure

---

[1]Bruce A. Ware, "Defining Evangelicalism's Boundaries Theologically: Is Open Theism Evangelical?" *Journal of the Evangelical Theological Society* 45.2 (June 2002): 202.

to look in the right place. We have noted that in the case of Boyd's statement about my earlier book. Similarly, however, Boyd complains that Ware
in his article has not taken note of, and interacted with, some of Boyd's
statements.[2] Ware, however, points out that he has indeed interacted with
those objections in a much larger work he has written.[3]

HERMENEUTICS

Much of the difference between the two views' appeals to Scripture in
support of their positions cannot be settled simply by citation of Scripture.
The deeper question is how the Scripture shall be understood or interpreted. A major difference here is how certain of the passages, such as God
"repenting," expressing surprise, and so forth, shall be understood. The
open theist understanding is that these shall be taken quite literally, or "at
face value"; while traditional theism has generally understood these as
anthropomorphisms or something of the sort. The question then is which
of these hermeneutics is the more adequate.

Traditional theism. In many ways, the traditional interpretations follow an approach that has been built up gradually since the church began
to break away from the allegorizing approach of some of the Fathers that
was widely held and practiced until the rise of higher criticism. The basic
premise of that hermeneutic has been to take passages in their "natural"
sense, which generally meant taking a passage literally unless there was
some good reason to take it differently. This meant that poetic passages
were interpreted as such, that similes were not forced to application in all
their points, that parables were understood as teaching a spiritual truth
rather than asserting actual historical occurrences. Interpretation was also
to be done in context, so that what was said was related to the situation in
time and culture, both broadly and narrowly, and the flow of the argument
in which it was placed.

This did not mean that the Bible was to be read as "flat," that is, that
all texts were to be treated as bearing equal weight. Some were to be
regarded as more influential than others in formulating the understanding

---

[2]Gregory A. Boyd, "Christian Love and Academic Dialogue: A Reply to Bruce Ware," *Journal of the Evangelical Theological Society* 45.2 (June 2002): 243.
[3]Ware, "Rejoinder to Replies," *Journal of the Evangelical Theological Society* 45.2 (June 2002): 255.

of a general topic. There were rules, or at least guidelines, for determining which passages were to be given priority in the formulation of any composite teaching. Included among these was the principle of progressive revelation, the idea that God has revealed himself over a long period of time, so that the later segments of the revelation should interpret the earlier, rather than the reverse.

The Traditional Approach. When we examine the two types of hermeneutic, we find relative strengths and weaknesses of each, although not necessarily equally. The traditional view is able to follow quite consistently its basic principle of taking Scripture in its natural sense. It treats some of the ignorance, surprise, and repentance passages as instances of anthropomorphism. In this, it is following the general principle that since the revelation speaks to us about God using human language, there must be a quality of what could be termed at least the anthropic about it. It should be noted that virtually all interpreters of Scripture see at least some references to God, such as references to his bodily parts, as being anthropomorphic. One problem for the traditional hermeneutic is that it has not necessarily worked out a clear set of criteria for how it classifies passages as anthropomorphic. It has seemed to some critics of the traditional view that these theologians must possess some knowledge of God independent of the biblical revelation that enables them to determine which qualities attributed to God in the Bible are literally true of him and which are not. To the critic, these criteria are derived from reading the Bible through the spectacles of Greek philosophy.

A further problem for the hermeneutic of traditional theism is that it must proceed by inference and extension in arriving at its conclusion of God's exhaustive foreknowledge. Critics have pointed out that no single text or combination of texts says that God's knowledge of the future covers everything that will ever happen. Since the statements that God knows a specific fact about the future would have to be exhaustive of every such event, the induction is only partial. The case for exhaustive foreknowledge requires an extrapolation from what Scripture does address to what it does not.

Open Theism. The great virtue and strength of the open theist hermeneutic is the ability to extend the natural meaning principle to some portions of the Scripture that have often been read otherwise. This enables the ordinary Christian, without a seminary education, to read and benefit from the Bible, taking it simply at its word.

The most significant single test of open theism's hermeneutic is whether it can be applied to all materials of a similar type. Thus, the practice of taking statements about God's discovering something or changing his mind straightforwardly should be extended to all similar references to God. Here some problems have occurred, since this leads to such conclusions as that God is mistaken on some matters, that he is ignorant of some past and present matters, that he is forgetful, that he becomes fatigued, and that he hates some people—to say nothing of the fact that he appears to possess a body. Some efforts have been made to avoid these implications of the hermeneutic by such means as treating passages as poetic or as obviously ridiculous if taken literally. Other efforts have been to say that the questions about the past and the present are rhetorical questions, and to claim that God's statements about matters that did not come to pass were merely assessments of the relative probability of options, rather than infallible statements of what must certainly come to pass, and therefore not mistakes. These qualifications of the apparent meaning at times become very contrived and certainly violate the principle of taking a statement "at face value."

One who has been willing to apply this hermeneutic consistently is Clark Pinnock, who consequently comes to the conclusion that God may have a body of some sort. While he does not necessarily accept this conclusion, the arguments that he advances for considering this possibility resemble rather strongly the arguments used by open theists in contending that the change of mind passages are to be taken literally. To my knowledge no other open theist has considered seriously this same conception, so Pinnock appears to be the most consistent practitioner of the hermeneutic.

Traditionally, conservative biblical interpreters have followed a principle known as the analogy of Scripture. This was the idea that the meaning of a given passage can sometimes be obtained by comparing it with other passages that address or at least touch on the same topic. Here a traditional theist, Bruce Ware, has sought to test the open theist thesis. He examines the open theist interpretation of Jehovah's statements in Jer. 7:31, 19:5, and 32:35 prohibiting offering of their sons and daughters as sacrifices in the fashion of Baal worshipers. In each of these passages, Jehovah says of the practice that it is "something I did not command, nor did it enter my mind." Open theists cite this as evidence that Jehovah did not anticipate this development. Ware, however, points out that in Deut. 12:31, 18:9–10, and Lev. 18:21, Jehovah explicitly prohibited their doing these things. Since these passages date to an earlier period, this certainly negates the idea that God did not imagine that they would do this. It also, incidentally, contradicts Boyd's "neo-molinism," which is the idea that God knows in advance all the possibilities, but not which of these will become actualized. It appears that, at least on this point, the open theist hermeneutic fails the test of *analogia Scriptura.*

A further problem with the open theist hermeneutic is also a matter of consistency. The open theists, and particularly Boyd, interpret the prediction of Peter's denial of Jesus on the basis of God's thorough knowledge of his character, a knowledge based on his past behavior. Yet he interprets the Gen. 22 passage as teaching that God truly did not know what Abraham would do, an interpretation also applied to the case of Hezekiah. This appears to be an inconsistent hermeneutic, or at least an inconsistent application of a theological principle. While it is not a failure to interpret one Scripture in light of another, it is a failure to interpret one Scripture in the light of the interpretation one has used on a similar type of passage or a similar issue.

In addition, Boyd in particular fails to apply to his own hermeneutic a logical requirement that he makes of the traditional view. He has correctly pointed out that no single Scripture passage or combination of passages asserts that God knows everything about the future. As David Hunt has observed, although Boyd has stated categorically that God has exhaustive definite knowledge of the past and of the present, there similarly is no Scripture or combination of texts that affirm this contention, either.

One issue that clearly separates the two theologies and two interpretive strategies is whether priority in interpretation is to be given to narrative or to didactic portions of Scripture. One place where this difference emerges is in 1 Sam. 15, where the narrative twice says that God repented of a given action, but there is a didactic statement to the effect that God does not repent. Open theists give precedence to the narrative statements and interpret the didactic statement in light of these, while traditional theists do the opposite.

In general, conservative hermeneutics has usually given primacy to the didactic portions of Scripture. It is interesting to note how frequently narrative is accompanied or sometimes followed by didactic portions commenting on or elucidating the narrative. One example that we noted is Ruth 4:1–12, where an explanatory didactic comment is inserted into the narrative to explain the narrative. A more frequent occurrence is Jesus' parables, where he often explained the parable, which was really a form of narrative, to his disciples. It is also interesting to note how many times Jesus appealed to an account of a historical event to illustrate the point he was making. In general, however, the principle of giving priority to the didactic seems sound, for without it, there can be confusion as to just what point the narrative is illustrating.

The open theists have acknowledged that there is a large amount of biblical material that supports the traditional view. They have insisted, however, that certain controlling metaphors should be given more weight in formulating one's understanding because they more closely approximate the overall or primary teaching of Scripture. When the Scripture is examined for its primary teachings, however, it is the Bible as interpreted through the lens of this model of interpretation: open theism. Thus, a clear circularity appears, a weakness that serves to vitiate the open theist hermeneutic.

It is apparent, however, that some motifs must be given more influence than others. We have suggested that some of these criteria, such as the emphasis, clarity, centrality, or frequency of certain teachings, are sounder and tend to support the traditional teaching. In particular, we noted that the number of passages favoring the traditional teaching greatly outnumber those supportive of the open theist view, or to put it negatively, there are many more problematic passages for the open theist hermeneutic to deal with than for the traditional view.

The issue of where those supporting passages are found is also an important consideration. The texts that the traditional view appeals to are basically rather equally distributed throughout the Scripture. It is notable, however, that every open theist who cites scriptural support for his view uses many more Old Testament than New Testament passages. It would appear that this contradicts the principle of progressive revelation, according to which a teaching should become more clearly and emphatically taught as the process of revelation unfolds.

HISTORICAL EVIDENCE

Traditional Theism. The strength of the traditional view lies in the fact that through the years of the church's history, this view has predominated. Almost without interruption, there has been a stream of testimony to belief in the exhaustive definite foreknowledge. This has been found among theologians who differed on a variety of other doctrinal issues. There also has been considerable difference about *how* God knows the future, but not necessarily about *whether* he knows the future.

One of the problems for the traditional view is that no council or other official authority has ever ruled on this issue. Surely, if this issue is as crucial as some in the traditional camp suggest, there should have been some definitive pronouncement or ruling on it. That, the open theists suggest, means that there is no official orthodox view on the subject, and that Christians today are therefore free to come to any conclusion on the basis of Scripture, without having to feel that they are departing from correct Christian doctrine.

Open Theism. There has been, nonetheless, a small but recurring alternative testimony. These, too, have been from a variety of thinkers, with the number increasing in recent years. It is notable, however, that these have not been from the mainstream of orthodox Christianity. Some, like Celsus, were persons who were not Christians at all or who, like Marcion or the Socinians, held heretical views in some other areas. Some were not theologians, but philosophers, psychologists, and scientists. Some were Christian theologians but were so obscure as to be virtually unknown and unnoticed, such as Calcidius, Billy Hibbert, and L. D. McCabe.

When these facts about those who have held to a view of less than exhaustive definite foreknowledge are taken into account, part of the enigma of the historical silence of the church is removed. Many issues of doctrine were never ruled on or even considered by official ecclesiastical deliberating bodies simply because there was no need. Within the mainstream of the church, no one who held to the other major tenets of orthodox belief denied them. Those who did also rejected major doctrinal tenets, and it was those doctrines that became the focus of the church's energy. So no action was taken. An example is the several statements of faith drawn up during the doctrinal disputes in the early part of the twentieth century. In the majority of cases, these made no affirmation of Jesus' humanity, not because those framing the confessions did not believe in that doctrine, but rather because no one was really disputing it. This seems like the best explanation also for the absence of statement from the major doctrinal pronouncements of any reference to foreknowledge.

This is not to say that the church has historically been unaware of the issue. It is quite impressive to see how early in the history of the church the major issues of the current dispute were raised. The question of the relationship of divine foreknowledge to human freedom, for example, was anticipated and dealt with by Origen in his dispute with Celsus, and it was also addressed by Tertullian. The point, however, is that the teaching rejected in those writings was never a sufficiently popular view that the church found it necessary to address it in an official way.

PHILOSOPHICAL

Traditional Theism. The issue of philosophy has arisen because open theists have charged that the traditional view has been influenced by Greek philosophy. The reason for the widespread belief that the Scripture teaches exhaustive divine foreknowledge, say open theists, is that the church early came under this alien influence and has subsequently interpreted Scripture through this cultural element or has blended the two factors into something known as classical orthodoxy. If this is true, it is a serious problem for the traditional view. It may be that it is more philosophical than biblical and that the open theist view is the truly biblically based theology.

Our examination of the evidence, however, cast heavy doubt on this thesis. For one thing, the Greek conception of God involved several attributes, so that a theology based on it should be expected to display all of those attributes as well. Yet when we look at contemporary examples of the traditional view, they do not hold the older view of impassibility, or the Greek philosophical conception of immutability for that matter. There is difference of opinion on the view of God as timelessly eternal or as everlastingly temporal. Open theists have insisted that because traditional theism has absorbed the Greek view it must also espouse these attributes. It may be that this absence should rather be taken as evidence that the traditional theology does not derive in any significant way from Greek philosophy.

It also appears that the distinction between biblical thought and *the* Greek view are at best exaggerated. A generation or two ago this was a common conception within the biblical theology movement, but the work of scholars like Martin Hengel and James Barr has seriously eroded if not eliminated this contention. Points of similarity between the two streams of thought may indicate, not influence of one by the other, but simply a common tenet.

One other objection to the perceived connection comes from an examination of the theology of the neo-orthodox theologians Karl Barth and Emil Brunner. Both made concerted efforts to purge their thought of any philosophical elements, especially from Greek philosophy. Yet both held to the traditional view of divine foreknowledge. Either they were not successful in thoroughly excising this influence, or it was not the source of belief in the doctrine of foreknowledge.

This is not to say that Greek thought has never been any influence on the classical view of God. Most contemporary conservative theologians admit as much and have taken steps to ensure that this influence is detected and rejected. This should be considered not a weakness but a strength of the traditional position. Nor is this to say that no current representatives of the traditional view incorporate elements of such philosophy into their doctrinal formulation. For example, Norman Geisler, a self-identified Thomist,[4] exhibits elements of the Greek synthesis in his doctrine of God and his arguments on the subject of divine foreknowledge.[5]

---

[4]Norman L. Geisler, *Thomas Aquinas: An Evangelical Appraisal* (Grand Rapids: Baker, 1991).
[5]Norman L. Geisler and H. Wayne House, *The Battle for God: Responding to the Challenge of Neotheism* (Grand Rapids: Kregel, 2001).

All theological systems and all exegetical methodologies work within some sort of philosophical perspective. Unfortunately, many traditional theists and most exegetes apparently do not recognize this or acknowledge it, or take conscious steps to compensate for any undue influence on their reading of Scripture. Despite this, it appears that the philosophical basis of most conservative traditional theism is less that of Greek philosophy than of modern realism, either commonsense or critical.

Open Theism. It is interesting to notice that open theism itself contains philosophical factors. There are even parallels between open theism and some early Greek philosophy.

There has also been considerable discussion of whether open theism may have been influenced by process philosophy. While no one suggests that open theism is an instance of what is generally meant by process theology, there are some indications of incorporation of some categories of process philosophy. While Gregory Boyd emphatically denies any connection between the two, he had earlier written of Charles Hartshorne's influence on him and had described his own thought as a modification of Hartshorne's process philosophy.[6] Several other open theists report being influenced by process philosophy, and there are indications of common themes and even common arguments in some cases.

It is significant that open theism's arguments are philosophical, as in the use of the problem of evil, or depend on clearly philosophical conceptions such as libertarian freedom, an A-theory of time, and the unreality of the future. This is not to say that open theism does not rely on Scripture, but rather to say that it is at least in part dependent on philosophy. Interestingly, although open theists have accused the traditional view of interpreting Scripture through Greek philosophical categories, none of them acknowledges any possible influence of philosophical influence on their reading of the Scripture. This, they maintain, is simply what the Bible says.

Open theism's philosophical stance leads it into several problems. At the heart of much of the difficulty is the conception of noncompatibilist or libertarian freedom. On this basis, God appears not to be free, and

---

[6]Gregory A. Boyd, *Trinity and Process: A Critical Evaluation and Reconstruction of Hartshorne's Di-Polar Theism Towards a Trinitarian Metaphysics* (New York: Peter Lang, 1992), preface.

humans will not be free in the life to come. While Hasker discusses the various views of freedom, he interprets compatibilism through the categories of incompatibilism, resulting in his caricaturing the traditional view in the imagery of robots, puppets, and ventriloquist's dummies.

There also is a problem for open theists in terms of how God can assure that his purposes are achieved. Each of them states that, if necessary, God can act unilaterally. This, however, appears to be a case of external coercion, something that even compatibilists reject. It thus is not a case of whether God coerces, but rather of how often he does so.

In *Satan and the Problem of Evil,* Boyd presents something of a change from his earlier position. While persons begin life with libertarian freedom, they progressively formulate their character to where their freedom is compatibilistic freedom. Thus, by the time of Jesus' prediction, Peter's character was largely fixed and predictable, as was that of Judas. There is a period of probation during which the person has the libertarian freedom given at birth, but after which the character is so solidified that God can both predict actions and is justified in acting on that character or causing the person to act in conformity with it. This accounts for the sinlessness of believers in heaven. Also, based upon Boyd's remark that Jesus had compatibilistic freedom, this seems to indicate that God's freedom is compatibilistic freedom.

Boyd is to be commended for seeing the problems with the libertarian view and moving closer to compatibilism. There is, however, an element of the contrived in this concept. It also casts doubt on whether this is consistent with valuing libertarian freedom as highly as open theism does.

The concept of the future is another area of difficulty for open theism. The open theist argument is that God's failure to know the future is not a lack of knowledge, because there is nothing there to know. The future has no reality. The analogy used by Boyd of God not knowing there is no monkey sitting next to him breaks down because traditional theists have never claimed that God's not knowing false propositions, such as this one, is a weakness. The idea that God knows some of the future suggests that on Boyd's terms, part of the future does "exist," which suggests an element of incoherence in the theory. Actually, it reveals an equivocation on the meaning of the term "exists."

Boyd also claims that open theism fits better with contemporary physics, particularly quantum mechanics and chaos theory, than does traditional theism. John Beckman, a scientist, has shown, however, that chaos theory in the form espoused by most scientists who hold this theory is actually a deterministic theory. Boyd seems to have moved from the epistemological indeterminability of movement of subatomic particles to their metaphysical indeterminacy, an unjustified leap of logic.

It appears that, contrary to open theist charges, traditional theism may not have been influenced by philosophy as much as open theism has. What is disappointing is that open theism has been reluctant to acknowledge this influence or any adverse effects it may have produced. It is as if influence by philosophy is a bad thing, but only in the case of certain philosophies. Consonance with certain current philosophies is claimed as a positive virtue.

Practical Issues

The Problem of Evil. Traditionally, this has been one of the most serious intellectual problems for the Christian faith. As the open theists correctly point out, this is especially a problem for the traditional view, which holds that God foreknows everything that is to happen throughout all of time. On this basis, God should have acted to prevent this happening or should not have willed for it to happen. Certainly this is a serious problem for the traditional view. Over many centuries, various efforts have been made to alleviate the problem, but it has never been satisfactorily resolved.

The open theist position is not as seriously affected by this problem since God cannot be blamed for not preventing what he did not know would occur. The problem still persists to some degree, however. For if, as Boyd contends, God knows all the possibilities that *might* occur, some of those possibilities, though perhaps slight in likelihood, are so horrendous that he surely should have acted to prevent their becoming actual. The atrocities committed by Adolf Hitler come to mind as a notable example. Moreover, at some point, the probability of these actions had become considerably greater (for example, after a few years of Hitler's regime) so that God should have acted to prevent more serious developments.

To some extent, the open theist is caught on the horns of a logical dilemma. Since God has granted irrevocable libertarian freedom, he cannot guarantee that his desired outcome will be achieved without his unilateral intervention. Such action, however, appears to be, if not a revocation, at least a suspension, of that freedom. Thus, either there is no assurance of a satisfactory disposition of evil, or open theism must compromise one of its cardinal tenets. It does appear, however, that the open theist treatment of the problem makes the problem of evil (but perhaps not evil itself) less severe than it is on the grounds of traditional theism.

Prayer. When we turn to prayer, the advantage certainly seems to be with open theism. Prayer, as most Christians practice it, and as the Bible describes it, seems to affect what happens. The open theist picture of prayer does seem to fit better the seemingly plain sense of the scriptural passages on prayer. It may well be that traditional theists' prayer practice is in contradiction to the theory. There are, of course, theologies of prayer that fit with the traditional theist theology, but they are not necessarily widely known on the popular level. Traditional theism needs to do a better job of articulating a theology of prayer that coheres with the rest of its doctrine of God and of relating it to this discussion.

Again we may observe that the open theist view, although it seems to fit more directly with the biblical teaching and with common Christian practice, is not free from difficulties. Because of the view of libertarian freedom, there is no guarantee that God will be able to answer certain types of prayers. Because he does not know free human actions in advance, God may not know what would be the best course of action to follow.

Guidance. Here the traditional view seems to have an advantage since there is a plan for God to guide his followers into. Because many of the decisions Christians make have far-reaching consequences, belief in a God who knows all of the future is an asset. By comparison, God's guidance, according to the open theist theology, is of necessity short-range and rather piecemeal. To the extent that God does offer guidance, it may turn out to be bad guidance, since he does not know all of the future.

One matter that should be examined is the use, primarily by Boyd, but also by other open theists, of the expression, "the myth of the blueprint."

Perhaps we should speak instead of "the myth of the myth of the blueprint." Apart from the fact that "blueprint" refers to a now technologically obsolete process, this conveys a conception of specificity that may be misleading. It suggests that there is one and only one way that God could accomplish an end, and that therefore the believer must find exactly the specific action to be followed. This leads to the type of situation where one must pray about every detail of one's life.

It should be observed that the idea that this is what traditional theism holds is itself something of a myth. Most Christians believe that God is working out his plan and that this plan includes the human's attempt to determine and conform to that will, but this does not necessarily entail that, from the human perspective, this involves all of the details or that all of God's plan involves direct and active decision and action on God's part. Plans used by workmen in constructing a building may be simply rough sketches, sufficiently detailed for their executing their work.

We have examined and attempted to evaluate the cases made by the two major parties in the present debate. In general, the open theist position seems to have the greater strength in the area of the practical issues of the Christian life. It also appeals to the current ethos of Western culture with its strong emphasis on human freedom and its aversion to external authority.

With respect to other considerations, however, the advantage appears to be clearly with the traditional view. It has done a more thorough exegetical treatment of Scripture and is supported by a much larger body of biblical texts than is the open theist view. The attempt to invalidate the traditional interpretation of some key passages on the grounds that the theology was under the influence of Greek philosophy has been difficult to maintain. Indeed, it appears that open theist theology incorporates significant philosophical material, while failing to acknowledge any influence of this on its interpretation of Scripture.

The open theist hermeneutic, when applied consistently, has led to conclusions that were unacceptable to open theists, resulting in some extraordinary efforts to restate the position. The logical problems created by this and by the philosophical positions taken have also rendered suspect the cogency of the position. The historical evidence indicates that even though the orthodox tradition was aware of the very problems raised by open theists, virtually no orthodox Christian theologian adopted the view of limited foreknowledge. Those who did adopt this view were very few in number and were not part of the major body of Christian thought.

On balance, then, while no single view has given final answers to the issues involved in the foreknowledge debate, the traditional view of God's exhaustive definite foreknowledge appears to have considerably more cogent intellectual support and fewer difficulties than does the alternative.

The debate will surely continue. The way in which it is conducted is important if there is really to be progress in the discussion. My single greatest wish is that the spirit of the conversations will be that of candor, courtesy, and fairness by both parties to the discussion. I would make the following suggestions to both parties.

1. It is important that the emotional tone of the debate be lowered.
2. The motives of the parties involved should not be questioned. It is not helpful for traditionalists to suggest that open theists are being insincere or for open theists to suggest that the issue is control.
3. The language employed needs to be watched carefully. Although the open theists have most loudly complained about the comments of the opposition,[7] sometimes justifiably, it has been they who have referred to their opponents as the Taliban and as mullahs conducting a fatwah, and have spoken of the traditional view of God as a divine rapist. Such language will not advance the discussion.

---

[7]Clark Pinnock, *Most Moved Mover: A Theology of God's Openness* (Grand Rapids: Baker, 2001), 10–18. Boyd, "Christian Love and Academic Discourse," 233–43. John Sanders, "Be Wary of Ware: A Reply to Bruce Ware," *Journal of the Evangelical Theological Society* 45.2 (June 2002): 221–31. Of the three replies to Ware, Pinnock's is the calmest, most respectful, and oriented to the intellectual issues.

4. Accurate portrayal of one's opponents' views needs to be pursued. Both parties have felt that their own view has been misunderstood, misrepresented, or even caricatured.
5. The real issues need to be identified and debated rather than the distracting false issues. For example, there should be no more suggestions that this is a Calvinist-Arminian issue, since traditional Arminians agree with Calvinists on the fact of foreknowledge, although not on its basis.

SUBJECT INDEX

Abiram, 113
Abraham, 22–23, 24–25, 34, 56, 61–62,
  63–64, 71–72, 240, 241
Adam and Eve, 30, 63, 65, 67
African-American theology, 128–30
Agabus, 28
Against Celsus (Origen), 111
Ahab, 30
American Psychological Association, 119–
  20
angelic beings, 225–26
annihilationism, 234
Aquinas, Thomas, 98–99, 131, 135–37,
  145, 194, 216
Aristotle, 139, 145, 148–49, 179
Arminius, James, 104, 106, 122, 131
atonement, 231–32
Augustine, 97–98, 101, 131
Aurelius, Marcus, 111

Babylon, 47–48
Baillie, John, 82
Barr, James, 18, 142, 250
Barth, Karl, 106–7, 109, 145, 146, 218,
  234, 250
Basinger, David, 69, 80, 151, 173, 174,
  204–5
Beckman, John, 182, 183, 184, 186, 253
Beethoven, Ludwig van, 194
Bible. *See* Scripture
Boaz, 75
body of God, 68–69, 245
Boman, Thorleif, 140–41, 142
Bowne, Borden Parker, 124, 125
Boyd, Gregory A., 18, 19, 21, 43, 45, 47,
  84, 128, 187, 241–42, 251; on
  African-American theology, 128–30;
  on the analogy of Scripture, 70; on
  angelic beings, 225–26; on atone-
  ment, 231–32; on conditional statements, 35–37; and consistency of
  principle in hermeneutics, 72; and

Boyd, Gregory A. *(continued)*
  criteria of verification in hermeneutics, 72–73; and directness and clarity
  of Scripture, 79–80; on divine foreknowledge in prophecies, 50–56, 220;
  on the dynamic nature of reality, 181–
  86; on errors by God, 64–65; on evil,
  150–51, 167; on frustration statements, 32–33; on God's ignorance
  about the future, 30–32, 221–22; on
  God's testing of people, 25–26, 29; on
  guidance from God, 254–55; on
  hermeneutics of, 246; on human freedom, 159–61; on inerrancy of the
  Bible, 229–30; on the influence of
  Greek philosophy, 134, 148; on Jesus'
  foreknowledge of Judas' betrayal, 54–
  56; on the justice of God, 218; on literal interpretations of the actions of
  God, 62–63, 67–68; on the nature of
  the future, 160–61, 176, 178–80; on
  the problem of evil, 190, 192–204; on
  process thought, 151–53; relative
  weight given to Old and New Testament materials by, 83; on the Socinians, 115–16; on the wrath of God,
  218
Briggs, Charles A., 18
Brightman, Edgar Sheffield, 124–26
Brown, Francis, 18
Brunner, Emil, 107, 145–46, 250
Bultmann, Rudolf, 144
Bush, George W., 16

Caiaphas, 185
Cain, 113
Calcidius, 113–14, 248
Calvin, John, 102–3, 131, 216
Calvinism, 12–13, 15, 102–3, 147–48,
  157–58, 218
Carnell, Edward John, 230

foreknowledge *(continued)*
terminology of, 48–49; Tertullian on, 93–94; Thomas Aquinas on, 98–99, 135–37, 145; time independence of, 43–44, 105–6, 108, 127, 137, 159–60; traditional view on, 39–40; and unilateral divine action, 57–58; William of Ockham on, 100–101; Wolfhart Pannenberg on, 107–9

freedom, human, 48, 50–51; compatibilist versus libertarian view of, 101–2, 163, 166–67, 175, 196–98, 251–52; cooperating with divine grace, 103; and evil, 167; Faustus Socinus on, 114–16; Gregory A. Boyd on, 159–61; influence versus constraint on, 122–23; and Judas' betrayal of Jesus, 55–56; liberal African-American theology on, 128–29; and the ongoing influence of God, 196–98; open theism concept of, 164–75; philosophical conceptions of, 157–61; and the problem of evil, 190–204; rejection of divine foreknowledge and, 114–16, 122–25; William Hasker on, 165–66

freedom of God, 167–69

Fretheim, Terence, 76, 78, 228

frustration statements in the Bible, 32–34

future, open theism concept of the, 176–81, 183–84

Garden of Gethsemane, 35, 37–38

Garrett, James Leo, 136

Geisler, Norman, 250

Gibbs, Karen, 11

God: body of, 68–69, 245; change of mind by, 22–24; conditional statements made by, 34–38, 58–59; divine love of, 14, 77–78, 112–13, 173, 213–18; doctrine of, 15, 213–25; errors of, 64–65; and failed prophecies, 27–30; foretelling the future, 30–32, 45–47, 79; freedom of, 167–69; frustration statements made by, 32–34; and the great flood, 66; guidance from, 209–12, 254–55; immutability of, 136–37, 138, 222–23; impassibility of, 135–36,

God *(continued)*
223–25; justice of, 218–19; literal interpretations of the actions of, 62–63, 66; middle knowledge of, 12; and the nature of universal statements, 84; ongoing influence of, 196–98; pain felt by, 18–22; prayer to, 204–9, 254; and the problem of evil, 189–204, 253–54; regret felt by, 18–22; simple foreknowledge of, 12, 39–60, 219–22; testing of people by, 24–27; timelessness of, 43–44, 105–6, 108, 127, 137, 159–60; triunity of, 14–15; unilateral divine action by, 57–58; will of, 101–2. *See also* Jehovah; prophecies of God

God of the Possible (Boyd), 115, 148, 152, 159

Green, Michael, 234

Griffin, David Ray, 154

Grudem, Wayne, 136

guidance from God, 209–12, 254–55

Hartshorne, Charles, 116, 117, 121, 126–28, 152, 153, 155, 183, 251

Hasker, William, 152, 154–55, 157, 167, 168, 252; on the concept of human freedom, 165–66

heaven, 234–35

Hebrew mentality, 140–44

Hengel, Martin, 143, 250

Heraclitus, 150

hermeneutics: analogy of Scripture and, 69–71; consistency of, 63–69; consistency of principle in, 71–72; and controlling metaphors in Scripture, 76–79; criteria of verification in, 72–73; directness and clarity of Scripture and, 79–80; and emphasis and cruciality of Scripture, 79; and the Hebrew mentality, 142–43; identifying issues in, 61–76; literal interpretations of actions of God and, 62–63, 66; narrative and didactic passages and, 73–76; and the nature of universal statements, 84; open theism and, 244–48, 255–56; progressive revelation and, 82–83; recurrence and frequency in Scripture

narrative passages in the Bible: and hermeneutics, 73–76; open theism on, 57–60; pre-identified individuals in, 49–51; prophecies of specific actions of individuals in, 51–57

Nash, Ronald, 137

neo-molinism, 221, 246

Nineveh, 28, 58–59

Nixon, Richard, 15

Ockham's Razor, Law of, 60

Olson, Roger, 134–35

On Interpretation (Aristotle), 148–49

Openness of God, The (Pinnock, Rice, et al.), 76, 135, 151, 210, 214, 217

open theism: on angelic beings, 225–26; on atonement, 231–32; change of mind passages supporting, 22–24; and chaos physics, 185–86; concept of human freedom in, 164–75; concept of the future in, 176–81, 183–84; conditional statements in the Scriptures and, 34–38, 58–59; correlation with certain philosophies and scientific theories, 186–88, 253; on the doctrine of humanity, 230–31; and the doctrine of the last things, 234–35; on the dynamic nature of reality, 181–86; and errors of God, 64–65; failed prophecies and, 27–30; frustration statements in the Scriptures and, 32–34; and God's apparent ignorance about the future, 30–32, 219–22; and God's regret, 18–22; on guidance from God, 209–12, 254–55; and hermeneutics, 244–48, 256–57; historical evidence supporting, 248–49; and the immutability of God, 222–23; and the impassibility of God, 223–25; and the influence of Greek philosophy, 133–35; influence of Greek philosophy on, 147–61, 251–53; on Jesus' prediction of Judas' betrayal, 54–56; on the justice of God, 218–19; on the knowledge of God, 219–22; on the love of God, 213–18; philosophical basis of,

open theism *(continued)* 163–64; and prayer, 254; on prayer, 204–9; and the problem of evil, 150–51, 154–55, 167, 190, 253–54; and process thought, 151–56; and prophecy, 57–60; recurrence and frequency of themes in Scripture and, 80–82; repentance passages supporting, 17–22; on revelation, 226–30; on salvation, 232–34; scriptural evidence supporting, 240–43; speech-act theory and, 31–32; and testing of people by God, 24–27; and unilateral divine action by God, 57–58

Origen, 94–96, 111

Orr, James, 14, 230

orthodox view on divine foreknowledge, 87–109

Padgett, Alan, 159

pain felt by God, 18–22

Pannenberg, Wolfhart, 107–9

panpsychists, 119

parsimony, law of, 60

Parunak, H. Van Dyke, 18–19

Paul, 28, 144, 211–12

Pedersen, Johannes, 140

Perrin, Norman, 144

Peter, 51–52, 51–54, 62, 71–73, 79, 84, 95, 171, 173–74, 199–201, 215, 242, 252

Pfleiderer, Otto, 120–21

philosophy, Greek: conceptions of human freedom, 157–61; and the Hebrew mentality, 140–44; influence on open theism, 147–61, 251–53; influence on the traditional view, 135–47, 249–51; influence on Thomas Aquinas, 135–40; logical versus systemic consistency and, 139; neo-orthodoxy's aversion to, 145–47; open theists on, 133–35; and the problem of evil, 150–51, 154–55; and process thought, 151–56; similarity of ideas with Scripture, 144–45

physics, chaos, 185–86

Picasso, Pablo, 194

Pilate, Pontius, 185

Stalin, Joseph, 194
Stewart, Martha, 16
Stott, John, 234
Strimple, R., 116
Swinburne, Richard, 167
sympathy, 224–25

Tatian, 91–92
Theresa, Mother, 194
Tertullian, 93–94, 131
testing of people by God, 24–27
Theophilus, 92
Timaeus (Plato), 113
time independence of God's knowledge, 43–44, 105–6, 108, 127, 137, 159–60
traditional view: aversion to philosophy, 145–47; didactic passages supporting, 39–49; on guidance from God, 211–12, 254–55; hermeneutics, 243–44; historical evidence supporting, 248; and the Law of Ockham's Razor, 60; narrative passages supporting, 49–57; open theism's response to, 57–60; philosophical influence on, 135–47, 249–53; of prayer, 254; on prayer,

traditional view *(continued)*
204; and the problem of evil, 253; scriptural evidence supporting, 238–40
Travis, Stephen, 234
Trinity, the, 14–15
Trinity and Process (Boyd), 115, 148, 153, 159
True Discourse, A (Celsus), 111
Truesdale, Albert, 130

Vincent of Lerins, 87
Viney, Wayne, 116–17

Ware, Bruce, 23–24, 29, 39–40, 42, 46, 62, 136, 169, 229, 239
Wenham, John, 234
Wesley, John, 106, 130
Westermann, Claus, 19
Whitehead, Alfred North, 117
Willard, Dallas, 220
William of Ockham, 100–101
Wolterstorff, Nicholas, 138–39
Zeno, 150

scripture index

what does god know and when does he know it?

We want to hear from you. Please send your comments about this book to us in care of zreview@zondervan.com. Thank you.

ZONDERVAN™

GRAND RAPIDS, MICHIGAN 49530 USA

WWW.ZONDERVAN.COM